PROSPECTS FOR PARTNERSHIP

INDUSTRIALIZATION
AND TRADE POLICIES
IN THE 1970s

PROSPECTS FOR PARTNERSHIP

INDUSTRIALIZATION
AND TRADE POLICIES
IN THE 1970s

A Seminar held at the
International Bank for Reconstruction and Development
October 5 and 6, 1972

edited by
HELEN HUGHES

THE JOHNS HOPKINS UNIVERSITY PRESS
Baltimore and London

338.9
P 96

Preface

Four years ago the Pearson Commission reported on the first two decades of the international development effort and suggested ways in which the emerging partnership between developed and developing countries might be improved. Its report* stressed the close link that exists between the capacity of developing countries to import and their overall potential for development. Maintenance of this link requires coordinated action on both sides of the partnership—to enable the developing countries to earn sufficient foreign exchange for their continued growth and to provide for the efficient transfer of capital assistance in cases where export earnings are not sufficient.

The principal source of foreign exchange for development is exports. In the long run the prospects for continued growth of trade between developed and developing countries appear excellent. Rapid expansion of mineral and manufactured exports from developing countries during the past decade has led to much less dependence on agricultural exports, for which growth of demand is relatively slow, than in the past. If advanced countries take measures to adjust their patterns of production, the rapid growth of manufactured imports into these countries should not pose a serious problem, since they will still represent a small share of the total supply of manufactures.

In the immediate future, these adjustment problems appear much more serious, and they may indeed threaten the development prospects of many industrializing countries. While the expansion of manufactured exports in the 1960s was confined to a handful of

---

*See Lester B. Pearson, *Partners in Development* (New York: Frederick A. Praeger, 1969).

small countries, several major developing countries have now entered world markets in a variety of industries. Absorption difficulties have already emerged for certain products, and some of the importing countries have threatened to impose further restrictions. Past experience does not suggest that there will be an easy and automatic adjustment of demand to supply. On the contrary, new approaches are needed to assist both developed and developing countries to formulate policies that will facilitate the structural changes required on both sides.

In October 1972 the World Bank invited a group of international economists to examine these aspects of the development partnership as part of its continuing research into development problems. Academic and practicing economists met to examine the nature of the adjustment problems affecting both developed and developing countries and the policies available to alleviate them. The present volume contains the papers presented at that seminar and a summary of the discussions that followed. We hope that their publication will contribute to a better understanding of adjustment problems and to the resolution of potential conflicts before they emerge as threats to development.

Hollis B. Chenery
Vice President for Development Policy
International Bank for
Reconstruction and Development

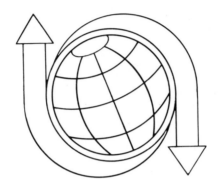

Contents

Seminar Participants

Ojetunji Aboyade, *University of Ibadan*
Edmar Bacha, *University of Brasilia*
Bela Balassa, *Johns Hopkins University*
Robert Baldwin, *University of Wisconsin*
Jean Baneth, *IBRD*
Haim Barkai, *University of Jerusalem*
Ferdnand Braun, *Commission of European Communities*
Hollis Chenery, *IBRD*
Max Corden, *Nuffield College*
Juergen Donges, *Kiel University*
Barend de Vries, *IBRD*
Charles Frank, *Brookings Institution*
Isaiah Frank, *School for Advanced International Studies*
Irving Friedman, *IBRD*
Nat Goldfinger, *AFL-CIO*
Craufurd Goodwin, *Ford Foundation*
Ravi Gulhati, *IBRD*
Philip Hayes, *IBRD*
Mahbub Haq, *IBRD*
David Henderson, *IBRD*
Gerry Helleiner, *University of Toronto*
Deane Hinton, *Council of International Economic Policy*
Helen Hughes, *IBRD*
Liz Jager, *AFL-CIO*
Harry Johnson, *University of Chicago*
John Karlik, *Joint Economic Committee, United States Congress*

Kiyoshi Kojima, *Hitotsubashi University*
Caroline Miles, *Nuffield College*
John Mutti, *University of Wisconsin*
Göran Ohlin, *Uppsala University*
Stanley Please, *IBRD*
Moeen Qureshi, *IBRD*
Jo Saxe, *IBRD*
Maurice Scott, *Nuffield College*
Ernest Stern, *IBRD*
Paul Streeten, *Queen Elizabeth House*
Jan Tumlir, *Trade Intelligence Division, GATT*
Pierre Uri, *Atlantic Institute*
Herman van der Tak, *IBRD*
David Wall, *University of Sussex*

Abbreviations

ECAFE	Economic Commission for Asia and the Far East
ECLA	Economic Commission for Latin America
EEC	European Economic Community
EFTA	European Free Trade Association
GATT	General Agreement on Tariffs and Trade
IBRD	International Bank for Reconstruction and Development
IMF	International Monetary Fund
OECD	Organization for Economic Cooperation and Development
UNCTAD	United Nations Conference on Trade and Development

Tables

Introduction

The purpose of the seminar on industrialization and trade policies in the 1970s was to focus on the demand aspects of the adjustment problems inherent in the increasing volume of manufactured product exports from developing countries. Supply issues had received a great deal of attention in recent years, and were therefore only to be considered in a secondary sense. Monetary aspects of the problem, while recognized as being of critical importance, were being discussed widely in other forums, and were not, therefore, to be central to the discussion.

The demand for developing countries' exports for manufactures can be seen as having three principal aspects. First, what is likely to be the rate of expansion of markets for various products, given free trade conditions (or at least the present level of price distortion) and worldwide income growth, that is, the income elasticity of demand. Secondly, given the developing countries' possible cost advantages, particularly in relatively labor-intensive goods, what the price elasticity of demand for such goods is, for this could lead to trade diversion, especially in third markets. Thirdly, what is likely to be the development of trade restrictions on the demand side, which factors influence these restrictions and how can the policy framework on the demand side be improved.

Existing knowledge of trade and policy trends suggests that a new movement toward diversification is accompanying the rising volume of the developing countries' exports. This is partly the result of the maturing of industrial development in the more economically advanced developing countries, but it is also part of a conscious desire to move into goods with a higher income elasticity and to spread export risks. A knowledge of the income and price elasticities of various products has thus become necessary to insure that the developing countries' export diversification efforts are directed toward the most favorable demand situations. Products for which income elasticity is high are likely to prove particularly important for developing countries because they are less likely to find themselves faced by restrictive import controls in rapidly growing markets than in stagnant ones. Price elasticity is unfortunately less likely to be a favorable factor in developed country markets, but it could be important in increasing trade in manufactures among developing countries. A supplementary knowledge of marketing and credit is needed. A general broadening and deepening of factual knowledge of demand could thus make a substantial contribution to the developing countries' ability to increase their exports of manufactures substantially.

However, even if developing countries are able to improve their export product mix in accordance with demand trends, they are still likely to face restrictive policies in developed countries unless there is an intensive effort to improve the developed countries' trade policies. Changes in trading patterns involve costs in the short run, while benefits only come in the long run. Neither the costs nor the benefits are evenly distributed within a community. Consumers usually benefit, particularly in the long run, but in situations of imperfect competition multinational corporations, importers, wholesalers or retailers may absorb price differentials in the form of high profits. The community may not benefit if such profits are lodged in tax havens. The costs to the producers, to investors, to entrepreneurs and to employers are immediate and direct. For these groups, and particularly for the workers, the problems of "adjustment" are proportionately acute, and unless they are solved they lead directly or indirectly to strong pressures for increased barriers to trade.

The adjustment problem has macroeconomic as well as microeconomic aspects. It seems relevant that the three principal cases of industry adjustment to new foreign sources of supply in recent years—the British and Japanese textile industries, and the European coal industry—occurred in periods of full employment and rapid economic growth. Conversely, it appears that adjustment assistance has run into grave difficulties in the United States because of high overall unemployment, and low growth levels. The workers least able to adjust come from among the most disadvantaged groups in a community, so that assisting them to adjust may not be primarily an economic problem, but a social one, and thus requires changes in social policies.

Because experience is limited, almost all the questions pertaining to the private and social costs entailed, and the administrative structure required, are yet to be resolved. Should adjustment assistance be confined to assisting resources to move out of a given competitive field? Should adjustment assistance be confined to demonstrable cases of disruption through trade, and if so, how can disruption be demonstrated and judged? What are the reasons of principle, as distinct from those of practical politics, for making adjustment assistance available to industries affected by international trade, but not by internal changes in technology, new sources of natural resource supplies or government decisions? To what extent can adjustment assistance be successful as a limited response to sectional pressures of industrialists and workers affected by imports or, indeed, by imports from developing countries, as Japan's legislation, tying adjustment assistance to the Generalized Preference Scheme, implies? Is adjustment assistance merely to be an alternative to foreign aid as some United States textile negotiations have suggested? What are the costs of adjustment assistance, and what is the best way of financing it? What are its benefits?

Changing trade patterns are not only a problem for developed countries. Given the gains from increasing trade, is there any scope, within the extremely limited resources of most developing countries, for adjustment as an accompaniment to their liberalization of trade? Would the benefits exceed the costs? Over what period of time?

The papers which follow, and the comments on them, address themselves to these questions from a broad range of viewpoints, first in terms of world trade and factor movements and, secondly, more specifically, in the light of the adjustment problems of leading developed countries. The discussion, which threaded together the various themes concerned with trade adjustment to changing international industrial patterns, sometimes in unison, but often divergently, is drawn together in the last paper to indicate directions which first analysis, and then policies might take.

I would like to thank the contributors and commentators as well as the other participants for spending two days at the end of a long summer of conferences focusing on these difficult if rather humdrum issues. I am grateful to Hollis Chenery and Bela Balassa for their support for the project from its inception, and to Max Corden and Harry Johnson who also advised me on how to carry it out. I owe thanks to the staff of the Economics of Industry Division for their support, particularly to Naimeh Hadjitarkhani, who did most of the checking of the finished manuscript. Ian Bowen's editing added clarity. I am especially indebted to Komola Ghose who, in spite of the considerable pressure of other work, organized the seminar and typed the manuscript.

Helen Hughes

Washington, D.C.
October 1973

PROSPECTS FOR PARTNERSHIP

**INDUSTRIALIZATION
AND TRADE POLICIES
IN THE 1970s**

1

Industrialization and Trade Trends: Some Issues for the 1970s[1]

Hollis B. Chenery and Helen Hughes

The trade problems of developing countries result to a large degree from their attempts to accelerate the pace of development. As between internal needs for resource mobilization and industrialization and the requirements for external balance, internal priorities are typically put first. It is only after the productive structure has become unbalanced and the balance of payments appears as an obstacle to further growth that trade receives adequate attention in overall development policy.

The developing countries as a group have been remarkably successful in achieving the goal that seemed to be paramount a decade ago, that of accelerated growth. The difference between success and failure has often hinged on exogenous factors affecting foreign exchange availabilities, such as the markets for primary exports and the supply of foreign capital.[2] In general, primary markets have improved over the decade and in only a few cases has the export pessimism of the early sixties proved to be justified.

1. The authors wish to thank Hazel Elkington, Naimeh Hadjitarkhani, John Eaton and Vinod Prakash for their assistance in the preparation of data.
2. A classification of "successful" development strategies based on trade considerations is given by Hollis B. Chenery. See "Targets for Development," in *The Widening Gap: Development in the 1970s,* ed. Barbara Ward (New York and London: Columbia University Press, 1971), pp. 27-47.

Although a number of smaller countries can continue to specialize in primary production until they reach fairly high levels of income, their population is less than a quarter of the total for the Third World. The bulk of developing countries must therefore industrialize at a rapid pace to sustain adequate rates of aggregate growth. Their principal choice is whether to focus on their domestic markets or alternatively to stress manufactured exports at some early stage.

Import substitution has provided the initial basis for industrialization in virtually all countries. It has stimulated overall growth and helped to close the gap between primary exports and import requirements over a period of ten to twenty years, when efficient import substitution has usually been completed. The negative effects have come from discriminating against both industrial exports as well as primary production as a means of prolonging import-substituting industrialization. Ten years ago there were virtually no exceptions to this generalization among the larger developing countries.

In the past decade a number of countries have shifted from import substitution to export promotion, both as a more efficient means of meeting their balance of payments needs and of sustaining rapid growth. The first group to do so—Hong Kong, Israel, Taiwan, Korea, Singapore—were often considered as special cases that could not readily be followed by countries with less education, skills and access to external capital. In the last few years, however, a number of larger and more typical countries—Yugoslavia, Pakistan, Brazil, Colombia, Mexico—have also shifted their external policies and started to promote industrial exports, with generally favorable results. Although the share of industrial production exported may still be low in this second group, the rate of growth of industrial exports now equals or exceeds that of the early leaders (see Table 1-2).

Since countries are becoming industrial exporters at different stages in their development and with widely varying factor endowments and technological skills, it is necessary to examine these internal aspects before turning to the potential markets for their exports. The relationship between industrialization and trade patterns is discussed in Section II, with a view to bringing out some of the uniformities in the two patterns as well as significant differences among countries.

Our examination of the supply side concludes that there is an enormous potential for expansion in the countries that are just becoming industrial exporters, and that they will be capable of supplying a wide range of industrial products at competitive prices. The limits to the growth of industrial exports from developing countries are therefore more likely to be found in the restrictions placed on them by the advanced countries.

The expanding export capabilities of the industrializing countries raise a new set of problems for trade policy. These have so far received relatively little attention. In the first-best world of pure trade theory, the developing countries would specialize in products having simpler technology and greater labor intensity, and the advanced countries would make available their markets freely to the mutual benefit of both. When we introduce immobile resources, uncertainty and other imperfections into the analysis, optimal policies for both sides become less clear, and the addition of political elements pushes us even further frcm the neoclassical solution. In the second- or third-best conditions of the real world, the arguments for diversification of manufactured exports to avoid market uncertainties are probably at least as strong as they are for primary commodities. The second part of the paper provides a framework for this type of analysis.

I. THE CHANGING STRUCTURE OF INDUSTRY AND TRADE

Poorest countries are alike in their extreme specialization in primary production and the absence of modern industry. Their limited demand for manufactured goods is largely satisfied by imports secured through the export of primary products. However, as per capita income rises from $50 to $100, the domestic manufacture of processed foods, beverages, textiles, clothing and other simple commodities is undertaken in response to growing local demand. By the time a country reaches a per capita income of $100, industry tends to approach 20 percent of total commodity production,[3] with its output going almost entirely to the local market. Once this common phase of natural import substitution is completed, however, there is greater diversity in the pattern of industrialization.

Alternative Patterns of Industrial Growth and Exports[4]

As development continues above the $100 income level, there is

_____

3. Industrial production is taken to include value added in manufacturing, the power and water sectors; agriculture and mining comprise primary production; together with construction all these sectors comprise commodity production.

4. The U.N. definition of exports of "manufactures," Total A, has been followed in this discussion. See U.N., *Trade in Manufactures of Developing Countries, 1970 Review* (New York: United Nations, 1971), pp. 1-2.

scope for increasing variation in the forms of specialization. The principal factors affecting the relative rate of growth of industry are a country's size, its geographical location and political affinities, its natural resource endowment and the economic policies followed by its government. Figure 1-1, in which per capita production of industry and primary products is plotted for income levels ranging from $100 to $1,500, clearly indicates the influence of size and natural endowment on industrial development.[5] Thus at one extreme, countries with rich natural resources and a strong comparative advantage in primary exports, such as Venezuela or New Zealand, may progress to high income levels by continuing their traditional orientation to primary production with only a limited development of industry for the domestic market. At the other extreme. countries without a significant resource base for primary exports, such as Japan, Taiwan or Korea, have had to begin specializing in industry for exports at relatively low income levels to earn foreign exchange for further growth.

The observed intercountry uniformity of production patterns can be largely explained by the similarity of changes in the composition of domestic demand with rising income, and the limited possibilities of supplying the rapid growth of demand for manufactured goods through the export of primary products. Both the internal and the external demand for primary products tend to rise less rapidly than income, and a shift from primary production to manufacturing is necessary.

In the past, the composition of exports showed a similar shift from primary to manufactured goods with rising per capita income, but the timing of the shift lagged far behind the change in production. Figure 1-1 indicates that industrial output has tended to equal primary output at an income level somewhat below $400. Figure 1-2 shows that the corresponding point in the composition of exports was reached only at an income level of $900. This tendency for the share of industrial exports to lag was accentuated in the 1950s and 1960s by the widespread adoption of policies favoring import substitution over exports.

The development of industry for the domestic market has been an important factor in a country's ability to export manufactured products. The usual infant industry arguments for protecting

5. These relationships are analyzed by Hollis B. Chenery and Lance Taylor. See "Development Patterns: Among Countries and Over Time," *Review of Economics and Statistics* L, no. 4 (November 1968): 391-416.

domestic industry are readily extended to the learning period in which product quality is raised to export standards and costs are reduced to competitive levels.[6] New industries specifically oriented toward the export market can only develop a comparative advantage after the physical infrastructure and commercial organization have reached a minimum "critical level," and skills and entrepreneurship have been acquired through some domestic production. Recent experience suggests, however, that this critical level can be substantially lowered by appropriate policies.

The development of manufactured exports has also been influenced by resource endowment and country size, which are important determinants of comparative advantage. Resource endowment and country size have been allowed for by classifying countries according to their size and trade patterns into three groups: large countries of over fifteen million population; small countries with relatively high primary exports, generally reflecting favorable natural resource endowments; and small countries with a relatively high proportion of manufactured exports. The last group is of particular interest here, since it consists of countries with poor natural resources which have thus had special incentives to adopt economic policies stimulating the exports of manufactured goods.

The average export patterns for each of these three groups of countries are shown in Figure 1-2 for the year 1968. The effect of a larger domestic market is to permit industries having economies of scale to develop at a lower income level.[7] The level of export per capita varies inversely with country size, being twice as great for a country of five million people as for a country of forty million.

Figure 1-2 is constructed to show per capita levels of exports of both primary and industrial products and hence the composition of total exports. These measures can be combined as an indicator of the shift toward industrial exports. For the average country of ten million population, industrial exports reach a level of $10 per capita at an income level of about $250. At this point, industrial exports are slightly more than 20 percent of total exports. The principal industrial exporters among the developing countries can be identified

---

6. The latter is stressed by Irving B. Kravis. See "Availability and Other Influences on the Commodity Composition of Trade," *Journal of Political Economy* LXIV, no. 2 (April 1956): 143-55; also Staffan B. Linder, *Trade and Trade Policy for Development* (New York: Frederick A. Praeger, 1967).

7. The data available are unfortunately at market prices, and therefore tend to overestimate the share of industry in commodity production in countries in which effective protection is high.

as those having either per capita industrial exports greater than $10, total industrial exports greater than $50 million, or a share of industrial exports greater than 20 percent. The thirty-nine developing countries meeting one or more of these criteria for the year 1969 are listed according to their trade patterns in Table 1-2, and are shown graphically in Figure 1-2.[8]

For the typical small country with high primary exports—represented by the curve *SP* in Figure 1-2—the threshold level of $10 per capita of industrial exports is not reached until income rises to a level of $350 per capita; at that point industrial products represent 10 percent of total exports. Jamaica, Malaysia and the Ivory Coast illustrate this pattern. At the other extreme, a country lacking in primary resources (as shown by the *SM* curve) usually has to attain this level of industrial exports before it can reach a per capita income level of $200. Singapore, Taiwan and Tunisia are three examples.

Large countries have a trade pattern quite similar to the small industry-oriented (*SM*) pattern, but with lower levels of primary exports. The shift in comparative advantage resulting from larger domestic markets has led to earlier import substitution on a broader scale, and hence to exports of intermediate goods and machinery as well as of consumer goods. As will be shown below, the composition of industrial exports tends to be quite different from those of the small countries at the same level of income.

Technology, Skills and Infrastructure

Although industrial growth has been focused on the domestic market to a very large extent, it has led to the accumulation of entrepreneurial skills, the creation of infrastructure in transport and power, and to other external economies that provide a basis for a shift toward industrial exports. Traditional "bazaar" traders have been transformed into business enterprises catering to the needs of manufacturers. New business groups have developed. Also, industrial growth has led to the expansion of auxiliary industries such as printing and packaging, all adding to an improved base for efficient production.

The evolution of entrepreneurial, managerial and technical skills has accompanied the growth of industry. Achievements vary

---

8. This analysis is taken from Hollis B. Chenery and Helen Hughes, "The International Division of Labor: The Case of Industry," in Society of International Development, *Towards a New World Economy* (Rotterdam: Rotterdam University Press, 1972), pp. 75-110.

greatly from country to country, but well-managed firms are evident in increasing numbers in many countries. (In countries with high protection, these intramarginal firms, of course, reap very high profits; some of these profits are being channeled into export promotion by export incentives.)

The level of technology has risen greatly. One of the most frequent criticisms of developing country industries is their failure to adapt technology to the prevailing factor prices. However, from the point of view of competing in exports, the rising level of technological expertise, whether acquired through patents, as part of a direct foreign investment package, or evolved locally, is a recently acquired characteristic for many developing countries.

Technology and management are frequently a part, and often the most important part of foreign investment. Multinational corporations initially invested in developing countries to gain access to markets hemmed in by import restrictions, but they were followed by corporations in search of a cheap production base. This trend grew with the development of electronics in the 1960s and spread to other industries. Some firms originally established in search of markets began to export manufactures on their own initiative or under pressure from host governments. While export limitations still exist, they no longer predominate as they did until the mid-1960s.

For multinational corporations in search of an export base, the cost of capital, as of technology, is often competitive with that in developed countries. But even local sources of capital have become relatively more available in many developing countries. Governments have made public funds available to industry at low cost. Capital has accumulated within firms, and the growth of banks and other capital market institutions has placed manufacturers in developing countries at less disadvantage in capital cost than they were ten years ago.

The greatest change has occurred in the supply and cost of labor. Over the years the industrializing countries have built up a labor force which has not only become accustomed to the regularity of factory work but has also acquired skills, often of a considerable degree. In many countries, rising rates of urban unemployment have given employees better labor selection and also reduced absenteeism. Labor remuneration has risen fairly slowly over the past twenty years, and in many countries productivity has grown faster. Labor costs per unit of output appear to have been falling in many cases while those in developed countries have been rising, so that developing countries achieved a competitive edge in a wide and increasing number of products.

The Composition of Manufactured Exports

We will now examine the composition of industrial production and exports in more detail. In general, light consumer goods and construction materials, particularly those which enjoyed natural freight protection, tended to develop first. These products were followed by consumer durable and some producer goods assembly, and only then by basic and intermediate goods production on a large scale. There are, of course, exceptions, but generally a clear pattern, determined by technology and the similarity of import replacement policies which dominated in the 1950s and 1960s, emerges in inward-oriented countries where domestic demand was the determining factor in industrial development.[9]

By the end of the 1960s a number of the larger countries had built up an industrial structure reaching from nondurable consumer goods through intermediates to basic and capital goods industries. Most of these industries were characterized by excess capacity due to the diseconomies of a limited domestic market and accentuated where groups of foreign investors had been encouraged by high protective duties to enter consumer durable and capital goods industries. Inability to reap economies of scale and low capital utilization were therefore general characteristics, particularly marked in the industries noted. These phenomena have encouraged a diversified entry into exports through marginal pricing by plants demonstrating excess capacity.

The varying stages at which entry into exports takes place add a number of elements to factor intensity in explaining international trade. Restrictions in advanced countries on processed primary and labor-intensive products, such as textiles, in which the developing countries have a comparative advantage, have also influenced the actual pattern of exports. The "international division of labor" is thus tending to be markedly different from patterns expected on the basis of simple theoretical models. Important as comparative advantage is as a principle for determining optimal trade patterns, it has been extremely difficult to forecast in practice.

The late 1960s saw a considerable change in attitudes as country after country turned its attention to exports. The initial develop-

---

9. Chenery and Taylor, op. cit., and Chenery and Hughes, op. cit.

ment of manufactured exports by small countries lacking natural resources has been followed by changing policies in some of the larger and more developed countries, which had locked themselves into their internal markets by high protection. Pakistan was the first of these, followed by Brazil, Mexico, Colombia and a number of smaller countries. The complete list is shown in Table 1-2. The list includes some countries with excellent natural resources, such as Iran and Malaysia, which are looking to exports to reduce the costs of inward-oriented industrialization and to increase employment opportunities. A number of international agencies are now assisting countries to begin manufacturing for export at a relatively early stage of their development.

The rate of export growth of manufactured goods from developing countries has been rising steadily. For the period 1962-67, the average rate of growth was 15 percent, but by the end of the 1960s it was averaging 18 percent per annum.[10] A number of large, relatively heavily industrialized newcomers to exports were already showing high average annual manufactured export growth rates in the late 1960s. The average annual growth rate of manufactured exports for 1967 to 1969 was 36 percent for Spain, 30 percent for Ireland and 29 percent for Mexico; for Colombia and Brazil it was 18 percent and for India it was 16 percent. A number of less industrialized countries starting from a low base also had high growth rates: Iran, 40 percent; Thailand and Ecuador, 32 percent; Ghana, 33 percent; the Ivory Coast, Malaysia and Nicaragua, 23 percent. The principal existing exporters, moreover, also maintained high rates of growth. Thus during 1967-69, Korea's manufacturing exports were still growing at 47 percent, Taiwan's at 37 percent, Hong Kong's at 23 percent and Israel's at 20 percent per annum.

The growth in volume has been accompanied by an even more striking development in the variety of exports. Table 1-1 shows high growth in machinery and transport equipment and in the miscellaneous category. These were the two fastest growing export product groups in the 1960s. They had a 30 percent and 24 percent rate of growth in 1967 and 1968 respectively. Textiles, in contrast, only grew at 8.7 percent in 1962-67, and 9.4 percent in 1967-68.

Further disaggregation indicates that Brazil is exporting clocks to Switzerland, refrigerators to the United States, furniture to Scandinavia, fashion garments to Italy, testing and measuring instru-

---

10. U.N., op. cit., p. 4.

ments to Germany and photo-electric cells to the Netherlands. Iran's exports consist not only of traditional goods such as textiles and footwear, but also sheet glass, trucks and buses. In 1969, intermediate and capital goods accounted for 10 percent of Iran's exports, and a major export program in machine tools and heavy equipment is planned.

The increasing sophistication of manufactured exports with a country's growing export experience, as well as the different levels at which countries begin exporting, are illustrated by Table 1-3, which shows exports of manufactured goods characteristic of "early," "middle" and "late" stages of export. These stages do not merely reflect simple changes in relative factor intensities, but rather a more complex group of explanatory variables which encompass entrepreneurship, technical and managerial skills and marketing ability in addition to factor intensities. For example, while relatively little management and marketing skill is required for the export of low quality cloth, and particularly of gray cloth, the requirements of supplying the clothing market in developed countries on a large scale are quite complex.

With few exceptions there has been some progression in the complexity of manufactured exports. The change in the composition of exports is most marked for countries such as Korea and Taiwan which have made the most sustained export efforts, supporting broad incentive measures with direct assistance programs for exporters. Several late-comers to export orientation—notably India and Brazil—showed little progress during the 1960s, but current indications are of very rapid change and move into technically complex goods, particularly in engineering. In some instances, however, for example in Pakistan, the failure of exports to develop in complexity throws considerable doubt on the efficacy of the export incentive schemes adopted.

These trends suggest that manufactured exports may be able to supply the bulk of the increase in foreign exchange earnings required by the developing countries for the next decade. To determine the demand for foreign exchange, the IBRD has conducted a study of the principal capital and commodity flows, in thirty of the largest developing countries (including Spain, Greece, Yugoslavia and Turkey) which account for some 85 percent of all developing country exports. The results suggest that developing countries will have to raise their export growth from the 7 percent per annum average of the 1960s to almost 10 percent in the 1970s to support a 6 percent rate of growth of gross national product. Assuming an 8 percent per annum increase in mineral fuels and a 5 percent per annum increase in all other primary products, manufactures would have to grow by some 15 percent to yield this total.

AVERAGE ANNUAL GROWTH RATE
(percent)

	Export Earnings	Export Volume	Export Unit Value
Primary Products (except fuels)	5.0	3.4	1.5
Manufactured Goods	15.1	13.4	1.5
Subtotal	9.8	8.2	1.5
Fuels	8.0	..	..
Total exports	9.7	..	..

··Not Available

If the more industrialized of the developing countries are able to perform somewhat better than the 15 percent average, aid funds can be concentrated on the least developed countries, particularly those without significant mineral resources. To achieve adequate foreign exchange earnings for developing countries thus requires a very substantial expansion in exports of manufactures with consequent shifts in international trade patterns and aid policies.

II. MARKETS FOR DEVELOPING COUNTRIES' MANUFACTURED EXPORTS

Table 1-4, showing the growth in developing countries' total manufactured exports by destination, indicates that the developed market economies have been their principal outlets throughout the 1960s. The socialist country markets grew more rapidly during this period, but from a small base. The growth of trade among developing countries lagged throughout the decade, with the exception of Latin America where internal trade growth was high (Table 1-5). Between 1962 and 1968 the developing countries' share of world trade in manufactured goods improved in total, and in each of the three market categories. The data suggest that there have been both income and price elasticity of demand. Many of the goods exported originally came in at relatively low prices to establish a share of existing markets.

Such aggregates cannot, however, throw a great deal of light on the demand elasticities for various types of goods. Table 1-6, showing imports of selected groups of manufactured products from developing countries per $1,000 of gross national product (1969) for market economy countries, suggests that many factors determine a country's propensity to trade, and in particular the propensity to import from developing countries. It is clear that in addition to per capita income, factors such as the size of a country, and trading policies already discussed in relation to exports of developing countries, tend to be the determining influence on import patterns.

Trends in International Trade Policies

The last twenty-five years have been dominated by two divergent and often contradictory trends in world trade. A strong reaction against the nationalist bloc protectionism of the 1930s led to an impetus towards greater freedom in the international movement of goods. The "Kennedy Round" led to substantial tariff reductions on industrial goods, but these mainly benefited developed countries because "sensitive" products, principally textiles, were at the last moment left out of the negotiations; the degree of escalation of effective protection on primary processed products was scarcely affected, and in some cases, indeed increased. The proposed new round of negotiations which is to begin, again under GATT auspices in 1973, is another step in the direction of reducing tariffs on industrial goods, and is to be welcomed as such. The increased variety of manufactured products which developing countries are producing for export is likely to make steps toward free trade in industrial goods of greater importance to them in the future than in the past. However, while developing countries as a bloc will benefit from such moves, the poorer, least developed countries will not. For the latter, conditions of trade in primary processed products and relatively simple, labor-intensive products such as textiles remain of prime importance.

The proposed round of negotiations is, moreover, being viewed with skepticism even among developing countries most likely to benefit, because of the limited role of tariffs in the overall determination of trade patterns. Nontariff barriers to trade have proved far more important than trade barriers in the past decade, and there are many indications that their importance is increasing.

Overt import quotas, particularly those imposed under the international Long Term Agreement on Cotton Textiles, are the best known. The cotton textile agreement was evolved because developed country tariffs on textiles proved no obstacle to efficient developing country producers, and their rigorousness has been increased over the years by the fragmentation of quota size for individual products. It is true that efficient producers, particularly in Hong Kong, have, in a sense, benefited from the quotas by being pushed into upgrading their products, by diversifying production, by investing in other developing countries and by entering new export fields. However, the fulfillment and overfulfillment of quotas as well as the relatively slow rate of growth of textiles and clothing exports suggest that both the formal and informal restrictions on quotas have quite significantly limited the developing countries' actual expansion.[11] Relative late-comers to the quota system, for whom textiles are the easiest point of entry into the manufacture of exports, have been mostly affected. Such new-comers' share of the developed countries' market typically represents only a few weeks' use of installed capacity.

While textile quotas have been in the forefront of quota formulation, quantitative restrictions, particularly of the "voluntary" type, are now becoming more pervasive. Indeed, a growing mood in the more highly industrialized developing countries suggests that no sooner do they attain a real comparative advantage in a mass consumption industrial product, tool up for expanded production, and invest in a trading network, than their endeavors are cut short by formal or informal quota arrangements. Thus footwear restrictions followed textile quotas, and the next consumer item in which developing countries appear to have achieved a comparative advantage, flatware, is subject to quantitative restrictions in most European countries and the United States. Quantitative restrictions are not restricted to labor-intensive consumer goods. Brazilian steel producers, for example, claim that they have had to limit sales in the United States to small lots under threat of import restriction.

The situation has been easier for products which are inputs into final goods manufactured in the developed countries, whether they be footwear or electronic components, and this has been particularly true where multinational corporations have been producers of both components and final products. Such imports are harder to identify, and they are often difficult to restrict because of the difficulty of specifying a variety of continually changing components. Another

---

11. The evolution of problems of the developing countries' textile exports are discussed by Geoffrey Shepherd. See "Exports of Cotton Textiles from Developing Countries to the European Economic Community and the United Kingdom, 1958-1967." IBRD Working Paper no. 111, mimeographed (Washington, D.C., 1971). See also Lucy Keough, "Export of Cotton and Cotton-Type Textiles from Developing Countries to the United States," IBRD Working Paper no. 122, mimeographed (Washington, D.C., 1971).

reason, however, may be that until recently such products, despite their importance as exports to a selected group of developing countries, have not had a major impact on domestic production. At present, however, there is a growing opposition to such imports in the United States. It is expressed formally in proposals for legislation seeking to eliminate double tax and value added tariff privileges for international corporations and, perhaps more seriously and effectively, through direct trade union pressure on the multinational corporations. Several corporations have responded, to some extent at least, by modifying or in some cases even abandoning plans for further operations abroad.

Several conclusions which emerge from the current situation require further elucidation. Perhaps the most worrying aspect is that moves for quantitative restrictions have appeared at relatively low levels of developing country exports to developed country markets. There appears to be a much stronger degree of opposition to developing countries on the ground of "unfair labor" competition than to developed country exports. In the light of rapidly increasing productivity in developing countries, such fears warrant far more serious investigation than they have received.

Quantitative restrictions are only a small part of the disabilities imposed on developing countries in international trade. The prevalence of restrictive practices by corporations is another. Most of the developing countries are still dependent on the technology of developed countries, and only the most advanced are now reaching the point where they can avoid bottlenecks in supply by copying or innovating. Many developed countries also have balance of payments problems, and some are guilty of mercantilist attitudes. Thus a developing country firm competing with a developed country parent, associate or even supplier for third country markets, frequently finds that it cannot obtain necessary components for export, or that they are priced unreasonably in direct competition for contracts between a developed country parent and developing country subsidiary. While export limiting franchises are not now as prevalent as they were in the 1950s and early 1960s, many still exist. Some multinational corporations are producing in lowest cost countries, but others prefer to concentrate as much as possible on production in their home country.

The price structure of international trade also tends to favor developed country exporters. There are many reasons why a large range of industrial products tends to be traded internationally at prices below those at which they are sold domestically. The desire to achieve the maximum benefits of economies of scale where these are important in production, supported by monopoly or a strong oligopoly in the domestic market which makes discriminatory pricing possible, is often the most important economic reason, applying to a variety of products from typewriters to steel and petrochemicals. Developing countries with small domestic markets are in a relatively unfavorable position for such discriminatory pricing, although some of the smaller countries without domestic industry potential have been able to benefit from discriminatory pricing by buying their raw material inputs cheaply; sophisticated export incentives such as "temporary admission" are now beginning to make this possible even for countries which for economic or political reasons wish to develop the basic input industries.

Discriminatory pricing has also been heavily encouraged, in both developed and developing countries, by measures exempting exporters from indirect and direct taxes, by special government subsidized export credit provisions and, in some cases, by cash subsidies. A variety of motives lie behind these measures. Where protective levels are relatively high—whether in developed or developing countries—it has, of course, been argued that the remission of duties on inputs, plus some general margin of assistance, is necessary to offset the protective bias against exporters. In some instances, however, through multiple exchange rate systems, credit and cash subsidies, exporting has been even more heavily subsidized than domestic production, achieving exports at considerable social economic cost, and without encouraging exporters to upgrade the quality and sophistication of their products. Some measures, such as the subsidy of long-term credits, begun as a competitive device by developed countries finding it difficult to enter foreign markets, have spread widely. Interest terms of 2.5 percent per annum with a repayment period of twenty years are not unusual for socialist countries which favor this form of competition in capital goods markets. GATT has accepted drawbacks of indirect taxes on the grounds that taxes should be paid at the point of consumption rather than at the point of production. But many such taxes contribute directly to lowering production costs through expenditure on the infrastructure, and can be argued to be a part of total production cost. As the discussion about the incidence of direct and indirect taxes is by no means resolved, it can also be argued that direct taxes, as well as indirect taxes should be subject to remission, and some countries, indeed do exempt exporters from such taxes. Under present GATT conventions, however, countries which prefer, for social reasons, to collect their taxes directly rather than indirectly, are under a disability.[12]

Increasing attention is now being focused on the transport cost component of international trade which often provides a form of subsidy on the part of fleet-owning countries. Conference freight rates are also coming under examination because they appear to favor the movement of manufactured goods from developed market economy countries to developing countries over those from other developing countries.

The Growth of Regional Markets

In Europe, the movement toward regional integration—sometimes running parallel, but often counter to a growing concern with world trade—has been a strong current in international trade during the last twenty years. Thus potential gains of lower tariffs have been reduced by the increased polarization of trade within the EEC trading bloc. Further tariff reductions would tend to reduce the tariff advantage of this trend, but a reduction of nontariff trade barriers within the enlarged EEC, and possibly in the West European Free Trade Association, could prove inimical to developing countries' trade expansion.

Developing countries are, of course, not alone in their fears of a closing European market. Japan and the United States, and other high-income countries, notably Canada and Australia, are equally concerned. In contrast, those of the developing countries which already have a "special relationship" to the EEC, or which hope to obtain it, may gain from the channeling of trade through duty free access to the developed country markets which "special relationships" promise. The overall effect is yet to be determined. At present there is little evidence that the African countries with special association to the EEC have benefited in terms of manufactured exports. It is true that for the most part these African countries are the poorest and least industrialized developing countries, with little export capability to date. However, there are now signs of policy change. A number of African countries are actively seeking subcontracting and other export opportunities. In the meantime the

---

12. The nontariff barriers to trade listed here are by no means exhaustive. See Robert E. Baldwin, *Nontariff Distortions of International Trade* (Washington, D.C.: The Brookings Institution, 1970).

reverse preferences which "special association" countries grant EEC countries, together with the tendency to continue trading through established channels, have meant that the developing countries have not always been able to purchase goods at minimum c.i.f. cost. They have also eschewed the advantages of low-cost imports, which might have been competitive inputs for exports, by import bans on low-priced East Asian manufactured exports. Developing countries not in special association with the EEC, that is, Asian and Latin American countries, are potentially at a disadvantage vis-à-vis the special association countries. Those which have in the past enjoyed privileged access to the United Kingdom market in terms of tariffs, quotas and trading association are likely to lose by the new arrangement.[13]

The Generalized Preference Scheme

For many economists the likely benefits of the generalized preference scheme have always been the subject of considerable skepticism. It has been argued that a minor rate of exchange adjustment by the developing countries could have achieved the same results. It has been recognized for some time that the relatively low tariffs of industrial countries were not an obstacle to countries which had been able to develop an export capacity. The scheme, it is true, has been limited in application to the EEC and Japan, and has only been in operation since 1971, but it already appears that most of the skepticism has been justified, and there is some danger of unfulfilled hopes turning to further discouragement. This is not to deny that the discussions, and then the introduction of the scheme turned the attention of some developing countries, which had previously shown little inclination to export, to export markets. However, it was found that the August 1971 devaluations and revaluations by developed countries were much more important than the tariff preference margins, that the problems of breaking into new markets were far more complex than the rather simple views implicit in the generalized preference scheme indicated and that concentrating on product and market development and on appropriate incentives to exporters vis-à-vis the domestic market, remained the real issues.[14] While it is true that the scheme has not had time to operate fully,

13. For a discussion of reverse preferences, see Naimeh Hadjitarkhani, "Preferential Trade Arrangements between Developing and Developed Countries, and Among Developing Countries," IBRD Working Paper no. 155, mimeographed (Washington, D.C., 1973).

14. David Wall, "The Commonwealth and the Generalized System of Preferences," mimeographed (a study prepared for the Commonwealth Secretariat, London, 1972).

this also means that its limiting aspects—the quotas—have not had to be widely invoked. Whether further energy should be devoted to the extension of preference schemes, or whether more appropriate steps may be taken to assist developing countries to gain access to developed country markets needs to be considered.

Regional Integration and Trade Among Developing Countries

The move toward regional markets has been paralleled among developing countries. There are some twenty nominal regional arrangements,[15] though to date only a handful can be said to be at all effective. The most advanced of these arrangements, the Central American Common Market, has, moreover, been showing signs of serious difficulty for some time. The principal arguments for regional integration have been well stated and require no repetition,[16] but more inquiry is required to indicate why, in contrast to the EEC, these regional markets have in general failed. Abstracting from the political difficulties, the principal reasons appear to lie in the chimerical nature of the economies of scale argument when applied to grouping of countries with low per capita incomes. The ensuing "economies of scale," as exemplified by the Central American Common Market, are still not adequate for reasonably efficient technological practice, and thus encourage high protection. A reduction of internal tariffs then tends to be matched by high external protection, with its concomitant problems. It is theoretically possible to postulate an arrangement maximizing the benefits of internal economies of scale with a minimum level of protection which could, at the same time, be offset by export incentives. However, in practice such arrangements are difficult when several countries are involved. It can on the other hand be argued that Singapore's separation from Malaysia in 1965, which forced a change from inward to outward manufacturing orientation was extremely fortunate, while Costa Rica and Nicaragua might have developed more rapidly independently of the Central American Common Market. Perhaps the most serious difficulty—the tendency of industry to locate in the most developed area and country of a developing country market grouping—can only be met with temporary transactions and various types of border taxes, as the East African Economic Community found. In practice these largely negate the common market concept.

---

15. Hadjitarkhani, op. cit., Table 6.
16. See Bela A. Balassa, *Economic Development and Integration* (Mexico City: Centro de Estudios Monetarios Latino Americanos, 1965).

Perhaps the aspect of trade which requires maximum stress, in relation to growing trade among developing countries for industrial goods, is the power of competition rather than the advantages of complementarity which underlie arguments for programming large units internationally. The advantages of the EEC were increasing competition — increased economies of scale followed from the specialization which such competition made possible. Thus, countries with the highest growth rates tend to be characterized by the high degree of imports and exports of the same type of goods. The importance of increasing trade gains through competitiveness moreover suggests that greater benefits are likely to accrue to the reduction of trade barriers among developing countries at similar levels of development. It is true that trade liberalization is more difficult for developing countries than for developed countries. The initial impact of increased mutual trade would likely be reflected in dislocation leading to unemployment, and each job is precious in countries with large and growing unemployment problems. The costs of adjustment which European countries could bear relatively easily in the full employment period of the 1950s and 1960s are problems of great difficulty for developing countries.

It seems likely, nevertheless, that developing countries have some of their most important trade gains to make in breaking down mutual tariff barriers which are much higher than those presented by developed countries. The first step in this direction was taken by a tripartite trade agreement applying tariff reduction on specified goods by Egypt, Yugoslavia and India. In 1971, sixteen developing countries, all at a relatively advanced level of industrial development, began discussions under GATT auspices for progressive multilateral reductions in tariffs which could lead to a long-run increase of trade among them. A major area for additional opportunities for mutual trade could grow from new developmental strategies seeking to move away from the patterns of consumption and production of the developed countries to those better suited to the economic and social needs of the developing countries. This would encourage the adaptation of production techniques to developing country factor costs and new opportunities for trade in capital goods among developing countries would be created.

III. CONCLUSIONS

Our analysis of the trends of exports of manufactures from developing countries suggests that their volume and variety can be expanded quite rapidly to meet foreign exchange needs. The particular resource characteristics of individual developing countries, the import substituting policies they have pursued, as well as the barriers to their exports erected by developed countries, have led to an export product mix which departs significantly from the labor-intensive, low-technology type of goods that a simple trade theory model would have predicted. While the actual exports emerging do not conform to a low labor cost advantage, they have other merits. There is less danger that commodity terms of trade will turn against developing countries in the trade in manufactured goods than might have been the case with a concentration on labor-intensive exports.[17] A greater variety of exports is likely to enable the developing countries to exploit income elastic and price elastic markets more easily than a narrower product range might have. Unfortunately, in spite of the growing variety of export products, a tendency toward the limitation of developing country imports, as distinct from other imports, may be seen in developed country policies. Such limitations tend to come into effect at relatively low levels of penetration of developed country markets. The nature of the developed countries' demand, of their trade policies, and of the possibilities of trade among developing countries thus requires much more attention than it has yet received.

---

17. Income terms of trade could have, of course, continued to improve, even if this were the case for some time. In the long run, however, elastic supply and inelastic demand could have led to a decline in income as well as commodity terms of trade.

FIGURE 1-1

COMPARISON OF PRODUCTION PATTERNS

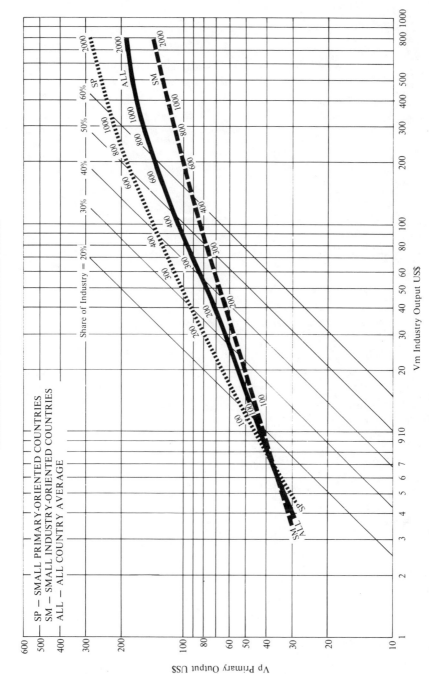

SP – SMALL PRIMARY-ORIENTED COUNTRIES
SM – SMALL INDUSTRY-ORIENTED COUNTRIES
ALL – ALL COUNTRY AVERAGE

Vp Primary Output US$

Vm Industry Output US$

SOURCE: "Uniform Analysis of Development Patterns", Chenery, H.B., Elkington, H. and Sims, C.: Harvard University Ec. Dev. Rep. No.148(1970).

FIGURE 1-2
COMPARISON OF TRADE PATTERNS

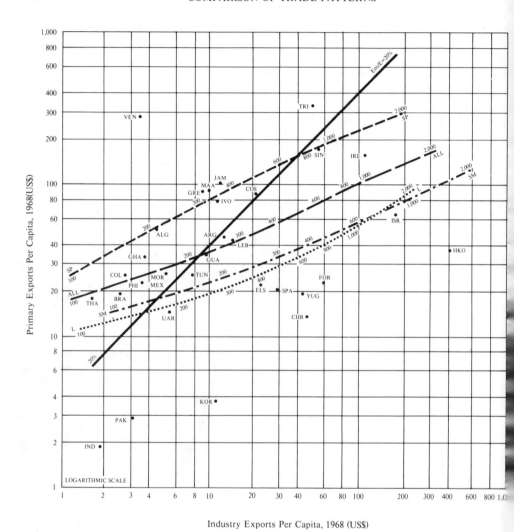

Industry Exports Per Capita, 1968 (US$)

SOURCE: "Uniform Analysis of Development Patterns", Chenery, H.B., Elkington, H. and Sims, C.: Harvard University Ec. Dev. Rep. No.148(1970).

TABLE 1-1

PRINCIPAL DEVELOPING COUNTRY EXPORTERS OF MACHINERY
AND MISCELLANEOUS GOODS: 1962, 1967 AND 1968

	Exports in Millions			Average Annual Growth Rate	
	1962	1967	1968	1962-67	1967-68
	Mns. US$			Percentage	
Machinery and Transport Equipment (SITC 7)					
Yugoslavia	85.1	63.0	87.0	−5.7	38.0
India	7.6	16.9	41.1	17.3	243.2
Brazil	8.1	28.0	30.4	28.0	8.5
Taiwan	3.6	22.8	29.2	45.0	28.0
Hong Kong	13.5	20.5	23.3	8.7	13.6
Mexico	4.7	11.8	11.1	20.0	−6.0
Argentina	3.3	9.7	11.0	24.0	13.4
Israel	1.6	7.5	9.1	36.0	21.3
Republic of Korea	0.3	5.5	5.8	80.0	5.4
All Developing Countries	417.0	855.0	1,029.0	15.4	30.4
Miscellaneous Manufactures (SITC 6 + 8 − 65 and 68)					
Hong Kong	105.1	134.5	151.0	5.0	12.2
India	27.3	72.4	102.1	21.5	41.0
Taiwan	21.7	75.4	70.8	28.0	−6.5
Israel	19.1	46.3	55.9	19.4	20.7
Yugoslavia	28.5	33.0	39.0	3.0	18.1
Brazil	2.4	36.5	29.3	72.5	−20.0
Mexico	13.0	22.7	24.8	11.8	9.2
Malaysia	15.8	21.6	··	6.4	··
Pakistan	4.9	10.8	17.1	17.1	58.3
Chile	5.3	19.2	15.4	29.3	−20.0
Colombia	2.2	10.9	12.9	37.8	18.3
Republic of Korea	1.2	8.5	12.2	48.0	43.5
United Arab Republic	··	7.5	··	··	··
All Developing Countries	1,415.0	3,338.0	4,137.0	18.6	23.9

·· Not available.

SOURCE: U.N., *Trade in Manufactures of Developing Countries, 1970 Review* (New York: United Nations, 1971).

TABLE 1-2

SOME CHARACTERISTICS OF LEADING DEVELOPING COUNTRIES IN MANUFACTURING AND EXPORTS

		GNP/N 1970	N 1970	M_v/C_v 1968	E_m/E 1969	E_m/N 1969	E_m/Mo 1969	E_m 1969	Average Annual Growth Rates 1960-69			E_p/N 1969
									E_m	M_v	GNP/N	
		(US$)	(Millions)	(%)	(%)	(US$)	(%)	(Mns. US$)	(%)	(%)	(%)	(US$)
Large Countries[a]												
INA	Indonesia	80	115.57	13.70	19.65	1.36	0.30	157.18	22.0	1.20	0.80	5.54
PAK	Pakistan[b]	100	130.17	19.20	56.35	3.03	15.58c	384.05	17.70	7.60	2.90	2.35
INA	India	110	538.13	20.70	51.91	1.85	6.30d	975.10	11.40	2.50	1.10	1.72
THA	Thailand	200	36.22	27.90	11.68	2.35	7.89e	82.58	9.80	8.10	4.70	17.79
PHI	Philippines	210	36.85	32.00	13.82c	3.64	4.52	130.75c	22.00f	4.30	1.90	22.71
UAR	U.A.R.	210	33.33	42.10	28.10	6.44	7.21c	209.30	15.80	...	1.20	16.47
KOR	Korea (Rep.)	250	31.79	33.00	76.20	15.25	13.77	474.30	66.50	14.20	6.40	4.77
TUR	Turkey	310	35.23	30.90	12.28	1.91	0.97c	65.96	6.20	8.60	3.40	13.65
COL	Colombia	340	21.63	33.00	10.65c	2.97c	1.88	59.48c	31.40f	4.50	1.50	24.94c
IRA	Iran	380	28.66	22.31g	3.95e	2.95e	3.20e	76.31e	6.60h	11.00f	4.90	71.57e
BRA	Brazil	420	92.76	56.30	17.54	4.39	1.39	405.49	12.60	6.60	1.40	20.64
YUG	Yugoslavia	650	20.54	60.60	74.33	53.73	30.28	1,096.08	35.00	7.80	4.60	18.55
MEX	Mexico	670	50.67	61.20e	25.12	7.35	6.36c	359.59	14.30	10.00	3.50	21.89
SPA	Spain	1,020	33.65	56.80	62.29	35.99	7.23	1,184.11	20.20	7.40	6.50	21.78
ARG	Argentina	1,160	23.21	61.80	21.81	15.29	0.80d	351.66	14.00	4.30	2.60	54.80
Small, Primary Trade-oriented												
*COR	Congo (Zaire)	90	18.80	9.30	0.98c	0.30c	10.00d	5.00c	21.00f	12.70	0.20	29.94c
MOR	Morocco	230	15.50	23.40d	21.97	7.06	2.50d	106.62	3.80	2.70	3.40	25.07
*PAR	Paraguay	260	2.38	32.60	7.18	1.59	4.05	3.66	-1.00	4.00	1.00	20.56
RHO	Rhodesia (Southern)	280	5.31	42.00d	34.59i	30.66i	21.75i	137.98i	16.30	5.50	0.40	57.98i
*ECU	Ecuador	290	6.09	32.30	1.41	0.44	0.58	2.59	-0.50	5.40	1.20	30.54
ALG	Algeria	300	14.33	26.70	18.32	12.31	13.68	171.14	-3.50	16.30	-2.80	54.89
GHA	Ghana	310	8.64	35.90	28.84	10.48	23.72d	86.95	32.60	3.70f	0.00	25.84
IVO	Ivory Coast	310	4.94	19.10	16.73	15.48	22.60c	75.84	40.80	11.20	4.70	77.00
*DOM	Dominican Republic	350	4.07	38.40	3.75c	1.52c	1.15e	6.08	-5.60f	3.60	0.40	38.94c
GUA	Guatemala	360	5.19	35.40	27.76c	12.82c	16.56c	62.93c	29.00f	7.90	1.90	33.42c

MAA	Malaysia	380	10.95	19.10[d]	13.18	16.40	16.34	175.53	12.40	12.00[f]	3.80	108.02
NIC	Nicaragua	430	1.98	31.00	14.41	11.76	4.90[d]	22.29	29.00	12.00	3.50	69.66
COS	Costa Rica	560	1.73	37.40[e]	20.11	22.45	8.99	38.17	28.00	..	2.90	89.14
JAM	Jamaica	670	1.89	35.60	13.79	17.88	3.52[c]	33.98	8.90	4.40	3.00	111.72
CHI	Chile	720	9.78	56.20	6.26	6.70	1.47[e]	66.90	3.50	5.60	1.70	104.27
*URU	Uruguay	820	2.89	51.20[d]	28.10	3.28	3.42[c]	9.51	1.80	..	-0.80	65.80
TRI	Trinidad & Tobago	860	1.03	30.90	13.97	66.34	36.41[c]	66.34	20.50	10.10	3.80	408.25
VEN	Venezuela	980	10.40	29.70	1.52	4.32	0.50[c]	43.18	60.00	7.00	2.50	284.96

Small, Manufacturing Trade-oriented

TUN	Tunisia	250	5.08	38.00	27.49	9.30	9.91	45.55	3.90	6.20	2.10	24.51
ELS	El Salvador	300	3.53	38.70	34.55	20.54	18.20	69.83	22.00	9.00	1.90	38.91
CHR	Taiwan	390	14.04	45.90	79.26	60.29	23.85	831.93	50.90	13.50	6.30	15.77
PER	Peru	450	13.59	39.40	30.43[c]	20.57[c]	11.45[c]	263.26[c]	14.60	2.90[f]	1.40	47.01[c]
LEB	Lebanon	590	2.73	48.70[e]	59.68	39.14	5.40[d]	101.76	35.00	..	2.10	26.43
POR	Portugal	660	9.64	61.60	79.55	70.69	29.07	678.64	11.60	7.90	4.90	18.16
*PAN	Panama	730	1.46	37.20	2.61	2.20	0.99	3.08	41.00	10.70	4.80	81.98
SIN	Singapore	920	2.08	65.90	28.03	217.08	31.19	434.16	6.40	19.00	4.50	557.23
HKO	Hong Kong	970	3.96	87.50	88.60	494.69	73.11[j]	1,929.30	15.00	14.30	8.70	63.65
GRE	Greece	1,090	8.89	39.60	49.76	31.32	7.20	275.66	29.30	6.20	6.20	31.52
IRI	Ireland	1,360	2.94	40.00[d]	44.67	132.44	16.12[c]	384.09	13.20	6.70	3.50	164.00
ISR	Israel	1,960	2.91	61.50	40.56	104.85	11.61	293.57	15.90	11.90	5.30	153.64

* Do not meet the criteria mentioned on page 7f.
a Over 15 million population in 1960
b Includes Bangladesh
c 1968
d 1966
e 1967
f 1960-68
g 1969
h 1960-67
i 1965
j M_o refers to 1970

GNP	Gross National Product in US$ at 1970 Market prices
N	Population in millions in mid-1970
M_v	Gross value added in manufacturing, which may be at factor cost or market prices; sometimes data may include other economic activities
C_v	Gross value added in commodity production, which includes agriculture, mining and manufacturing, as well as electricity, gas and water
E_m	Exports of (nonresource-based) manufacturing, defined as Total A in UNCTAD, *Trade in Manufacturing of Developing Countries: 1970 Review*
E	Total merchandise exports
M_o	Gross value of output in manufacturing, usually in large size establishments only
E_p	Exports of primary products; E_p has been obtained as a residual, i.e., $E-E_m$.

NOTE: The average annual growth rate of E_m is calculated at current prices, whereas the same for M_v and GNP/N are computed at constant prices. As far as possible, local currencies have been used in the time series for E_m and M_v.

PRINCIPAL SOURCES: U.N., *Yearbook of International Trade Statistics,* 1960; U.N., *Yearbook of National Accounts Statistics,* vol. 1, 1969 and vol. 1, 1970; U.N., *The Growth of World Industry,* vol. 1, 1970; IBRD, World Tables, January 1971; IBRD, *Atlas,* 1972; country data.

TABLE 1-3

THE CHANGING COMPOSITION OF EXPORTS FROM SELECTED DEVELOPING COUNTRIES

	Currency Unit	Year	Early[b] Industries	Middle[c] Industries	Late[d] Industries	Exports of Manufactures	Total Merchandise Exports	Share (%) of Total Merchandise Exports		
								Early Industries	Middle Industries	Late Industries
Large Countries[a]										
BRA Brazil	Mn. US$	1960	62	19	5	86	1,269	4.9	1.5	0.4
		1968	173	56	76	305	1,881	9.2	3.0	4.1
COL Colombia	Th. US$	1964	15,964	12,502	3,455	31,921	548,136	2.9	2.3	0.6
		1968	18,800	23,532	20,794	63,126	558,278	3.4	4.2	3.7
IND India	Mn. Rs.	1960	2,649	151	68	2,868	6,239	42.5	2.4	1.1
		1968	4,288	356	1,854	6,498	13,542	31.7	2.6	13.7
KOR Korea	Th. US$	1960	2,894	1,988	88	4,970	31,832	9.1	6.2	0.3
		1968	104,173	72,485	163,532	340,190	455,399	22.9	15.9	35.9
MEX Mexico	Mn. Pesos	1960	638	427	253	1,318	9,541	6.7	4.5	2.6
		1968	687	1,368	1,198	4,762	15,721	4.4	8.7	7.6
PAK Pakistan	Mn. Rs.	1960	451	14	54	519	1,905	23.7	0.7	2.9
		1968	1,400	43	265	1,709	3,430	40.8	1.3	7.7
PHI Philippines	Mn. US$	1961	25	15	15	55	530	4.7	2.8	2.9
		1968	30	53	41	124	946	3.1	5.6	4.4
SPA Spain	Mn. Pesetas	1961	8,071	4,520	6,021	18,613	42,575	19.0	10.6	14.1
		1968	19,961	11,182	38,721	69,864	111,244	17.9	10.1	34.8
YUG Yugoslavia	Mn. Dinars	1960	31,818	15,158	60,149	107,125	169,848	18.7	8.9	35.4
		1968[e]	2,241	1,526	8,192	11,959	15,796	14.2	9.6	51.9
Small Primary Oriented										
COS Costa Rica	Th. US$	1962	256	1,124	240	1,620	92,970	0.3	1.2	0.3
		1968	6,827	13,016	14,148	33,991	170,821	4.0	7.6	8.3
Small Industry Oriented										
ISR Israel	Th. US$		20,619	32,335	33,955	86,909	245,280	8.4	13.2	13.8
		1968	61,850	77,694	125,628	265,172	639,642	9.7	12.1	19.6
SIN Singapore	Mn. S$	1960	240	290	331	834	3,477	6.9	8.3	8.7
		1968	339	268	512	1,120	3,891	8.7	6.9	13.2
CHR Taiwan	Mn. NT$	1962	1,941	1,696	1,080	4,717	8,738	22.2	19.4	12.4
		1968	6,923	5,539	10,953	23,414	31,578	21.9	17.5	34.7
Other Industrializing Countries										
IRA Iran	Mn. Rials	1960	..	..	..	..	..	..	..	..
		1967	4,644	634	489	5,767	146,200	3.2	0.4	0.3
TUR Turkey	Mn. Liras	1961	232	22	24	278	3,121	7.4	0.7	0.8
		1968	363	91	2	455	4,467	8.1	2.0	0.0

[a]Over 15 million population in 1960.
[b]*Early industries* are those which supply essential demands of the poorest countries, require simple technology and increase their share of GNP relatively little above income levels of $280 or so; they consist of food, leather goods and textiles.
[c]*Middle industries* are those which double their share of GNP in the lower income levels but show relatively little rise above income levels of $400-$500; nonmetallic minerals, rubber products, wood products and chemicals and petroleum refining fall in this category.
[d]*Late industries* are those that continue to grow faster than GNP up to the highest income levels; they typically double their share of GNP in the later stages of industrialization (above $300); this group includes clothing, printing, basic metals, paper and metal products.
[e]New dinars introduced on January 1, 1966 with a value of 12.50 new dinars per US$ (1 dinar = 8.00 cents).

SOURCE: Calculated from U.N., *Yearbooks of International Trade Statistics, 1961-69,* (New York: United Nations, 1962-1970).

TABLE 1-4

EXPORTS OF MANUFACTURES (SITC 5-8 LESS 68) FROM THE
WORLD AND FROM DEVELOPING COUNTRIES: 1962, 1967 AND 1968

	Destinations			
	World	Developed Market-Economy Countries	Developing Countries	Socialist Countries of Eastern Europe and Asia
Exports from (Mns. US$)				
World:				
1962	75,110	44,008	19,272	9,593
1967	123,160	79,392	28,148	14,971
1968	141,200	92,084	31,976	16,485
Developing Countries:				
1962	3,204	1,680	1,324	175
1967	6,427	3,583	2,167	611
1968	7,592	4,517	2,428	623
Annual Growth Rates (%)				
World:				
1962-1967	10.4	12.5	7.9	9.3
1967-1968	14.6	16.0	13.6	10.1
Developing Countries:				
1962-1967	15.0	16.4	10.3	28.4
1967-1968	18.1	26.1	12.0	2.0
Share (%)				
Developing Countries:				
1962	4.3	3.8	6.9	1.8
1967	5.2	4.5	7.7	4.1
1968	5.4	4.9	7.6	3.8

SOURCE: U.N., *Trade in Manufactures of Developing Countries, 1970 Review* (New York: United Nations, 1971).

TABLE 1-5

EXPORTS OF MANUFACTURES (SITC 5-8 LESS 68) FROM DEVELOPING COUNTRIES: 1962, 1967 AND 1968

				Destination				
					Developing Countries			
Exporting Countries	World[a]	Developed Market-Economy Countries	Socialist Countries of Eastern Europe and Asia	Total[b]	Latin America	Africa	Western Asia	South and East Asia
All Developing Countries								
Value of exports (Mns. US$)								
1962	3,204	1,680	175	1,324	185	262	143	691
1967	6,416	3,583	611	2,167	421	398	271	1,010
1968	7,592	4,517	623	2,428	519	423	304	1,077
Annual growth rate (%)								
1962-1967	14.9	16.4	28.4	10.3	17.8	8.7	13.7	7.9
1967-1968	18.3	26.1	2.0	12.0	23.3	6.3	12.2	6.6
Latin America								
Value of exports (Mns. US$)								
1962	279	176	5	91	79	—	—	10
1967	750	365	17	364	343	4	1	7
1968	905	444	20	441	421	5	1	9
Annual growth rate (%)								
1962-1967	21.9	15.7	27.7	31.9	34.1	—	—	−6.8
1967-1968	20.7	21.6	17.6	21.2	22.7	25.0	—	28.6
Africa								
Value of exports (Mns. US$)								
1962	358	234	17	125	6	87	22	4
1967	683	377	88	205	5	160	26	12
1968	774	402	108	239	4	190	31	11
Annual growth rate (%)								
1962-1967	13.8	10.0	38.9	10.4	−3.7	12.8	3.4	24.9
1967-1968	13.3	6.6	22.7	16.6	−20.0	18.8	19.2	−8.4
Western Asia								
Value of exports (Mns. US$)								
1962	225	171	8	68	1	12	31	18
1967	558	363	14	170	5	29	90	37
1968	623	415	16	180	7	29	90	40
Annual growth rate (%)								
1962-1967	16.9	16.3	11.9	20.1	38.0	19.3	23.8	15.5
1967-1968	11.6	14.3	14.3	5.9	40.0	—	—	8.1
South and East Asia								
Value of exports (Mns. US$)								
1962	1,886	937	42	901	60	136	61	612
1967	3,468	2,045	133	1,263	39	184	106	915
1968	4,224	2,709	148	1,367	57	189	126	951
Annual growth rate (%)								
1962-1967	12.9	16.9	25.9	7.0	−8.3	6.2	11.7	8.4
1967-1968	21.8	32.5	11.3	8.2	46.1	2.7	18.9	3.9
Yugoslavia								
Value of exports (Mns. US$)								
1962	344	112	104	128	31	21	28	47
1967	706	234	355	114	14	13	45	39
1968	748	271	331	145	16	9	53	63
Annual growth rate (%)								
1962-1967	15.5	15.8	27.8	−2.3	−14.7	−9.2	9.9	−3.7
1967-1968	5.9	15.8	−6.8	27.2	14.3	−30.8	17.8	61.5

[a]World total includes special category exports, ships stores and bunkers and other exports of minor importance whose destinations could not be determined. Therefore, the world total, in general, is greater than the sum of exports to developed market-economy countries, Socialist countries of Eastern Europe and Asia and all developing countries.
[b]The sum of exports to Latin America, Africa, Western Asia, South and East Asia and Yugoslavia may not add up to the total of developing countries because of rounding, or because there are exports to other developing countries, mainly islands in the Caribbean and Pacific areas.

SOURCE: U.N., *Trade in Manufactures of Developing Countries, 1970 Review* (New York: United Nations, 1971).

TABLE 1-6

IMPORTS OF SELECTED GROUPS OF MANUFACTURED PRODUCTS FROM DEVELOPING COUNTRIES BY INDIVIDUAL DEVELOPED MARKET ECONOMY COUNTRIES PER $1,000 OF GROSS NATIONAL PRODUCT: 1969 (U.S. CENTS)

Importing country or area	Total*	Food	Drink and tobacco	Wood and furniture	Rubber	Leather and footwear	Textiles	Clothing	Chemicals	Pulp, paper and board	Non-metallic	Iron and Steel	Worked non-ferrous metals	Engineering and metal	Miscellaneous light manufacturing
Total 21 Developed Market-Economy Countries	346.8	44.5	9.3	37.5	1.4	17.9	55.3	58.4	22.3	2.3	3.3	10.7	9.3	39.5	35.0
EEC Total	401.7	62.8	30.6	43.0	1.3	31.4	56.2	51.4	31.6	5.4	3.4	20.0	23.2	24.5	16.8
Belgium-Luxembourg	336.7	53.7	7.3	69.5	0.6	16.8	66.6	14.9	21.8	4.7	2.0	13.0	26.3	21.0	18.5
Federal Republic of Germany	483.6	64.4	9.2	39.2	2.3	35.4	88.2	114.5	21.9	3.6	3.1	11.7	32.9	30.8	26.6
France	335.3	65.5	82.5	29.0	0.5	24.8	23.4	10.3	29.4	4.5	0.9	26.8	18.2	11.4	8.1
Italy	297.3	27.3	1.0	47.2	0.8	48.8	41.5	3.5	26.3	11.6	5.4	34.0	20.2	20.9	8.9
Netherlands	699.9	161.7	5.4	104.5	1.8	9.6	84.5	84.2	123.2	3.2	13.5	1.7	5.5	71.3	29.7
EFTA Total	596.0	93.2	10.2	61.5	3.6	41.3	98.5	114.2	47.1	3.4	2.1	4.9	17.1	50.1	48.5
Austria	342.8	40.8	2.0	30.2	3.8	25.1	57.9	46.1	25.4	2.8	5.1	24.0	16.5	43.8	19.5
Denmark	415.0	28.9	5.9	95.8	2.3	21.9	77.3	101.8	16.3	0.5	0.9	0.7	10.1	19.9	32.7
Finland	220.1	32.2	5.7	10.0	2.5	11.2	30.5	17.0	20.6	0.2	0.2	4.1	7.7	59.6	18.6
Norway	330.1	17.2	4.3	44.4	2.0	9.1	30.7	107.4	7.0	—	2.1	2.0	15.6	67.9	20.4
Portugal	250.2	33.9	0.7	43.5	0.6	12.6	46.4	9.6	27.8	0.4	12.3	3.5	0.6	36.3	22.2
Sweden	410.3	32.6	6.0	26.7	0.8	25.3	56.9	170.4	17.7	0.1	2.4	7.7	20.4	17.3	26.0
Switzerland	459.0	87.9	22.4	24.6	0.7	16.9	90.5	76.9	50.8	1.1	1.9	3.1	13.0	29.0	40.3
Iceland	175.0	:	:	:	:	:	38.6	56.7	:	:	:	:	:	:	:
United Kingdom	790.7	138.5	12.1	82.6	5.3	60.7	132.0	129.6	67.2	5.9	1.6	3.4	19.7	64.9	67.2
Australia	438.4	22.5	7.3	63.2	2.6	10.1	176.5	38.9	14.6	4.6	7.0	4.9	—	32.2	54.1
Canada	331.7	50.7	5.9	31.3	1.1	16.2	74.8	78.3	13.3	0.3	3.5	0.2	0.9	22.1	33.3
Ireland	552.5	69.8	8.9	143.0	:	4.7	118.5	10.6	79.8	:	:	:	:	29.8	55.9
Japan	196.0	35.2	2.0	23.0	0.4	8.3	30.9	10.2	21.6	2.3	0.5	25.0	11.7	12.1	12.7
New Zealand	746.2	34.4	11.9	25.4	4.6	18.5	521.2	12.9	13.7	0.1	0.9	14.6	0.3	61.0	27.6
United States	289.1	27.4	1.1	31.5	1.1	8.9	41.3	57.6	13.6	0.7	3.8	6.2	1.9	50.2	43.7

*Excludes pearls, gemstones, nonelectric power-generating machinery, ships and boats (except from Yugoslavia), silver, petroleum and related products and unworked nonferrous metals.

SOURCE: U.N., Trade in Manufactures of Developing Countries, 1970 Review (New York: United Nations, 1971).

Comment

Göran Ohlin

Anyone contemplating the trade prospects of developing countries in the 1970s is likely to raise much the same issues: the need for a rapid expansion of exports, the special importance of manufactures and the resistance to imports of manufactures by the rich countries. My principal question is only whether the gloomy mood of the paper is quite warranted.

The defensive attitude in industrialized countries is to some extent a measure of the remarkable success which some developing countries have scored in exporting manufactures in recent years. It is striking to what a large extent this accelerated growth of exports has occurred outside the field of early and simple manufactures such as textiles and footwear. As the paper comments, there has been a most impressive expansion of exports in the machinery and miscellaneous categories.

The question now is whether in the 1970s there is going to be the same resistance to these new types of exports as has been mounted, for example, against textiles. We know rather little about the process of structural change and the refusal to abide by the market in rich countries. I would nevertheless suspect that the situation in the engineering industries is going to be rather different. Large parts of the textile industry have been completely wiped out, and resistance has naturally enough been rather desperate. In engineering, the absorption of structural change promises to be a great deal easier, if only because the possibilities of shifting resources into other products are greater, sometimes even within the individual firm and definitely within the industry, so that there is little reason to fear an absolute contraction.

Another circumstance which presumably facilitates the expansion of exports of nontraditional manufactures is that much of it is under the aegis of multinational companies. For better or for worse, this makes the absorption of such exports easier than if they come from independent producers.

There is now more and more talk about adjustment assistance policies which are seen as a way of overcoming the resistance to imports of developing country manufactures. So far, however, we have not seen any example of genuine adjustment assistance policy.

There has been much talk of it but what we have had are a number of ad hoc responses to the many strains and stresses in industrial structure. We have regional policy, sectoral policy, industrial policy and so forth, but one of the questions before this seminar is whether it makes sense even to imagine a specific adjustment assistance policy designed to cope exclusively with the displacement of production by foreign trade. I submit that it is futile to expect such specific policies, not only because it is politically unthinkable but also because it is intellectually impossible to draw a hard and fast line between the displacement arising from trade and that which arises out of rapid growth and structural change in general.

One may nonetheless ask to what extent structural change in rich countries will emanate from trade expansion and to what extent it will simply be a consequence of rapid increase in productivity, shifting demand patterns et cetera. Caroline Miles has much to say about this in her paper, which confirms my impression that the overall problem of structural change has been overwhelmingly dominant in the past and is likely to be so in the future, and that the adjustment made necessary by the growing export capacity of developing countries is very small in comparison.

This is not to say that such adjustment cannot be very painful if it is concentrated in one narrow sector. But that seems less likely to the extent that the growing diversification of developing country exports spreads the impact over a wider range of products.

If adjustment policies are likely to be pursued in the context of structural and regional policies, as I suspect, one has reason to ask precisely how they are likely to be designed. If one takes a gloomy view, one must expect them to take the character of neoprotectionist, nontariff barriers. Instead of phasing out production to make room for new imports, it may to a large extent stimulate modernization and conversion and try to make producers competitive again. Measures of this kind are also, if past experience is any guide, quite likely to be uncoordinated and ad hoc, reflecting no particular logic or concern and benefiting no one except the industry immediately involved. What the advocates of adjustment assistance seem to have in mind are policies involving actual buying out of capacity in order to close it down, but the prospects of such policies being carried out seem relatively small.

Measures of this kind would affect trade among the rich countries at least as much as imports from developing countries and a great deal of effort to coordinate these and other nontariff barriers to avoid or at least reduce discrimination is therefore necessary. There is also already much talk about creating multilateral safeguards. Such developments would presumably also be of benefit to developing countries; at least they would more or less know what they could count on.

Occasionally there is discussion about the income and price elasticity of various developing country manufactures in rich countries. But the important elasticities, it seems to me, are not the ones pertaining to total demand but the ones faced by the foreign producer, that is, the elasticity of substitution of imports for domestic products. Both in recent times and in earlier economic history, one frequently observes how high these elasticities can be and how rapidly the switch to new sources of supply can be made. In textiles in the sixties, we have the dramatic example of Japan, and for that matter the way in which Germany broke into the export markets before World War I. When comparative advantage was secured it only took a reasonably short time to move into other markets. Is there any particular reason why this process should be checked more effectively now than in the past?

There are perhaps a number of reasons why the rich countries are now more sensitive. In particular, the labor force is much less likely to tolerate excessively rapid displacement and has a much bigger political influence. Nevertheless, one must remember that by historical standards trade has probably never been so free and that a stupendous amount of adjustment has been taken in stride in the last decades.

This is also a warning not to exaggerate the extent to which even protectionist structural assistance policies are likely to hold up the process of change. The biggest instance of modern structural policy is, of course, agricultural policy, but all that agricultural policy achieves is to slow up by some indeterminable amount the rate at which resources are shifted out. I would expect this also to happen in manufactures. Even on pessimistic expectations about the scale and nature of neoprotectionism, the impact is likely to be only marginal. It will be a matter of slowing down the rate of contraction and decline in some industries, not of halting it.

This is why I find the authors' pessimism excessive and offer instead a qualified optimism based on the experience that protectionism means only a marginal modification of the pattern of world economic change.

Comment

Paul Streeten

It is often said that one of the most important conditions for successful adjustment assistance is full employment in the developed countries, because if you have full employment you provide jobs for those thrown out of employment by freer access of imports. One could go further and say that full employment is not enough: overfull employment is necessary, so that there are always more vacancies than men seeking jobs. We know from wartime experience that overfull employment creates strong pressures to reemploy men and speedily eliminates so-called frictional, structural and technological unemployment, however intractable it had appeared to be in peacetime. In addition and by the way, overfull employment widens the range of choice of workers and enables women and old people to choose between leisure and part-time work—a welfare gain that is rarely cited in this context by the advocates of widening the range of consumers' choices.

But this is not the point I wish to make here. The point I do want to make—and this is usually omitted from discussions of this problem—is that, however desirable full employment policy is on other grounds, while it removes some reasons, it creates its own new reasons for trade restrictions and for limiting access of labor-intensive products from low-income countries.

I can think of at least three (not equally good) reasons for restricting access in conditions of full employment; perhaps there are others. The first and most obvious reason is the fact that full employment policies (and even more so overfull employment policies) make for stronger inflationary pressures and therefore tend to aggravate balance of payments problems if the country's inflation is greater than average. Balance of payments difficulties resulting from inflation are perhaps not good reasons, but they are often used as excuses for trade and foreign exchange restrictions. This is one reason (and I think there are others) why I do not think that we either can or should hive off the international aspect, and concentrate on the national aspects. The two are closely related and we shall succeed in adopting proper national adjustment policies only if we do so in an appropriate international framework. An attempt to solve adjustment problems on a purely national basis will run into these international obstacles.

My second reason is that very often full-employment policies are interpreted (some might say misinterpreted) as policies that guarantee particular groups of workers their present jobs. Transitional unemployment is not easily distinguished by its victims and their representatives from lapses from full employment. While it would be clearly a mistake to identify full employment in a growing and changing society with a prescriptive right to existing jobs in particular occupations and regions, I have some sympathy with those who argue that change and transition have social costs. The better off a society is, the more it can afford to forego extra increases in production for the sake of less disruption, particularly if such disruption continues to be called for repeatedly or if its benefits are mainly enjoyed by others. If full-employment policies are interpreted in this way, they will present a new motive against admitting more imports.

The case made by the trade unions in this context is twofold. First, there is the cost of disruption and temporary unemployment and the temporary duration will be prolonged if repeated adjustments are necessary. Second, there are the changes in domestic income distribution resulting from freer access. Even if full employment were maintained, more imports of labor-intensive goods would, according to a well-known theorem in international economics, tend to reduce the incomes of unskilled and semiskilled workers. Unless we have a perfect system of bribes, it is understandable that these groups resist the removal of trade restrictions. The implications for income distribution are quite distinct from those for unemployment. This is an important point to bear in mind for those advocating adjustment assistance. Here again, there need be no distributional loss in conditions of general unemployment.

My third point is that, in conditions of full employment, the terms of trade argument for tariff restrictions, also called the optimum tariff argument, comes into its own. If resources are unemployed, the nation can export more and simultaneously raise everybody's income. But in conditions of full employment national gains may be at the expense of other nations. In particular, it becomes important to keep the prices of imported necessities as low as possible. I do not suppose that many governments impose tariffs in order to improve their terms of trade and, in any case, trade restrictions imposed for other reasons must often lead to higher barriers than those indicated by the optimum tariff argument. Nevertheless, there may be conditions in which the restrictions are not above the optimum and when governments are reluctant to remove them because this would lead to a deterioration in the terms of trade below the optimum. To wish to avoid a loss is rather different from trying to snatch a gain at the expense of others.

It should be remembered that all three reasons (or excuses) for trade restrictions in conditions of full employment are *national* arguments which can be met by appropriate *international* rules or arrangements. It is for this reason that I do not see how we can divide the subject too neatly between monetary and trade problems. Rules about international adjustments and possibly about international compensation are necessary in order to remove the nationalistic demand for trade and payments restrictions, particularly on labor-intensive products, in conditions of full and overfull employment.

My second comment refers to the typology part of the paper. It is very helpful to have a typology of developing countries which provides a guide to the choice between "outward-" and "inward-looking" policies and between manufacturing and primary production for export. Such a fourfold typology takes into account size of country and income levels (relevant to economies of scale in import substitution) and resource endowment (relevant to primary exports). It might also provide a qualification to indiscriminate enthusiasm in advocating manufactured exports for all countries, irrespective of market size, stage of development and resource endowment. The lessons to be learned from Hong Kong, Taiwan, Israel and Korea are valuable but cannot be directly applied to India or Nigeria.

The point I should like to make here is to suggest that it might be useful to include in the categories of this typology some of the variables that we do not normally regard as strictly economic ones. The level of administrative skills will determine the ability to change the structure of production through public policies and the time this is likely to take. The political structure and the interests and allegiances of the ruling elites will determine what actions are possible and where the political and sociological constraints operate. The particular constellation of interests and power will itself be the result of the economic, social and political history of the country. A country which has industrialized through import substitution behind high tariff walls will have to be treated differently, in analysis and prescription, from one which has neither started to industrialize nor departed from the principles of free trade. All policies are bound to hurt some interests. Regimes will differ according to their readiness to violate the interests of urban industrialists or large land-owners. It would be naive to assume that policies operate in a sovereign sphere outside and above the social system. Policies often decried as stupid by the standards of economic textbooks are the expression of powerful interests in a society.

Thus, the limits to import substitution set by the size of the domestic market, the wealth of indigenous raw materials and foodstuffs, the level of human skills, the efficiency and honesty of the civil service and the interests reflected by the ruling elite, are important determinants of the appropriate strategy. A typology along such lines will qualify easy generalizations from the recent experience of successful exporters. If the heavy emphasis on manufacturing import subsitution in the 1950s went too far in one direction, the new conventional wisdom of advocating "outward-looking" policies of manufactured export promotion may have gone too far in the other direction.

We tend to identify far too readily the interest of a country with the interest of its government, whereas in fact policies which on this assumption appear to be rather stupid turn out to be comprehensible when they are seen to promote the interest of a particular powerfully organized group. Such an analysis embracing social and political forces is useful not only for purposes of analysis but also for policy-making. Policies can be framed more effectively when it is clear where the common interests lie and where one can recruit or harness supporting political power groups, some of them running across national boundaries.

The paper is also concerned with the limits of export expansion. They are to be found not only in such obvious obstacles as tariffs and nontariff barriers and the absence of appropriate design or export credits or sales and marketing organizations; they lie also in a host of policies pursued by importing countries, such as the direction of their research and development expenditure, their science policy, government contracts, tax structure et cetera. By propping up industries that ought to contract or by seeking, through research and development, to defend our dwindling comparative advantage, we impede the export efforts of the developing countries, often under the name of "adjustment assistance."

I take it that it is not part of our agenda to focus on the difficulties on the side of supply such as why do some countries but not others enjoy entrepreneurial capacity that can spot quickly products the demand for which is highly income elastic and how do they readily discover new and expanding markets for their products. Some of these limitations lie somewhere between supply and demand—for example, the institutional arrangements that facilitate supply to meet demand.

But in addition to the problems of the *limits* of export growth, there is the important problem of the *distribution* of the gains from more manufactured exports. On this issue the paper does not say very much. The distribution of gains is itself related to the various strategies for export promotion. Thus, to invite the multinational corporation may overcome some obstacles by helping to organize sales and marketing, to raise credit and, in the case of the vertically integrated firm, to overcome resistance to imports. Against this must be set the fact that a part of the profits and other incomes will be accruing to foreigners. In the extreme case, the host country will gain only the wages of unskilled labor previously unemployed, while the whole surplus of the value of the product of that labor goes abroad.

There are also problems of internal distribution within the developing countries. How do shares of the various groups within these countries differ according to different export strategies? Relevant points are raised in one or two places. Oligopolistic price formation may mean that cost reductions are not passed on either to consumers in rich countries or to workers and other suppliers in poor countries. Again, tax concessions, tariff concessions, trading estates and other incentives to attract foreign companies have national costs, as well as benefits. For a nation to try to encourage its own indigenous entrepreneurs and management in export industries by various export incentives may, on the other hand, present precisely the same danger in the outward-looking strategy that we have been warned against so much in the inward-looking strategy of import substitution; that is, although the country is increasing its exports and earning more foreign exchange, it may find that the value added is negative or very low, lower than in alternative lines of production. There is also the danger that a generalization for all developing countries of the recommendation to increase exports will tend to lead to a lowering of the income terms of trade, so that a rising volume of exports leaves some countries with few benefits. All this is only to suggest that, in addition to discussing the limits to export expansion, we should consider the distribution of the gains from increasing exports, both internationally between exporting and importing countries and internally between different economic and political groups.

2

Trade, Investment and Labor, and the Changing International Division of Production

Harry G. Johnson

It has become generally accepted in recent years that the underlying philosophy concerning the promotion of economic development that prevailed during the 1950s and 1960s has proved inadequate in many crucial respects, in the light of adverse experience. Its inadequacy is in large part associated with an initial misunderstanding of both the scale and the complexity of the development problem.

That philosophy largely reflected the experience of the great depression of the 1930s. What happened in the 1930s, as we now know from subsequent research and analysis, was a massive collapse of international liquidity and of domestic money supplies, triggered by the failure of the United States Federal Reserve Board to prevent a sharp collapse of the United States domestic money supply, but communicated to the rest of the world directly via the effects of the United States's depression on world trade and indirectly via the vulnerability of the gold exchange standard to liquidity crises. In the industrial countries, owing to the rigidity of wages and prices characteristic of the industrial system of production, the collapse of demand resulting from the liquidity collapse led on the one hand to mass underutilization of installed capacity and a consequent collapse of net investment which worsened the situation; on the other hand, to mass unemployment. In the primary producing countries, where production proceeds on the basis of flexible prices and producer incomes, there was a collapse of prices and incomes, carrying with it an increase in the real burden of interest on past debts, at the same time as the supply of new loan capital for "infrastructure" investment virtually dried up.

In the advanced countries, mass unemployment of men and machines developed to complement one another in the production process, strongly suggesting that production could be vastly increased by somewhat more intelligent economic management, centralized to remedy the apparent failure of the capitalist market competition system to match unemployed men and unemployed resources. The apparent success of Russia on the one hand and Germany on the other in providing full employment reinforced this belief. In the less developed regions, the collapse of primary product prices, and its consequences in raising the real burden of interest payments on past debts, strongly suggested the necessity of planned industrialization financed by domestic resources as the only way of raising living standards. Planning was, moreover, conceived in terms of planning a national economy, assumed usually to be of continental size and variety of resources and virtually self-sufficient.

The plausibility of these views after the Second World War was initially facilitated by the fact that the war produced a massive shift toward self-sufficiency in both the belligerent and the nonbelligerent countries, and required centralized economic planning of natural resource use and careful management of foreign exchange reserves by the major belligerents. Subsequently, they were further reinforced by the success of the Marshall Plan in reconstructing the European economies and establishing them on a path of rapid economic growth by means of a relatively small injection of capital and technical assistance.

The philosophy of development promotion inherited from the 1930s Great Depression experience has proved extremely disappointing—though one must not overlook the fact that in most of the developing countries concerned a process of self-sustaining growth has been successfully started up, even though the rates of growth are not generally spectacular enough to satisfy the policy-makers. The actual methods of planning have generally been extremely inefficient, with respect to both the promotion of growth and the effective utilization of currently available capacity. Self-sufficiency and "the infant industry" argument have been disappointing in results, usually because applied by countries with too-small market areas. Industrialization has frequently proved a bad prescription for this reason and also because, in a generally prospering world economy, primary products have regained their comparative advantage. In addition, it has not produced the expected growth of employment and more equal income distribution hoped for. Finally, development aid has been disappointing for a variety of reasons, of which the mixed motives for aid-giving, the absence of factors complementary with capital funds and technical assistance, and the trivial magnitude of the real resource flows involved relative to the size of the problem, are the most general.

All this suggests the need to rethink the philosophy of development inherited from the special political and economic circumstances of the 1930s, and to return to a more fundamental philosophy looking to the working of longer-run economic forces making for the stimulation and diffusion of economic development in the world economy.

I. COMPETITION AND ECONOMIC GROWTH

Put very crudely and briefly, the forces in question are the classical forces of competition. If there were freedom of movement of goods across distance and cultural barriers to trade, freedom of movement of capital to natural resources, cheap labor supplies and markets and free movement of labor to higher-wage regions, there would be both maximum stimulus to economic growth and maximum diffusion of it.

This general proposition has to be qualified, however, in various important respects — respects which make it impossible to maintain (except, perhaps, in constructing a straw man to knock down) that laissez faire would suffice to produce an ideal world. First, as regards trade in goods, distance costs in moving goods from production point to market may mean that labor costs and incomes in particular locations will have to remain relatively low in order to attract the capital required to produce the goods and employ the labor; while the economic, social, and other costs for labor moving to higher-wage areas may prevent labor from moving to where the markets and the capital are. This factor would give rise to regional wage differences, and possibly also regional unemployment differences of a persistent kind, but would not by itself give rise to growing wage inequalities. On the contrary, as has happened in the experience of developed countries with high factor mobility, the levels of wages rise more or less in step, even though the differentials remain; the differentials may even narrow as general incomes rise. Note in passing that competition can only be expected to tend to equalize prices for the same productive contribution, involving the same labor skill or the same amount of capital invested. Incomes per capita will vary with the possession of labor skill, and the ownership of capital per capita. This brings us to another and more serious qualification: the influences that tend to make regional wages abnormally low (and regional unemployment rates abnormally high) may create a vicious circle of increasing unequal incomes per capita among regions. Specifically, initially low wages and high unemployment rates may reduce both the incentives to acquire skills and the ability to finance their acquisition, and also involve barriers of both inadequate skills and resources and cultural differences in work attitudes, discipline and so on to migration to higher-wage regions.

One should note in this connection that governmental policies or other acts of man, well intentioned as they may seem to the political and social process in the context of reducing inequality, may aggravate the problem in the long run. For example, trade unions, acting ostensibly to raise wage standards in poor regions but effectively to protect themselves from low-wage competition, may help to create a social milieu of relatively high unemployment rates in those regions and induce labor attitudes that make these workers relatively unattractive to outside or even local capitalists as prospective employees. Similarly, minimum wage laws and social security systems geared to the higher-wage regions may contribute significantly to creating a social environment inimical to efficient and disciplined reliably full-time work. Regional policies of subsidizing firms to make do with an awkward labor force may also contribute, by perpetuating inefficient practices and attitudes that would otherwise be forcibly cured by penury and migration in search of better opportunities.

A further major problem in the field of labor supply and migration has become increasingly apparent in recent years, as a result of the experience of both the less developed countries and the advanced countries (notably the United States) with the general problem of trusting for the relief of poverty to migration from poor to rich regions, and economic centers. The process cannot work, and may even worsen the poverty problem, if the people of the poorer regions simply multiply more copiously as some are drawn off into the more prosperous regions and sectors. This problem has two dimensions, in both contexts—the growth of an urban unemployed army, culled from the rural sector, and the continuation of poverty in the rural sector and/or in the backward industrial sectors. The problem calls for a two-pronged attack. One is designed to restrain the rate of population growth in the poor sectors, both rural and urban. (There is a well-known historical generalization that metropolitan areas only maintain and increase their populations by immigration from the country.) The other is to provide through education the skills required for the rural and backward-sector industrial populations to fit into the higher-wage and more rapidly advancing sectors. The two attacks have to go together, because the cost of the necessary education is high and largely has to be borne by the richer sectors, and because population restraint programs are only likely to be successful if they produce clear economic gains for those conforming to them. Unfortunately—to put the point in perhaps unnecessarily technical terms—children tend to be regarded by their parents as producers' goods in the rural sector and as consumers' goods in the urban-industrial sector, so that the one sector has incentives to breed an oversupply while the other has ample economic incentives for family limitation.

There is a final and very difficult problem which has been emerging both from experience and from research on industrial organization and international trade—the problem created by current institutional arrangements for producing and applying new industrial technology. The general principle stated above about the growth-promoting and growth-diffusing functions of competition assumes that everyone has access one way or another to comparable technology—through competition in the supply of goods embodying such technology, or through migration of either capital or labor or both, or through the free availability of knowledge in written form or in the "oral tradition." But society is faced with a dilemma—that the production of new knowledge costs resources, and investment in it must be paid for somehow, but that optimization of its use requires that it be freely available to all potential users. The uneasy compromise society has chosen, at least for most commercially useful knowledge, is to grant a limited monopoly to the inventors of new knowledge, protected either by patents or by commercial secrecy, and trust to time and competition gradually to erode the monopoly. The result is both an alliance of technological superiority with the ownership of capital, especially in the large national and multinational corporation, which generates political and social tensions, particularly in less developed countries playing "host" to direct foreign investment in order to acquire better technology; the persistence of long technological lags among the more and the less advanced countries both reflects the slowing down of the diffusion of new technology by monopoly, and preserves inequalities of factor prices. One should observe, however, that such technological lags among nations may reflect the existence of barriers to the free movement of goods, capital and labor, rather than anything inherent in the nature of technology itself. If, for example, there were no barriers to the free movement of goods, one would expect production with a new technology to locate itself in regions with the lowest cost of factors of production; and if capital were free to move, these would be the regions with the lowest labor costs. But with barriers to trade on both sides, the transplantation of technology for production for export back to the home market is impeded; production for sale in the market of the "host" country becomes profitable only when factor prices, tariffs, or income levels make it profitable—and the transplant can easily be uneconomically premature.

II. COMPETITION AND DEVELOPMENT

The foregoing presents a general picture of how competition would tend to promote and diffuse world economic growth. It should be reiterated that it would still leave plenty of problems in fulfilling various people's standards of Utopia, and in particular that if emphasis is placed—as some have recently come to place it—on equality of income distribution rather than on growth of income per capita as the essential definition of development, there is no reason to believe that competition will produce results considered acceptable. Competition means equality of opportunity for those comparably placed, and a tendency for equality of returns for comparable inputs into production. Equality of income distribution means equality of shares in the overall output, regardless of contribution, which is a very different thing. It may be pointed out in this connection that those who are now criticizing economic development for its failure to reduce inequality are criticizing methods of promoting economic development that were on the whole either deliberately designed, or politically warped, to generate inequality as a means of providing incentives or rewards for growth. Moreover, many of those who are now vociferous critics of the failure of development planning to produce greater equality of income distribution and a more pervasive satisfaction of "basic human needs" were in the past equally vociferous advocates of the need for centralized planning to increase the rate of economic growth; one senses a change of intellectual fashion without a change in underlying nationalistic objective, reflecting the failure of development planning to deliver results it was never intended to produce, and perhaps also the growing disillusionment in the western world with the "quality of life" produced by national affluence.

To turn from general principle to the development problems of this decade, we may note that the development strategy of the past has paid very little attention to the beneficial effects of competition in promoting it. To caricature it slightly, but not ridiculously so, it preserved and did not seriously question the prevailing restrictions on the mobility of goods, labor and capital—restrictions whose level was sharply levered upward in the interwar period, and in the case of agricultural trade in the postwar period as well. Instead, the strategy relied on offsetting the effects of these restrictions by allowing the less developed countries to impose fresh restrictions on their imports from (and exports to) the advanced countries on the strength of the ancient "infant industry" argument, suitably generalized into an "infant economy" argument, and transferring capital and technology to them in the form of "foreign aid"—including some subsidization on both sides of private capital investment, especially direct investment. Two things have gone wrong with this strategy.

First, it has come to be recognized that industrialization for most countries has to be based on the export market rather than on import substitution. This has been reflected both in export subsidization of a notably indiscriminate and generally inefficient kind, and in the demand for preferences for less developed country exports in the markets of the developed countries—which seems in practice likely to mean the restriction rather than the expansion of export opportunities.

Secondly, the willingness of the advanced countries both to give direct foreign aid as capital and technical assistance and to subsidize private direct investment through their own tax systems or to tolerate subsidization of it by the less developed countries, has been drying up—and, as mentioned, the direct resource transfers were never in any case very significant in relation to the size of the problem. (They also contained important elements of protection for domestic interests, disguised as help to the poor countries.)

The implications for the future are that development will have to rely relatively more, and perhaps virtually exclusively, on the classical mechanisms of market competition; for these to be successful in promoting development, they will have to be consciously assisted and promoted by reforms of both national policies and the structure of the international economic system.

At this juncture, the most important reform almost certainly lies in the field of international monetary organization. Specifically, the international monetary system needs to be reformed to provide—and insure that nations actually use—more efficient and smoothly operating mechanisms of adjustment. For it is the balance of payments disequilibria that result from a defective set of adjustment mechanisms that face deficit countries with the "dilemma case" choice between a deficit and a domestic inflation of income and employment, or the need to arrive at some combination of the two. The obvious way out is to try to improve the balance of payments by interventions in the already restricted international flows of goods and capital, or to improve domestic employment by further restriction of imports. The chronic deficits resulting from a faulty adjustment mechanism induce and are held to justify resort by advanced nations to such devices as "voluntary" export restrictions, nontariff barriers to trade and controls on capital exports, which interfere with the process of diffusion of economic development. Balance of payments deficits induced by currency overvaluation, uncorrected by the appropriate devaluation, it may be noted, also lead to policies in the less developed countries that may be inimical to their growth—for example, indiscriminate import substitution and export promotion, and indiscriminate bidding at times for foreign direct investment whose immediate capital contribution helps the balance of payments and whose ultimate productive activity it is hoped will strengthen the current account. A better adjustment mechanism would remove the justification at least for the more extreme of those resource-allocation-distorting and growth-diffusion-impeding policies.

There also needs to be a substantial movement in the direction of genuinely free world trade. This is a complicated negotiation problem for many reasons, of which three are most important. One is that any such negotiation will have to include international trade in agricultural products, since various nations have varying interests in such products as compared with industrial products. But agricultural protectionism is much more explicitly an income-redistribution and poverty-relief policy than industrial protectionism. Further, government-intervention to protect agriculture includes not only quotas and similar arrangements in addition to tariffs, but also subsidies to exports as a means of disposing of farm surpluses not domestically marketable at the support-price levels. Thirdly, the negotiations will have to deal with nontariff barriers to trade, which have become both more visible and employed by governments to an increasing extent, as tariff barriers to trade in industrial products have been negotiated downward. One might even argue that governments have been willing virtually to eliminate quotas and negotiate down tariff barriers on industrial products because they have increasingly realized that these methods of intervention are far less efficient and effective in securing the objectives of protection than more direct methods such as subsidization through tax reliefs or offsets of, for example, modernization of equipment, research and development expenditure and investment in depressed regions, or more generally through governmental provision of research and development as part of "science policy."

If the advanced countries are effectively to open their markets to imports from the less developed countries, it will be necessary for them to devise both domestic adjustment assistance programs and safeguards against disruption of domestic markets, production and employment by too-rapid acceleration of specific categories of exports from the less developed countries. Both are necessary and complementary—a reasonable and politically acceptable adjustment program must be designed for some expected maximum rate of displacement of domestic production by imports, which can only be insured by some sort of safeguard against market disruption, while safeguards against disruption can only be designed to allow a reasonable expansion of imports, consistent with broadly liberal principles of international competition, if adjustment assistance is provided on a fairly generous and consistent scale. (It is unreasonable, in the light of past experience, to insist that there should be no safeguards against market disruption and that the whole burden of adjustment should fall on adjustment assistance. In practice, not only will this result in demands in the advanced countries for some other form of protection against market disruption, but it implies that the whole burden of adjustment to changes in comparative advantage should be borne by the importing [advanced] countries.)

The danger with both adjustment assistance and safeguards against disruption is that each may become a new instrument of protection in disguise. For safeguards this is obvious. But adjustment assistance can easily take the form of subsidies to equipment modernization, upgrading of labor skills and so on which keep the assisted industry in apparently competitive but actually subsidized existence. This danger could be substantially reduced by the negotiation of a code of international principles covering the joint use of the two policies.

Thirdly, there is the need to devise some sort of international code governing relations between the national state and the multinational corporation. Much of the difficulty in this area stems from what I consider an outmoded political and economic ideology that identifies the corporation both with being alien and the ownership of capital pure and simple. The assumption of alienness is one party's view of the difference in the decision-taking domain between the government of a nation-state and the management of a corporation; the multinational corporation may well prove a far better servant of both the political and the economic interests of mankind than governments elected (sometimes merely self-appointed) as the administrators of what a particular national constituency currently considers to be its own interests. The identification of the corporation with the ownership of capital ignores the role of the corporation in producing, applying and transmitting knowledge. Nevertheless, there are bound to be problems and tensions when on the one hand large corporations have the power—by taking actions of a widely varying degree of legitimacy to topple small governments—and when governments from time to time find it necessary—for immediate reasons of growth or the balance of payments or resource exploitation—to make bargains with large corporations which they (or their successors) are later under political pressure to renegotiate for more favorable terms to themselves. If the process of promoting growth by the diffusion of more advanced technology is to be enlisted in the service of world economic development, the corporation, as the major instrument to this end in the modern world, should be given a reasonably settled and accepted place in the system of international economic relations.

III. THE MOVEMENT OF LABOR

Finally, my assignment calls for me to discuss the role of labor movements in changing the international allocation of production.

(I interpret "labor movements" in the sense of international mobility of labor; the "labor movement" in the sense of trade unions may militate against the diffusion process both by demanding protection against imports and by seeking to get wages raised in less developed countries.) In the eighteenth, nineteenth and early twentieth centuries, international movements of labor were probably at least as important as capital and technology movements in promoting growth and change. One thinks of both the vast outflows of people, skilled and unskilled, from Europe to the "regions of recent settlement" and the colonies, and the flows of nonwhite labor within and between continents. In connection with the latter, however, one has to remember the population question, and note that for various reasons expanded economic opportunities were largely — though not entirely — soaked up by an expansion of the numbers that could be supported at an acceptable minimum standard of living. This fact, in turn, has been largely responsible for the clamping down of immigration barriers in the advanced countries, largely to prevent or control competition of immigrants with domestic workers used to far higher standards of living, and also for the clamping down of immigration barriers among the less developed countries, and in even more extreme form the expulsion of racial and religious minority groups from them. Such expulsions are usually motivated by the desire to benefit the majority group in the short run by some form of expropriation of the property of the expelled and the opening up of economic opportunities created by the forced vacation of them by those expelled. In the longer run, the effect is almost invariably to reduce productivity and efficiency. (It does, however, sometimes have the incidental beneficial effect of forcing the advanced countries to admit to participation in their affluence immigrants who otherwise would not be allowed in.) Relaxation of the severity of the restrictions imposed by the immigration laws of the advanced countries, and especially of the discrimination now exercised in favor of educated and skilled immigrants and against unskilled immigrants, by permitting permanent or long-period entry of the less skilled, could help to accelerate the process of technological diffusion. (In this respect, the influx of large numbers of southern European workers into the EEC under labor permits will probably have a significant long-run effect in modernizing the Mediterranean.)

A final point pertains to professional and technical labor. The international circulation of "human capital" in the form of such people, both as students and on foreign missions or managerial assignments, is an important aspect of the process of diffusion of technology in a broad sense. Hence efforts to restrict this circulation for nationalist reasons—for example, by imposing quotas on foreign students or by insisting that a high proportion of the top management of affiliates of foreign firms operating in a country must be nationals of that country—are fairly certain to impede the diffusion process.

IV. ADDENDUM: TRADE LIBERALIZATION AND UNITED STATES SKILLED LABOR

One of the main recurring issues of the trade controversy is whether trade liberalization by the United States can be injurious to the welfare of skilled American labor. It is obvious that if, in the short run, skilled and unskilled labor cooperate in production, trade liberalization and other changes that displace domestic production by imports cause short-run unemployment of both types of labor, and so are adverse to the interests of existing labor in the industry affected. This provides the case for adjustment assistance and safeguards against market disruption. The more important longer-run question is whether, after reallocation of production and the labor force have been made, skilled labor may still be harmed. This question is treated in very sketchy outline here.

As a preliminary, several points concerned with unionization need to be noted. First, "union members" are not coterminous with "skilled workers," because a substantial fraction of the labor force is not unionized and because "general" unions contain both skilled and unskilled workers. For the latter reason, particularly, harmful effects on union members may reflect harmful effects on unskilled rather than skilled workers. Second, as H. Gregg Lewis has shown,[1] the economic effect of unions is to establish a monopoly premium (of the order of 10 percent) for union wages over the wages of comparably skilled workers in nonunionized occupations; hence, harmful effects on union workers may be socially beneficial in eroding a position of monopoly privilege that is inconsistent with the principles of competition. Third, union officials, whose existence depends on membership dues reflecting their services to members in organizing and enforcing this monopoly, stand to lose from reductions in employment and union membership even though, after the resulting redeployment of labor, the former members themselves would be better off.

1. H. Gregg Lewis, "Relative Employment Effects of Unionism," *Industrial Relations Research Association Proceedings* 16 (December 1963): 104-15.

For related reasons, union officials are likely to be far more concerned about losses of jobs (and dues) in the import-competing section of their industry than attracted by the prospect of gains of jobs in the exporting section of their industry—and not impressed at all by the prospect of gains of jobs in exporting industries organized by another union.

These considerations apart, superficial but plausible reasoning based on the assumption that America's comparative advantage lies in skilled-labor-intensive industries, and her comparative disadvantage in unskilled-labor-intensive industries (and implicitly making use of the Heckscher-Ohlin model of international trade), leads to the conclusion that liberalization of international trade, or other, external changes leading to reduced prices and increased quantities of imports from abroad, should benefit skilled United States labor at the expense of unskilled United States labor. This follows from the so-called Stolper-Samuelson relation, according to which an increase in production of one of two commodities producible by the use of two factors, with fixed total supplies of the two factors, must raise the real wage of the factor used intensively in the production of the commodity whose output has increased, and reduce the real wage of the other factor. The same system of analysis concludes that if (with given trade barriers), the supply of skilled workers in the rest of the world increases, the wages of skilled workers everywhere must fall both absolutely and relative to those of unskilled workers. Also, United States exports would fall absolutely, or relative to trend, and the terms of trade would turn against the United States. This holds true whether "skilled" and "unskilled" workers in the United States and outside are exactly alike, or whether United States workers differ from foreign workers by a "productivity factor" (which may be different for skilled than for unskilled workers). An easy extension of the analysis shows that if the productivity differential for skilled United States over skilled nonworkers is eroded by the transfer of superior United States skilled-worker "know-how" to foreign skilled workers, the same result of a reduction in both absolute real wages of United States skilled workers and of real wages of United States skilled workers relative to United States unskilled workers will ensue. (Foreign skilled workers' real wages may move either way relative to foreign unskilled workers' wages, since the relative price of the product using them intensively will have fallen but their marginal product in terms of that product will have risen.) On the other hand, the transfer of superior United States unskilled-worker "know-how" to foreign unskilled workers will increase the supply of imports, improve the United States terms of trade and raise the real wages of skilled United States labor both absolutely and relative to the (now lower) wages of United States unskilled labor. (Foreign skilled labor will lose from the shift of production toward unskilled-labor-intensive exports; foreign unskilled labor will lose from the fall in the price of the export product but gain from the increase in its productivity.)

In summary, the model indicates that while, with constant total supplies of skilled and unskilled labor in the United States and abroad, United States skilled labor will gain from trade liberalization, it will tend to lose from the growth of skilled labor supplies abroad and from the transfer of "know-how" to skilled foreign labor. But, perhaps paradoxically, its best defense against these adverse effects (within limits) would be still further trade liberalization, which for the reasons given above would tend to raise its absolute and relative real wages and so offset the adverse effects of these external changes. Trade liberalization would also increase the favorable effects of the transmission of superior "know-how" from unskilled United States to unskilled foreign labor. This is the best defense, however, only if defense is restricted to the trade policy field. If the transfer of "know-how" can be policy-controlled, the proper policy for United States skilled labor would be to prevent the transfer of skilled-labor "know-how" (the objective of the United States union movement) or to transfer unskilled-labor "know-how" only (the policy of Japan, that is, invest only in the exploitation of other countries' natural resources, and the industrialization of their resources of cheap labor, for export to Japan). A third alternative, suggested by the analysis, is to suppress the growth of skilled as compared with unskilled labor supplies abroad (one aspect of so-called colonialism). Note that while the analysis has been cast in terms of the real wages of skilled labor, in absolute terms and relative to those of unskilled labor, in the country whose policy we are concerned with, it could equally well be cast in terms of the number of skilled-labor jobs available, at a given differential of skilled-labor wages over unskilled-labor wages.

The foregoing model is superficial but plausible, as mentioned, because while it bases itself on skilled and unskilled labor as the only factors of production, the concept of skilled labor can be stretched to include the influence of capital and technology, and the export of capital can be treated as a simultaneous reduction in the amount of skilled labor available in the capital-exporting country and increase in the amount available in the capital-importing country. A more satisfactory model would have to include the direct role of technology, material capital and human capital in the form of professional, managerial and other executive personnel as well as of skilled and unskilled labor. It would have to disaggregate production into the production of many goods in an interdependent input-output system. It would also have to treat skilled labor explicitly as involving an investment of resources in raising the skills of labor that would otherwise be unskilled. Each would involve a complex mathematical-theoretical exercise. A few brief remarks may help to point up some of the relevant considerations.

Disaggregation into an input-output system producing many goods obviously requires resort to the concept of "effective" as distinct from "nominal" protection. It also raises the question of what is meant by "skill-intensity." Consideration of skilled labor as resulting from investments in upgrading otherwise unskilled labor suggests that (on the initial assumption that United States exports are relatively skill-intensive) the rate of return on such investment is increased in the United States and reduced in the foreign countries by trade liberalization, thereby increasing the supply in the United States and reducing the supply abroad. However, if capital is also introduced as a factor of production, and investment in human capital is assumed to be carried to the point where its rate of return is equated with that on capital, the problem becomes more complicated.

Consideration of other factors can be expressed in terms of a very simple model:

$$C_X + S_X + U_X = 1$$

$$C_Y + S_Y + U_Y = 1$$

where quantities of commodities X and Y are measured in pre-trade-liberalization United States dollar values, C stands for capital inputs, taken to include technology and managerial services, S is skilled labor input and U unskilled labor input, into the subscripted industry, measured in per unit dollar terms.

Note that we have an initial difficulty with the concept of relative skilled-labor intensity, which may be defined in terms of ratios of skilled-labor input to output, skilled-labor input to capital input and skilled-labor input to unskilled-labor input. The first is most relevant to the effect of changes in the production pattern of the economy of factor prices, but the last is the sense in which the term seems usually to be employed, and will be employed here, Now assume that X is the export good and Y the import good, that $S_X/U_X > S_Y/U_Y$, and that a small reduction in the tariff shifts production away from Y towards X. Then we have four possible cases.

1. $S_X < S_Y$, $U_X < U_Y$, $C_X > C_Y$. Trade liberalization creates an excess supply of both skilled and unskilled labor and an excess demand for capital. On normal assumptions, capital gains in rent while both skilled and unskilled labor lose, in terms of real wages.

2. $S_X > S_Y$, $U_X > U_Y$, $C_X < C_Y$. Trade liberalization creates an excess demand for both skilled and unskilled labor and an excess supply of capital. Under normal assumptions both skilled and unskilled labor gain in real wages while capital loses rent.

3. $S_X > S_Y$, $U_X < U_Y$, $C_X > C_Y$. Trade liberalization creates an excess demand for skilled labor, an excess supply of unskilled labor, and an excess demand for capital. Under normal assumptions skilled labor wages rise, unskilled labor wages fall and the rental rate on capital increases.

4. $S_X > S_Y$, $U_X < U_Y$, $C_X < C_Y$. Trade liberalization creates an excess demand for skilled labor and an excess supply of both unskilled labor and capital. Under normal assumptions, the real wage of skilled labor rises and the real wage of unskilled labor and the rental rate of capital fall.

In the first case skilled labor loses from trade liberalization even though the export industry is more skilled-labor-intensive than the import-competing industry (on the definition selected). In the other three cases it gains, but in only two of the three does unskilled labor lose by trade liberalization; in the other it also gains, at the expense of capital. Thus, the finding in the two-factor (skilled and unskilled labor) model that skilled labor gains and unskilled labor loses from trade liberalization corresponds to only two of the four possible cases. (If we take seriously the "Leontief paradox," whereby United States exports are labor-intensive and capital-unintensive, only cases 2 and 4 are relevant; skilled labor must gain, and unskilled labor may gain or lose, from trade liberalization.) Disaggregation into an input-output system, with purchased inputs entering the equations and having their own coefficients for capital and skilled and unskilled labor, would make the possibilities even more complex to specify in terms of characteristics of the production process.

Comment

John Karlik

In the absence of Harry Johnson's paper until today, I was obliged to sit down earlier this week and write out some of my own thoughts on the subject of this seminar, just to be sure that I would have something to say. So what I shall do first is to present my own viewpoint to provide a background for some subsequent remarks on Harry Johnson's paper.

The fundamental presumption behind this seminar seems to be the proposition that developing countries need to be able to sell their manufactured goods in the markets of industrial nations in order that the former will be able to raise their standards of living. Hence our concern about prospects for the next decade and about problems of adjustment in the northern hemisphere.

Why do developing countries need the markets of the industrialized world? Speaking as an economist to a group with a similar orientation, I would offer a couple of reasons. Efforts to explain differences among poor nations in their economic performance have been formulated in terms of the ability of these countries, either through their own initiative or as a result of assistance from abroad, to close two or more gaps. One of these gaps relates to the balance of payments constraint and to the need of a growing economy for sophisticated capital goods and other essential inputs from abroad. Growth would be stymied if poor countries were unable to export to industrialized nations and if essential imports were therefore not available.

According to our common religion of comparative advantage—a conviction that seems to have stood the test of time better than most—it seems to make sense that the rich industrialized countries should export computers, aircraft, diesel electric locomotives, power plants, and the like to developing countries, while the latter obtain these goods in exchange for agricultural products, raw materials and, increasingly as a focus of our concern, simpler manufactured goods. For economists this is a convenient and comfortable way to order the world.

Immersed in a political environment, however, as the international economist for the Joint Economic Committee of the United States Congress, I am bound to view the issue of the ability of developing countries to sell their manufactures in industrial markets somewhat differently. I have raised the issue because, first, I know some astute and responsible politicians either have or will and, second, because political leaders will implement whatever plans economists devise to improve market access for the benefit of the less fortunate. This implementation will invariably color, probably strongly, the ultimate result.

Hence, aside from the need to service existing debt burdens, a special issue, is it really reasonable to assert that the developing countries vitally need improved access to the markets of the industrial world? After all, there is a huge untapped potential market in these low-income countries, which include approximately two-thirds of the world's population. Secondly, there is considerable diversity among the nonindustrial countries in their levels of per capita income and industrial capabilities. According to standard comparative advantage, the relatively more advanced of the developing countries could trade with the more backward, and growth might proceed smoothly. Under this argument, only the most developed of the nonindustrialized really need access to the markets of Western Europe, United States and Japan. But it is precisely those nations that ought to be competing quite strictly on the basis of their own capabilities and not enjoying the benefit of preferential access. Finally, there are a number of developing countries that have been independent for a long time, some for over a century, that have been richly endowed with natural resources and educated, skilled immigrants, but which nevertheless have not made it. If they did not make it with all they have got, why should we expect that a little more assistance from the industrial world, of whatever type, is going to make any difference?

I raise these questions because I suspect that the reasons we have some preferential trade agreements today reflect basically political objectives overlaid with economic rationalizations. The six founders of the EEC have a political interest in close trading ties with the countries surrounding the Mediterranean and with the former French colonies in Central Africa. The same type of political consideration, admittedly in a limited and diluted form, is responsible for the extension of similar benefits to the developing members of the Commonwealth. In a comparable way, Japan has a special interest in assured supplies of raw materials from Southeast Asia. The counterpart of these imports are shipments for Japanese steel, capital good and consumer products to the primary producers. In addition to being the economic giant of the area, Japan, through trading relationships, is to an increasing degree becoming a powerful political influence.

I point out these political links, not to denigrate economic considerations and the importance of economic planning. In fact, because of the significance of political motivations on the part of industrialized countries, we should probably be even more concerned about assuring that trade and investment flows do in fact bring economic benefits to the less developed countries. Instead, I have called attention to political considerations on the part of Western Europe and the Japanese to point out what I believe is a contrast between the forces that drive other industrial countries, and those that are relevant to the United States.

The United States used to feel, as I see it, a special responsibility towards Latin America, but no longer does. While these ties are sometimes emphasized rhetorically, we have not done anything for Latins lately. The failure of the Administration to introduce legislation enacting special trade preferences for imports from developing countries indicates the absence of United States concern about assisting either Latin America, or low income nations in general. Certainly part of the Administration's reluctance to present legislation for tariff preferences is the fear that such a proposal would be greeted by a mixed reaction at best from the Congress. More seriously, such a bill could become a vehicle for protectionist amendments. Preference legislation might presumably be adopted as a small part of the statutory authority for a major United States initiative to liberalize trade. Aside from this possibility, my estimate is that the likelihood for acceptance of trade preferences by the Congress is extremely low.

I have mentioned the loss of a feeling of responsibility in the United States for what happens in Latin America, as well as in the rest of the developing world. Undoubtedly there are a number of reasons for this shift in attitudes, including disillusionment with foreign involvement and domestic budgetary problems. But I would like to mention just one other reason that seems important to me and is in contrast to the policies of other industrial countries.

In the United States, there has been a minimal concern for helping workers and firms adjust to changes of any type in the economic environment. We do not even have the type of weak regional assistance and income redistribution policies that exist in the EEC, in the United Kingdom and, to a lesser extent, in Japan. We hold a strange set of attitudes in the United States. Domestically generated economic hardship—whether the consequence of obsolete technology, transfers of industry to areas where labor costs are lower, exhaustion of natural resources deposits or the abrupt termination of government procurement—seems to be regarded by the national bodies which jointly produce economic policy as being "good for the soul." Workers and businessmen in depressed areas of course do not have the same attitude. On the other hand, any loss of employment or market disruption resulting from import competition, even though the aggregate disruption may be only one-twentieth of that resulting from domestic causes, is presented in Washington as a serious threat to the economic vitality of the entire nation. Until there is a change in the attitudes of the economic policy-makers, both in the executive and legislative branches toward the virtues of adjustment assistance to ease transitions as opposed to the desirability of import restrictions to deal with trade problems, the developing countries, to the extent that they rely upon the United States, may do best by cultivating their own markets.

Happily the developing countries are not exclusively dependent upon the United States, and fortunately the United States can benefit from the examples of the other industrial nations.

Turning specifically to Harry Johnson's paper, I share his critical attitude toward efforts to develop patterned after the Marshall Plan model. By contrast with post-World War II Europe, minimal inputs of real resources and technical advice are unlikely to produce dramatic results in nations that have never known industrialization.

When, after a discussion of general principles, Harry Johnson focuses on the problems of the current decade, he initially notes "that the development strategy of the past has paid very little attention to the beneficial effects of competition" in promoting economic growth [p. 46]. His "implications for the future are that development will have to rely relatively more, and perhaps virtually exclusively on the classical mechanism of market competition; for these to be successful in promoting development, they will have to be consciously assisted and promoted by reforms of both national policies and the structure of the international economic system" [p. 47]. He cites three desirable reforms: altering the mechanism of the international monetary system to insure that exchange rates change smoothly and efficiently to eliminate balance of payments disequilibria, "a substantial movement in the direction of genuinely free world trade"; and the introduction of "some sort of international

60 / *John Karlik*

code governing relations between the national state and the multinational corporation" [pp. 47, 49].

To those familiar with his writings, it is no surprise that Harry Johnson comes out in favor of increased reliance upon the forces of market competition. However, his recommendations fail to go beyond what in much of the industrial world at least is the present conventional wisdom. Nor does he offer any guidelines in determining how far policy-makers should go in introducing and enforcing competition. This absence of guidelines is disturbing because he himself recognizes that some of the consequences of competition can retard, rather than promote, economic development.

In discussing competition and economic growth as part of the general introduction to his paper, Harry Johnson criticizes regional assistance policies. He says, "Regional policies of subsidizing firms to make do with an awkward labor force may also contribute, by perpetuating inefficient practices and attitudes that would otherwise be *forcibly cured by penury and migration in search of better opportunities*" [p. 43, emphasis added]. The previous paragraph, however, states that the "influences that tend to make regional wages abnormally low (and regional unemployment rates abnormally high) may create a vicious circle of increasingly unequal incomes per capita among regions. Specifically, initially low wages and high unemployment rates may reduce both the incentives to acquire skills and the ability to finance their acquisition, and also involve barriers of both inadequate skills and resources and cultural differences in work attitudes, discipline and so on to migration to higher-wage regions" [p. 43].

The contradiction between these two statements brings us squarely against the typical problem of politicians and policymakers. In Harry Johnson's context, how much competition is enough? How much competition is needed to induce a degree of penury and unemployment sufficient to promote migration and a more rational use of productive resources, but at the same time, avoid discouraging such a transformation through the creation of excessive poverty and ignorance of opportunities elsewhere? This absence of practical guidelines is to me the most unsatisfying aspect of Harry Johnson's discussion.

My observation that developing countries should perhaps look to trade among one another as an alternative to assured access to the markets of industrial countries might conflict with Harry Johnson's plea for greater competition. But to what extent should burgeoning industries in developing countries be obliged to compete against experienced manufacturers of the same products in industrial nations? Again, Harry Johnson offers barely a hint of an answer.

Comment

Charles Frank

Harry Johnson has provided us with an interesting overview of the relationship between economic growth and development on the one hand and the smooth functioning of a competitive, world trading economy on the other. He sees the needs of growth and development in the less developed nations as being met best in a world of highly competitive markets, expanding opportunities for trade and reduced barriers to movement of capital, technology and skills. He identifies the reforms required to bring about such a desirable world economic environment. They are: reform of the international monetary organizations, further removal of tariff and nontariff barriers to trade through multilateral negotiations, devising a set of rules of the game for multinational corporations which permits them to function in a socially effective manner and more effective programs of adjustment assistance tied closely to safeguard mechanisms.

It is hard to find an economist who would not agree to the proposition that such a competitive world economy as described by Harry Johnson would be in the interest of most of the nations of the world and particularly in the interest of some of the more advanced, less developed countries. Yet within the United States there is significant opposition to this kind of world and there is a rising swell of protectionist sentiment which threatens full United States participation in the world economy. For the developing countries this is especially unfortunate, since the United States provides the largest market for their exports. Exchange rate adjustments, relatively full employment in the United States economy, substantial reform of the international monetary system, and improved programs of trade adjustment assistance are necessary if the system of liberal trade and investment is to be maintained and expanded. But even if the world were all set right by exchange rate adjustments, monetary reforms, full employment and improved adjustment assistance programs, would this be sufficient to stem the rising tide opposition to liberal trade and investment policies?

In order to answer this question, we must broaden our view of the trading system and go beyond the Heckscher-Ohlin frame of reference. Despite the fact that economists are quite willing to modify the Heckscher-Ohlin view of trade flows by adding factors of production other than labor and capital and allowing for differences in technology, I would argue that there is a basic tendency for many economists to stick to that frame of reference in analyzing policy alternatives. This tendency may lead to wrong conclusions about policy problems. Let us briefly review where the Heckscher-Ohlin approach has led us.

One major conclusion of the Heckscher-Ohlin theory and one of very fundamental policy significance is the factor-price equalization theorem. This theorem implies that with free trade, the price of labor falls and the price of capital rises in a country with abundant supplies of capital relative to labor. Most of the theoretical advances in trade theory have tended to dispute the importance of factor-price equalization.

It has been shown that the theorem seems to hold only under very special assumptions and these assumptions are unlikely to be satisfied in the real world. The conclusion derived from this extension of the theory is that although there may be a tendency toward factor-price equalization under free trade, there is no reason to believe that equalization of returns to capital and labor will be complete.

Recent empirical work on the Leontief paradox for the United States economy has indicated that United States exports are skill-intensive rather than capital-intensive. This research supports the view of trade in the context of a modified Heckscher-Ohlin theory in which labor skills are a separate factor of production. However, since labor skills are embodied in the worker, the implication is that wages in the United States can be maintained at higher levels than abroad because of the greater relative skill endowment and the greater rate of skill acquisition in the United States, both of which give the United States a comparative advantage with respect to skill-intensive products.

Another methodological advance in trade theory, which is consistent with a modified Heckscher-Ohlin approach, is the product-cycle theory. This theory reinforces the optimistic view of United States wage trends. The United States is presumed to be the most tech-

COMMENT: TRADE, INVESTMENT AND LABOR /63

nologically advanced nation and to introduce new technologies much earlier than the rest of the world. The technological lead enjoyed by the United States enables it to produce and export many products at an early stage in the product cycle. The returns to United States factors of production, including labor, are certainly enhanced by this alleged lead in technology.

With these most important modifications to classical trade theory, the Heckscher-Ohlin view of comparative advantage as stemming from differences in relative factor endowment is still the basic intellectual underpinning of modern trade theory and the policy recommendations which stem from it. There is a growing concern that this type of trade theory is no longer relevant for analyzing trade problems and policies. The growth in the extent and speed of transport and communications has facilitated the growth of multinational corporations which operate with little regard to international borders. Capital is much more mobile than it used to be. Technology is transferred from country to country more rapidly, and the product cycle has become shorter. High-level management skills are no longer location specific and are applied without regard to borders. In such a world, it is argued, the theory of comparative advantage and the gains from trade no longer apply.

If we accept the reality of relatively free movement of capital and transfer of technology, then a quite different model of trade may be applied. The theory that one might use in analyzing this kind of world is more akin to location theory models. Production of particular commodities is localized and trade takes place because of economies of scale in production; local availability of raw materials, skilled labor supplies or legal, financial, marketing accounting services; the necessity to be located close to major marketing areas; the existence of important social and economic overhead facilities; or a particularly favorable climate or environment. One would not necessarily predict less trade with a model of capital mobility and rapid technology transfer as compared to a Heckscher-Ohlin comparative advantage model. On the contrary, we might expect more trade, given the fact that within the United States the various states are very dependent on trade with each other.

The gains from trade in a location theory model are not necessarily less than the gains from trade in a Heckscher-Ohlin type model as some critics of the latter might have us believe. With capital and technology free to move from countries where returns are low to countries where returns are high, total world product should be enhanced. That is not to say, however, that the gains from trade will accrue equally to all factors of production. The returns to a particular factor of production in a particular country may decline as the result of trade.

This brings us to a most important difference between the Heckscher-Ohlin frame of reference and the location theory approach. In the Heckscher-Ohlin model, as modified through the years, we can expect only a tendency toward factor-price equalization. The free movement of capital and technology, however, implies complete factor-price equalization in the long run. Equilibrium in this kind of model is achieved only when the marginal productivity of factors is the same everywhere, and factor returns are equalized everywhere. Of course, skill differentials may persist and keep wage rates higher in the United States than in other countries. But this analysis implies that skill levels will have to increase much more rapidly in the United States if United States workers are to maintain the same relative rate of growth in worker incomes. It also means that other ways of redistributing income may have to be found. If a free and competitive economy will shift the relative returns in the United States in favor of capital, we must find ways of giving workers some share of the increased returns to capital, that is ways in which labor can share more equitably in gains from trade.

I would not accept the location theory frame of reference as a completely accurate description of the world economy. There are still many barriers to the movement of capital, technology and managerial skills. But these barriers have been drastically reduced in the last decade or so. There are many reasons to expect the barriers to become less important in the future. We are moving toward a world which is better described by a location theory framework—a world without borders.

The developing countries have much to gain from this type of world. They can be the major recipients of capital and technology from the capital- and technology-rich countries. Their economic growth can be much more rapid. The productivity of their workers can be enhanced. Their exports can grow more rapidly, and they could be able to afford a larger volume and variety of imports. Not all developing countries, however, stand to gain equally. Some countries have already benefited substantially in terms of rapid economic growth and growth in trade. Korea, Taiwan, Mexico and Brazil are some of the familiar examples. Some countries cannot participate as fully in the world trading economy because their labor markets are not well developed, they lack basic education and skills among the labor force, they cannot provide adequate ancillary services and social and economic overheads, and their internal markets are too small or they are too remote from major world markets. This is true of many of the sub-Saharan African countries. Still other countries could participate in the growth of the world economy but they choose not to do so. They have chosen to develop with inward looking strategies and install a wide range of barriers to free trade and investment from abroad. This is characteristic of the development strategies of India and some Latin American countries.

The trend toward a freer, more competitive and trade-oriented world economy has occurred not so much because of the lowering of tariff and nontariff barriers to trade but because of a reduction in transportation and communications barriers, the rise of the multinational corporation and the long period of relative peace and political stability among the world's largest and most powerful trading economies since World War II. The United States, despite the decline in its relative importance in world trade and its relative economic power, still plays a very important role in the continuation of these trends toward a more integrated world economy. Yet political resistance in the United States toward these trends is growing. The strongest resistance comes from organized labor.

The resistance of organized labor is based on a number of factors. Some of these are short-run and may be eliminated if the United States's balance of trade begins to improve in the seventies due to exchange rate adjustments, improvements in international payments mechanisms and shifts in relative rates of economic growth and inflation among the major trading countries. A reduction in the current high rate of unemployment will also mitigate labor's concern with import competition. Another reason for labor's resistance is the particular structure of the organized labor movement in the United States. There are very great differences in the representation of import competing industries as opposed to export industries. Steel, textiles, glass and electronics are overrepresented relative to the major export industries. Furthermore, union leaders may be interested in maintaining membership and see foreign competition as a threat to their unions as institutions. They may also see basic trends toward a service economy accelerated by liberal trade and investment policies and view this as a threat to the political power of organized labor. Finally, organized labor may be reflecting the fears of the workers that rapid movement of goods and investment will increase movement from job to job and increase the level of unemployment due to frictional factors. Workers may attach a great amount of value to job stability per se.

These short-run and bureaucratic factors and the desire for job security, however, may not be the most fundamental with which policy-makers will have to deal. The soundest intellectual rationale for labor resistance to free trade is more basic and long-run in nature. It is the fear that export of United States capital and relocation of production facilities abroad will have adverse effects on the relative share of labor in total United States national income and returns to labor in the United States relative to wage rates in the rest of the world. Labor unions do not want to bargain with corporations which are becoming increasingly multinational and can use the threat of overseas relocation or production facilities at the bargaining table. As we tried to illustrate, there is a good deal of intellectual justification for the fear that labor's relative position in a capital-rich country may worsen in a modern, competitive, world economy. From this point of view, the support of organized labor for controls on trade may not be just an attempt to protect vulnerable workers and industries from import competition. Rather it may be an attempt to insure that the United States economy forms one vast protected market in which there is a reduced incentive to export capital and technology abroad to take advantage of low-cost labor. Firms locating abroad would not be able to reenter United States markets because of import controls. Import controls would be only one aspect of this grand strategy of protection. Controls on United States investment abroad would be another major element.

It is often suggested that trade adjustment assistance is a major policy tool which can be used to compensate individual workers for losses that they might incur as part of a liberal trade policy which is in the general national interest. It should be kept in mind that relative·to a decade or so ago, although adjustment assistance may have increased in absolute importance as a policy tool, it has probably decreased in relative importance as compared to other policy tools. In a world in which capital and technology move freely among countries, exchange rate adjustments and improvements in international payments mechanisms become relatively more important. Terms of trade can shift more rapidly and this must be reflected in exchange rate movements. Otherwise trade deficits are likely to widen more rapidly with an adverse impact on employment—directly through slower growing job opportunities in export industries, and indirectly through the negative effect of trade deficits on aggregate demand.

Adjustment assistance becomes relatively less important as a means for compensating United States labor for losses it might incur in a free-trade world. While adjustment assistance might mitigate the losses in income and welfare for workers who lose their jobs as a *direct* result of import competition, it does very little to redress the deterioration of labor's perceived bargaining position with multinational firms and the general tendency for downward presssures on returns to labor relative to returns to capital. There are ways in which labor's complaints might be met. Most important are full employment policies, manpower training programs and measures for income redistribution. Losses in labor incomes from unemployment probably far outweigh the effect of any downward pressures on wages due to free trade and capital flows. Despite the increase in trade volume and the tendency for capital movements, their effect on equalizing factor incomes probably operates very slowly. Increasing labor skills through training may raise labor incomes rapidly enough to offset these trends. Measures for income redistribution can offset the trend toward reduced labor income completely by enabling all income groups to have a share in the gains from trade.

More specifically, there are some things which can be done which are directly related to trade and investment policy and can help in satisfying the concerns of organized labor. First, we could remove preferential treatment of taxes on income of corporations who operate overseas. These corporations often do not pay taxes on overseas income until they are repatriated. Even when profits are repatriated they are not necessarily taxed equally with income originating in the United States. The law provides for equal treatment on federal income taxes only; it does not take into account other federal, state and local taxes which discriminate in favor of foreign income. Second, organized labor has been opposed to sections 806.30 and 807.00 of the United States tariff code which provide incentives for United States firms to invest capital in assembly facilities overseas. The elimination of these codes, which are discriminatory and difficult to administer appropriately, may be a small price to pay for a more liberal United States trade policy. Finally, another reform that might help in meeting labor objections to free trade is to require that companies which relocate production facilities overseas bear some part of the costs of the training and relocation of workers displaced by the shift to overseas production.

Adjustment assistance programs, while possibly becoming less important in relation to other measures in promoting free trade, may at the same time become absolutely more necessary. In a world of rapid movement of capital and technology, changes in patterns of production and trade can shift much more rapidly than when barriers to movement are greater. The need for more rapid adjustment and greater amounts of adjustment assistance is obvious. In order to achieve better programs of adjustment assistance, substantial reforms in the present United States system are necessary. It has been inadequate in terms of the amounts of assistance which are given to injured parties and the time between application for assistance and delivery of adjustment assistance benefits.

In an addendum to his paper, Harry Johnson correctly points out that organized labor and labor in general are not the same and that the special interests of labor union leaders are not necessarily synonymous with the interests of all laborers. He also analyzes the effect of free trade in a two-factor Heckscher-Ohlin model in which skilled and unskilled labor are the two factors. Using this analytical framework, he shows that skilled labor in the United States will gain from free trade because it is the relatively abundant factor of production and the United States may tend to specialize further in skill-intensive commodities. The conclusion he reaches is that it may pay labor to support liberal trade policies.

When a third factor, capital, is introduced into the model, however, the movement of relative factor prices becomes ambiguous. The returns to both skilled and unskilled labor may deteriorate relative to that of capital. Furthermore, the export of technology may have "external effects" by raising labor skills abroad. This may lead to a reduction in relative returns to skilled labor in the United States. Harry Johnson points out both of these possible effects. If, in addition, we open the model to allow free movement of capital, we increase the tendency for returns to both skilled and unskilled labor to decline relative to capital and technology.

It is an empirical question as to whether the net result of all these tendencies is to favor workers in general as opposed to owners of capital and technology. I would simply argue that we must confront the latter possibility in a serious manner and that there is substantial casual evidence to indicate that we are moving toward a world economic environment which is relatively more favorable to owners of capital and technology.

3

The Role of the Multinational Corporation

Pierre Uri

The literature on multinational corporations is becoming voluminous and of a baffling diversity. It extends from passionate pleas — either indiscriminate eulogies or outright condemnations — to massive descriptions of trends, strategies and conflicts, to the building of models which assemble all the positive and negative factors relevant to an exhaustive cost-benefit analysis, whether retrospective or prospective. The great virtue of such models is to take the steam out of the debate, to dispose the defenders and the attackers in favor of a case-by-case assessment. The trouble is that, complicated though they are, they are nonetheless condemned to oversimplification: they must ignore some of the most relevant but nonquantifiable elements, mainly of a political nature, which may have a decisive economic feedback. Moreover, a good part of the data necessary to fill the boxes is generally not available, and some parts are by nature bound to be the subject of sheer guesswork, particularly when they relate to the potential effects of alternative solutions. The factual work has shed a good deal of light on the diversity of circumstances in which multinationals are involved and the rationale of their disparate, and often evolving types of internal organization. This is helpful in preventing one from jumping to conclusions, but at the risk of limiting clear-cut practical answers. It is tempting to ignore all those efforts and to try to restate some basic points even if they appear trivial. The elaborate models will serve as a reminder of the pros and cons which should enter into a final appraisal. The accumulation of factual evidence will provide examples and illustrations. The main attempt will be to appear as dispassionate as the scholars who have followed both those painstaking approaches, but to find and justify, if possible, several proposals for action.

In that vein, the paper will be organized around two main themes. In the present context of the world economy, the existence of the multinational corporations which could be an instrument of the most efficient allocation of resources, is likely to lead to distortions of all kinds. How can these be minimized or prevented? Multinational corporations both contribute resources and are a drag on resources in terms of balances of payments; they may carry along other sectors of the national economies or stifle them. What are the likely ways of increasing the benefits and reducing the costs?

I. A TRANSPARENT OR A DISTORTED MARKET?

The concept of direct foreign investment is not clear-cut. The only obvious feature is that the investment has to be entered into by a firm. A majority ownership by an individual would not qualify for the appellation. This, however, is a necessary but not a sufficient condition. There is no doubt in the case of a 100 percent ownership of a subsidiary or of an absolute majority which, for some decisions and in some countries, may require more than a mere 51 percent. In that case, full control is assured. However, it can also be acquired with a much smaller proportion of the ownership, depending on how the rest is distributed. If there is one local partner who holds the majority, even a block of shares as large as 49 percent, raises doubts.

Why could it not be treated as portfolio investment by a company? In fact, some other elements are always present in that kind of situation. Often there is an agreement whereby the minority interest is protected and its concurrence is required for the strategic decisions, sometimes it is effective participation by management, sometimes the supply of patents, licenses and know-how, sometimes arrangements for joint production or joint marketing. Thus a dividing line between direct and portfolio investment according to the percentage owned in the stock of a foreign company is arbitrary and irrelevant whether it is the 20 percent threshold adopted in the statistics of the United States Department of Commerce, or the 10 percent which exonerates American investors from the interest equalization tax. Moreover, if any degree of ownership were relevant, it would have to be gross, not net. The dissociation between direct investment and movements of capital is a major new phenomenon. A large part of the funds used to acquire participation in another country's firm, or to create a subsidiary from scratch, may be borrowed in that country. Thus, much more should be known about minority investments for the computation of statistics. Do they involve effective control, or what additional arrangements supplement them to gain an effective influence on the management and orientation of the "subsidiary" firm?

The notion of multinational corporations is not much more definite. In the strict sense, they should be independent of any particular country and incorporated with some international body. The spread of stock among shareholders of various nationalities is in no sense an approximation to that condition. The presence of people of various nationalities on the board, a practice the largest oil companies and some others are beginning to introduce, is a positive step forward. Although this is a legalistic aspect, it may have some important economic feedbacks, inasmuch as political reactions to foreign investment, irrational though they may be, are part of the picture; truly multinational companies would make a better contribution to world affairs than the present pseudo-multinationals.

The practical criterion is not the ownership of the management, but the geographic spread of operations. A convention according to which a company would qualify as multinational when it begins to have its own facilities, wholly or jointly owned, in something like six different foreign countries is now gaining ground. Why not begin with one operation or important participation in another country, since a multiplication of such situations would already create quite a flow of investments? Odd as the drawing of the line may look, it makes sense inasmuch as at some point a quantitative increase makes for a qualitative jump. A company which is organized to operate in several countries constitutes a network of information far beyond that in which local companies may have an interest, even if their exports are sizable.

In theory this feature could make the multinational corporation the most efficient vehicle for the world wide allocation of resources.

This applies firstly to the division of labor. Because of the abundance of its information, the rapidity of communications, the concentration of decision-making, such a company should be in a position to exploit the local advantages in a swifter way then the most perfect system of pure competition. In the manufacturing sector, one can witness the specialization of plants, the full use of the possibility of making parts in the most appropriate location for production, and assembly at the best place from a market point of view. Seen in a dynamic perspective, this allocation of resources also takes the form of a prompt transfer of new techniques wherever they can be successfully applied. The distribution of investments tends to maximize profitability, and it can be argued that the capital exporting country enjoys a gain if the rate of return is higher on investments made abroad than at home. Such corporations are also able to borrow in the cheapest markets, and to invest their short-term funds in the most remunerative.

Inducements and Difficulties

Even these simplistic economics cannot overlook a major change which is taking place in the relative importance of the factors which determine the international division of labor. Land proper plays less of a role as agriculture represents a dwindling fraction of national products, and as yields grow so fast that in the most advanced parts of the world there is not too little, but too much land under cultivation. Raw materials are increasingly obtained by the main countries from the same overseas sources, and freight rates fluctuate in unison for all users, except for the companies which operate their own transport facilities. If capital and management are more readily transferable, neither the immobility of factors nor the relative factor endowment can be assumed as the bases of fundamental international trade theorems. The one factor which does remain relatively immobile is labor. Thus a great simplification is tending to take place. The decisive and almost unique element is the relation of productivity to wage costs. Taking into account the nontrade elements of balances of payments, any overall difference in that ratio is tantamount to an exchange rate disequilibrium. That ratio varies among industries, so that, even if in a modified sense, the law of comparative advantage retains its validity.

The real issue lies elsewhere. It is the contradiction between the existence of companies with elbowroom to move and adjust, and partititoned and administered national markets. Hence the distortions in the location of economic activities, as well as in the functioning of financial markets, and the deviations from comparative advantage in its classical or modified sense.

The first and overriding point is, of course, the extreme difference in the degree to which foreign investments, and particularly multinational corporations, are welcomed in the various countries. Nationalism can assume quite contradictory aspects, and justify quite contradictory practices. It may be bent on attracting funds and firms in a beggar-my-neighbor policy, or rejecting them for fear of loss of control and exploitation or competition to local interests. Such impulses, in short, are then glorified under the guise of "industrial policy." Either consciously or not, industrial policy tends to determine the share of global output a country tries to gain for itself as well as its form. This becomes the decisive factor in where the multinational corporations locate their activities.

Strange as it may look, even the member countries of the EEC have not managed to agree on a common attitude vis-à-vis foreign firms in a span of fourteen years. Some countries are granting tax holidays, subsidized interest rates, and even free land to firms from third countries. The avowed purposes are, of course, growth, employment and technology. The net effect is that foreign investment and multinational firms are used as an instrument of competition against the other partners in the EEC. Some on the other hand have tried to apply restrictions according to the nationality of the firm, to the economic sector or to the character of the operation, by pretending to distinguish between creations and acquisitions. Thus, an asymmetrical effect is evolving: the favors tend to spread from country to country in a kind of auctioneering process; the restrictions are circumvented through the territory of the other members. Thus the more restrictive countries feel the impact of competition without the corresponding benefits of increased production and employment.

The differences are even more striking in the developing countries. They usually have to grant more discriminatory advantages if they want to attract foreign firms and, on the other hand, the deterrents they apply are also more extreme. Nationalization without compensation may appear initially as a nice gain, but this remains true only if the operation was, and remains, profitable. It also kills the chance that firms would again venture to that country. The Andean code agreed upon in the Pact of Cartagena not only cuts firms from local credit when there is a foreign majority ownership, but it also blocks their entry into some activities, makes entry into others conditional upon a plan for future divestment, and enjoins the divestment of "excess" foreign interests, or their complete withdrawal, even for already established firms. Nevertheless, the multinational corporation might perhaps have adjusted to such rules if they were for the future. However, the retroactive character of some of the provisions leads to the fear of other such sudden and arbitrary changes in years to come. It is true that there is an enormous loophole in the Pact, and each country may discard the rules as it deems fit in its own interest. The "auctioneering" process is in fact now at work in a series of waivers.

Some other rather well-known points can be dealt with even more cursorily. One is the effect of protection. The higher it is and the narrower the market, the more the producer is likely to enjoy a monopoly position. It is a fact that one of the incentives for the entry of United States companies into the EEC was to place themselves *behind* the wall of the common external tariff, rather than outside it. In this case, however, the level of protection is quite low, and competition from local firms, or other multinationals, makes itself felt. The case is completely different in developing countries, however small, which try to launch a process of autarkic industrialization. The multinational corporations may, moreover, be able to bargain for higher protection than a local company would obtain.

The overvaluation of a currency, frequent in developing countries, particularly in Latin America, enhances the nominal rate of profits when they can be repatriated, although, of course, the scope for making profits, particularly on exports, is considerably reduced.

Perhaps the most intractable difficulty lies in disparities in taxation among countries. A multinational corporation finds itself in the best position to exploit such differences to its advantage, because there is little possibility of controlling or challenging the transfer prices charged by a firm's plant to another. It would usually be difficult to set a standard unless there were some outside sales. The rule of nondiscrimination would require that the price to the buyer in the family should be the same as the one paid by the outsider, with due regard to the volume or regularity of deliveries, but the leeway letting profits appear where taxation is the lowest is very large indeed. The advantages accruing from this practice are somewhat reduced when a country such as the United States taxes a company on its worldwide profits after deducting the taxes paid to local governments. But profits abroad are not always taxed at the time they are earned, and the use of tax havens is not barred. It is interesting to note that the United States, with, as would be expected for the largest industrial producer in the world, a large surplus on its balance of patents and licenses, has an apparent deficit on that score with Canada. It seems highly probable that royalties are paid to subsidiaries in order to benefit from tax differentials. Artificial incentives to invest abroad are even greater in a country such as France which taxes only those profits made by French companies on its territory, but allows them to consolidate their balance sheets in case of losses incurred by their foreign subsidiaries, which can thus be written off.

An inducement to make acquisitions abroad rather than at home has until recently been provided by the United States's antitrust policy. It enjoined the largest corporations from acquiring other firms in the United States in fields in which they were already active. This led them to make similar acquisitions in foreign countries, particularly in the EEC. Now the rule has been extended to those external operations, thus creating a curious case of extraterritorial application of American jurisdiction.

Even independently of differences in taxation, vertical integration may lead to a distorted policy as to the apportionment of profits. A classic example is provided by the major oil companies. A time-honored policy, dating back to John D. Rockefeller, places the nominal profit as close as possible to the production of crude oil; the structure of prices was meant to discard the competition of independent refiners or distributors who had not the same direct access to th₂ basic resources. With the ever-increasing pressure of the oil-producing countries to obtain a larger share of the proceeds, following the effort of the independents to go to the sources by offering more favorable terms, this policy pays its belated penalty, which, of course, is passed on to the consumer.

It would take an infinitely detailed inquiry to discover what distortion of competition the new form of concentration represented by the utterly diversified conglomerates brings with it. The crisscross subsidization from profitable to less profitable activities which this structure makes possible may benefit some consumers, hurt others or displace competitors irrespective of true cost. (However, the same effect may obtain inside one national market as well as between markets.)

So much for the division of labor. In matters of finance, the treasurers of multinational corporations have been charged with creating turmoil in the various currencies and being the arch speculators. One non-American chairman said flatly that he had a duty, vis-à-vis his shareholders, and would consider it a major fault if he left his money where he thought the currency might be devalued or let go a possible profit where a currency appreciated. As a matter of fact, the multinationals with their ability to borrow funds and to move them may play the role of an amplifier. But the accusations of speculation usually mistake effect for cause. The fact is that convertibility was reestablished among the major currencies without any attempt at a coordination of monetary policies. More often than not, governors of central banks have to make up for the reluctance of governments or parliaments to resort to fiscal policies. Thus interest rates often move in directions completely alien to those the equilibrium of balances of payments would require. When, moreover, exchange rates are kept out of balance, or changed in an abrupt way, it is no surprise that such enormous masses of funds should move from one market to another. Multinational corporations have more freedom than bankers to play a game prompted by a preoccupation with avoiding losses even more than one of making profits. It has also long been known that one of the fields in which competition was most imperfect was in the ability to obtain funds: large companies are at an advantage over small ones, and for some time now, the Euro-currency market has widened the gap. The role of banks which also obtain resources on that market and are able to relend them to smaller customers has, however, reduced this inequality.

Controls

The existence and spread of the multinational corporations create a clear obligation on public authorities to counter the distortions which this across-the-border activity may create.

In some developed countries it may be argued on infant industry lines that some initial protection may be necessary to avoid foreign control of advanced technology. But those countries cannot at the same time protect themselves against the products and against the firms. The door should remain open to foreign firms to move forward new technology and research in the country concerned. Protection for products should be given only on a declining basis. A more dramatic case appears when multinational corporations themselves are able to exact from developing countries a high degree of protection as a condition for starting an operation. Again, unless this protection is progressively lowered, this new industry may be faced with a limited domestic market, no prospects for export, and a regressive effect on income distribution.

It should be clear that regional integration, particularly among developing countries, offers one of the best chances of attracting foreign investment without having to grant an unjustified degree of protection. Corporations would benefit from larger markets, and the ensuing possibility of specialized component plants. The difficulties, however, should not be underrated. Disguised unemployment serves as a justification for creating even the most uneconomic types of production. Industries which have been started in a narrow market create vested interests. This is not the place to go into possible schemes and inducements for regional integration in developing areas. Suffice it to mention one proposal which tried to pay full regard to the special difficulties of developing countries. Developing countries do not have the same certainty as EEC members that dynamic and diversified exports will be able to pay for any increased imports which the process of lowering obstacles to trade might entail. Hence the idea that those countries which experience an increase in their overall exports should pledge themselves to increase the share of their imports coming from other countries of the area which undertake the same commitment. This would set in motion a cumulative process, pass on trade concessions or increased purchases by the industrialized countries in the form of a better productive structure among the developing countries.

An accompanying step could reduce the differences in risks which distort the location of foreign investment. Developing countries engaging in a process of regional trade cooperation or integration should try to set up jointly administered guarantees. They would undertake to prevent defaults on the servicing of loans, and expropriations without proper compensation, by any member of the group, or together to indemnify the party affected. Again the difficulties cannot be overlooked as countries of different leanings in the same area may be reluctant to warrant and underwrite each other's action. But the political and economic advantages should not be ignored. It is less detrimental to be under one's own partner's pressure to keep one's commitments, than to be exposed to retaliations by powerful countries or international organizations dominated by the rich. A joint guarantee board would be in a better positon vis-à-vis powerful corporations to negotiate the terms under which they may operate than a single and often small country. It would also avoid the "auctioneering" process by which countries may grant undue favors to foreign firms at their own, and their neighbors' expense. It could thus be an instrument not only for eliminating distortions, but also for applying the rules which are likely to maximize the benefits and minimize the costs of the presence of multinational corporations for the countries concerned.

The key to a better allocation of resources is of course that some ground rules of industrial policy should be laid down, first and foremost among the industrialized countries, to prevent the retention of activities which are not in their best interest, and to use multinational corporations as an instrument to export industries where they belong. This requires the correct concept of competitiveness. An industry is not competitive because it is able to attract cheap labor; on the contrary, the reliance on low wages is a sign of weakness. Differences in the distribution of wage rates among industries in the industrialized countries are striking. The ratios are roughly from one to two and a half even excluding the capital-intensive industries such as oil or electricity generation, where labor costs, whatever the rates, are insignificant; for instance, the gap between the textile and garment industries at one end, and engineering, chemical or electrical industries considered as a unit at the other end, as well as electricity generation in which labor costs play a very limited role. Obviously, and subject to alternative employment opportunities, it would be in the interest of labor, and it should be the policy of the unions, to move away from low-wage branches. Adjustment policies including retraining should receive much more money from public authorities than they have been given hitherto. Experience shows, however, that there is also an adjustment problem for the owners and managers. This explains the extent of what could be called defensive investment, for example, when the textile industry in high wage countries tries to automate at all costs. This is a waste of the saving capacity without preserving employment. For the owners and managers of an industry, it is also much better to transfer production facilities to areas where they are consonant with a normal level of wages. Another consideration which should be given full weight is the new preoccupation with excessive urban and industrial concentration and ensuing pollution. This could lead to a more effective geographic redistribution of industry, if the social costs of such concentration which tend to grow exponentially are charged to the responsible industries rather than blindly covered by the community through the confused practices of public finance.

It has already been mentioned that the artificial incentives for making acquisitions abroad have been lessened by a change in United States antitrust policy. But by prohibiting the purchase of foreign companies by a dominant American company, the United States authorities were obviously interfering with the sovereignty of another country. A more balanced situation emerges now that the EEC is coming to grips with the problem of a misuse of a dominant position, to the point of forcing divestment when there is a threat that a monopoly position could be acquired in the Common Market. Thus some kind of harmonized antitrust policy might evolve at an international level.

A harmonization of taxation, that would prevent a distortion in investments and artificial transfer pricing among the various branches of a multinational corporation is, however, still distant. The rule of thumb proposed by Raymond Vernon,[1] that taxes on the worldwide profits of companies should be apportioned among the various countries in which they operate—for example, according to the sales made in or from each territory—remains the only specific proposal in this area.

The elimination of distortions emanating from the imputation of profits to various stages in the case of vertical integration, or to various activities in the case of conglomerates, would require a degree of control over the internal operation of companies which few if any countries, and even less so the international community, are prepared to exercise.

II. BENEFITS AND COSTS

The balance of benefits and costs to the host country of the installation of a multinational corporation is delicate. It can be viewed in its contribution to growth including technological progress, and its effect on the external accounts including its incidence on public finance which in turn may affect external equilibrium.

In a chapter contributed by the OECD Secretariat to a large-scale study of its Development and Assistance Committee's Development Centre,[2] a significant correlation has been evidenced between the inflow of foreign investment and the rate of growth in the developing countries. Even a superficial comparison of countries

---

1. See "Economic Sovereignty at Bay" in a collection of Raymond Vernon's essays, *The Economic and Political Consequences of Multinational Enterprise, An Anthology* (Boston: Harvard Graduate School of Business Administration, 1972), pp. 3-19.

2. See Grant L. Reuber and Associates, "Private Foreign Investment in Development" (forthcoming).

seems also to confirm that point. This of course is not surprising: foreign investment supplements inadequate internal savings, providing additional real resources and know-how. The correlation is much higher than with the amount of aid, be it in the form of outright grants or concessional lending. Again this is no surprise. The way aid has been distributed from different sources according to political rather than economic criteria, its application to such objectives as education, housing or infrastructure which, even if rationally done, has a much more indirect and long-term impact, is enough to explain this *prima facie* failure. As regards direct investment, however, the case is not that simple. It is obviously essential to distinguish between periods, as there is both an inflow and an outflow, and to measure the effects by comparison with other alternatives, either domestic investment or other forms of external resources. Thus the net benefit varies from case to case and is extraordinarily difficult to assess.

Impact on the Country and Its Economic Sectors

The Pearson Report, in a chapter devoted to private foreign investment,[3] comes to the conclusion that it is on the whole beneficial to the host countries and should be encouraged by them through special facilities. The Herbert May study for the Council of the Americas goes even further in attributing to it extreme advantages.[4] In a provocative paper which happens to be limited to Latin America, Albert Hirschmann, on the contrary, makes a case for gradual divestment.[5] He points out not only the balance of payments costs which occur when the repatriation of profits and other remittances outpaces the inflow of capital, but he even doubts the contribution to growth. His main argument is that foreign investment is a facile solution which stifles the inducement to internal savings and local entrepreneurship. He states that in the periods, notably between the two world wars, when certain countries had to liquidate their external assets, the Latin Americans proved easily able to provide the savings necessary to repurchase them. And although multinational corporations employ local personnel even in responsible positions, there is a difference between the problems of decision-

---

3. See Lester B. Pearson, *Partners in Development* (New York: Frederick A Praeger, 1969), pp. 99-123.

4. Herbert K. May, *The Effects of United States and Other Foreign Investment in Latin America* (New York: The Council for Latin America, Inc., 1970).

5. Albert O. Hirschman, *How to Divest in Latin America, and Why,* Essays in International Finance, no. 76 (Princeton, N.J.: Princeton University Press, 1969).

making for an independent firm and for a subsidiary. Thus local managers, even if they are nationals of the host country, are deprived of the proper training in what constitutes the essence of management, that is, strategic reorientations. However, Hirschmann's main preoccupation was political. He was bent on avoiding the frictions and rash reaction which the presence of large foreign firms may bring about. In order, however, to avoid any abrupt withdrawal of capital which would not be sustainable for the host countries, he was suggesting an international organization which would acquire the assets and resell them only gradually to local interests.

In terms of policy there is nothing shocking about Hirschmann's proposal. By the end of the last century, European investment in the United States may have represented as much as 15 percent of the total capital stock. It is now an almost negligible proportion, although portfolio investment is very sizable. Thus a divesting process has taken place through repurchase by Americans. It is, however, necessary to state the assumptions underlying the proposal. It implies that there are always preferable alternatives and, moreover, these are of a domestic character. That a better fiscal and particularly tax policy could be pursued, that capital markets could be developed, is not to be denied. But on the balance of payments side, the difficulties experienced cast some doubt on the possibility of doing away altogether with a new inflow of foreign capital, let alone financing regular, even if protracted, repayments. One should also remember Raymond Vernon's warning with regard to management, technology and marketing: the displacement of foreign by local companies not only may cut some sources of funds, but also may sever very valuable links and a constant inflow of information and know-how.

The external alternatives are not easy to appraise. Borrowing to obtain the funds will be discussed in relation with the balance of payments aspects. Management contracts are a broad category and may extend from mere advice to direct conduct of a firm which, however, in a capitalist system, may lead to conflicts with the shareholders. There are complaints about the high cost of licenses as a way of acquiring know-how. Finally the greatest difficulty may be in the field of marketing where the multinational corporation is likely to be a much more effective instrument than local firms or intermediaries.

The key question regarding growth is whether the sector occupied by the multinational corporations will carry along the rest of the economy or remain an enclave. Worse still, there is a distinct possibility that the creation of a modern sector may hamper the development of the rest of the economy. The oil industry has in most cases apparently been of the enclave type. It is not unreasonable to argue that, for instance, in Venezuela, the wages oil was able to pay, and the external proceeds that it earned, led to an exchange rate and a level of wages which made the creation of other industries more difficult. True enough, this contradiction may just as well occur in the case of domestic as of foreign investment. It will be interesting to watch the Algerian experience. Will the energetic effort to create modern industries such as steel and petrochemicals diffuse its effects on other activities? Is there not the risk that this advanced segment will not create enough direct employment, will not find all the outlets for its capacity of production, will absorb the resources which might have been necessary for a proper diffusion of progress and finally by its very presence be a hindrance for other more modest activities? Such wide dualism may be an obstacle to development. Probably a key factor in the economic success of Japan has been its original way of dealing with dualism. The system of lifelong employment in the large corporations, while attracting more manpower away from the traditional firms or sectors, avoided any depressing effect on those sectors. It established a barrier and let the levels of wages differ greatly between the two categories of firms. Under such conditions, the diffusion of progress takes place through the gradual and orderly channeling of manpower from the traditional to the modern sectors. In the absence of such a partition, the traditional sector may wither away and concealed unemployment is likely to grow. This lack of adjustment to the overall conditions may be more serious in the case of multinational corporations than of a national effort and, paradoxically enough, even more so if their operations are geared to exports rather than to the domestic market of the host country. The risk of high protection and the ensuing maldistribution of income would then be replaced by the risk of using advanced techniques with comparatively low-wage labor. The spread of progress internally might be halted, while the effects on international competition might be more than industrialized countries are prepared to bear.

Impact on the Balance of Payments

Competition from advanced countries is thus all the more severe if there is an enclave of modern high-productivity industries in an economic environment of low standards of living and money wages in underdeveloped countries. It goes without saying that an over-valued currency may also lead to excessive foreign investment. The export of jobs which was blamed by the United States labor unions on the multinational corporations was just another expression of the disequilibrium in exchange rates. But the key problem is to assess the balance of payments impact of multinational corporations on the countries in which they establish themselves. There is a very discernible trend. Profit remittances or royalties to United States companies may already in some countries, particularly in Latin America, more than offset the inflow of direct investment and aid. The growing indebtedness is due partly to former overborrowing, partly to the necessity of filling that gap. This tends to make Latin America a net exporter of long-term capital, whereas at the same time there is a continuous net inflow of United States investment in industrialized countries, particularly in Europe.

The reports presented to the Development Centre of OECD[6] have clearly distinguished all the elements which have to be taken into consideration, and discarded some oversimplifications or falla-cies. The obvious items are, of course, the inflow and outflow of capital. The ploughing back of profits on the spot may be considered as a positive item inasmuch as it saves additional foreign borrowing or is the equivalent of an inflow of foreign capital which would otherwise have been necessary. The difference between the inflow plus the reinvested profits and the outflow cannot however be taken as the only measure of the contribution to, or the drain on, the bal-ance of payments. The exports attributable to the multinational cor-porations have to be taken into account. But here also there is a great measure of uncertainty. It is only the excess of such exports over the alternative, that is what a domestic corporation may have sold abroad, which should be credited properly to the foreign-owned operations. This item may even be negative. Moreover, there must be a deduction for the import content of exports, which again has to be compared with what purely domestic production would have re-quired. Beyond the direct import content, the import multiplier— that is, the additional imports induced by the increase in internal in-come and demand— come into play. A very moot question is that of import saving which can be credited to foreign investment. Herbert

---

6. See Reuber and Associates, op. cit., and [Hendricus C. Bos], "A Quantitative Study of the Macroeconomic Impact of Private Foreign Investment in Less Developed Countries," Netherlands Economic Institute, mimeographed (Rotterdam, n.d.).

May goes so far as to consider all production of the United States subsidiaries as automatic import saving.[7] This is obviously contradictory. Imports are a function of income, and the same imports would not take place if a given volume of production were not present to generate the income. Although they should be viewed more in the context of total resources than in their balance of payments effect, the taxes paid and the subsidies received by foreign corporations have to be taken into account. The higher the taxes, or the lower the subsidies, the more the net inflow of capital. Those taxes and subsidies must also be compared with what an alternative domestic operation would have contributed or received. It is also essential to know how much of the foreign operation is financed locally, particularly by drawing on the credit system.

Paul Rosenstein-Rodan focused on the conditions of financing and on a link between the inflow and the outflow.[8] His first point is that the return on direct investment is normally higher than the interest rate on borrowing, so that when the profits are remitted abroad, the drain on the balance of payments is particularly high. He was suggesting that direct investment should be accompanied by loans as was the case in the nineteenth century. The difference, however, is that, given the present world, and particularly the condition of the developing countries, the loans would have to be provided by the public sector—governments or international organizations—rather than by private investors. There is in any case a drawback to that solution. The service of loans is due whatever the economic situation of the country concerned, whereas profits vary with the level of activity, and largely, with that of exports. There are also some periods in which the rate of interest, except on concessional lending, may jump very high indeed. The other proposal is, rather than setting an arbitrary limit on profit remittances as is, for instance, foreseen in the Andean Pact, that they should be linked to what has been effectively imported as capital as distinct from what has been obtained locally. The difficulty, however, is that if foreign investment cannot obtain the leverage of internal borrowing, this again may act as an undesirable deterrent.

Ideas of this kind at least indicate a way ahead. They do not attempt to list and measure in each case all the benefits and costs of a foreign investment project, or of the presence of multinational cor-

---

7. May, op. cit.

8. Paul N. Rosenstein-Rodan, *Multinational Investment in the Framework of Latin America Integration*, Massachusetts Institute of Technology monograph (Cambridge, Mass., March 1968).

porations, because if the comparison were to be made with more or less real alternatives, this would in most cases defy any attempt at adequate measurement. But there are general orientations which are more likely than not to be beneficial. Thus one should tend to what might be called a probabilist policy. It may not be the optimum, which would require placing an exact value on all the parameters, actual and potential, present and future. But it would be so geared as to maximize the chances of increasing benefits and reducing costs.

III. SOME PROPOSALS FOR CONTROL OF
MULTINATIONAL CORPORATIONS

To that effect a general set of policies seems to be valid for developed and developing countries alike. It should be supplemented by the setting up of a particular type of multinational corporation most appropriate for the developing areas.

The general policies and rules will be presented first. They stem from two or three simple principles. The first is that the foreign corporation should behave like a local one, if not better. The second is that foreign investment should make all the contributions to the host country which in theory may be expected from it. In a world where pure competition does not prevail, definite rules will in most cases be required to bring this about. The third idea, which applies mostly to the developed countries, and even more to the EEC, would be to face up to the competition of foreign multinationals, and give local companies the same means and the same status.

From the first principle some corollaries can be derived. There is always a fear that multinational corporations being steered from an outside center of decision will entail a loss of control on the part of the host country over its own direction and, as the case may be, on the implementation of its internal planning. The argument is much too broad. Any country which is engaged in international trade depends unavoidably, to a large extent, on outside markets and outside competitors. For instance, the closing down of a plant by a multinational corporation is not different in essence from the effects on employment of the loss of an external market. The problems are more specific. There is no dispute on the subjection of foreign subsidiaries to the direction of a national plan, if any. One particular application is the location of plants. It is recognized that in that respect foreign companies are usually more flexible than local ones which already have their roots in a particular place. Some mistakes have been made in the field of labor relations, such as abrupt dismissals by foreign companies which did not pay full regard to the local customs, to requirements for advance notice, and the need to find alternative jobs. But the multinationals have usually learned from such errors.

There are, however, two points which are more difficult to observe. One relates to exports, the other to research.

On the export side, there may be two kinds of conflicts. One was particularly evident in the days of strict restraint on the export of particular items from the United States to Eastern countries, and still is, in the embargo applying to Cuba. There was an unavoidable dilemma. Either the subsidiary was acting contrary to the policy of the host country, or the injunctions of the United States Government were circumvented through the foreign subsidiary of the United States company. The first course had particularly serious consequences in the case of a takeover. For example, a company might have sold some equipment to China, and its new owner would interrupt the delivery of parts. The United States has finally decided in favor of the second course, and exempts subsidiaries from restrictions on exports applying to the parent company. But even when that conflict is solved, another one is latent in the very existence of the multinational corporations. There is an essential difference between subsidiaries and independent firms. The latter ignore the losses which their own activity may provoke for their competitors. A multinational corporation aiming at the maximization of its overall profits is bound to coordinate the activities of its branches. This may go as far as prohibiting exports by some of them to some markets, and in particular reducing the competition to the parent company in its own market. In these circumstances, the host country may reasonably refuse to be bound by such limitations and may insist its export policy has precedence over the internal arrangements of the multinationals, because this is not only a question of sovereignty, but of the superiority of competition over monopolistic practices.

Research is rightly considered as an essential element of progress, almost a new factor of production. It is, of course, profitable to draw on the results obtained abroad, but in a dynamic sense, it is essential for a country to be associated with the process of research itself in some kind of learning-by-doing. Some of the multinational corporations have made attempts at decentralizing their research facilities not only with a view to forestalling the objections of host countries, but also to draw on local talent. In many cases, however, there is a technical advantage in centralizing research so that communication is established between various specialists, and one line of research may benefit from the work done on another. Host governments may insist nonetheless that part of the research should be carried out in their territories and by their own people.

The second principle takes stock of the usual arguments in favor of foreign investment: it is supposed to bring with it capital, technology and know-how, management and the training of local staff, and foreign companies also appear as a kind of voluntary taxpayer.

In the actual transfer of funds, one should emphasize again the divorce between foreign investment and movements of capital. This does not create a serious problem in the case of Europe, which has a high savings potential, although some companies complain that large United States corporations are in a better position to borrow on the Euro-currency market than they are themselves. In come cases, the fact that European companies do not have the same access to the New York market as the United States companies creates a distortion of competition. Suppose that two corporations, one from the United States and the other from Europe, are bidding against each other to acquire a third. The United States firm may draw both on the European and United States capital markets, whereas the European company would face the interest equalization tax and the limitations on bank credits abroad. When it comes to developing countries, they are justified in insisting, as Argentina and also the Andean Group have begun to, that the foreign companies should bring funds with them.

It is not easy to comply with the insistence that a foreign corporation should produce its latest models and apply its most modern techniques in the host country. In some cases, at the start, the market may not be large enough. In developing countries, a premature application of new techniques might even be contrary to their own best interest, as it would not provide a combination of capital and labor best suited to their economic structure. It is, however, normal to require that at some point the more advanced techniques be introduced, and the stages could be agreed upon in advance. Local companies would benefit by training high level personnel and management in multinational corporations.

Taxes raise intricate problems. There is no assurance that a multinational corporation will not manage, through its transfer prices, to push the profits to the place where tax rates are most advantageous. Thus it would be a normal course of action on the part of a country, or of the EEC for that matter, to limit the right of establishment to companies depending either on local headquarters or directly on the parent company in its country of origin, and to exclude those which are run from a base located in some third country likely to be a tax haven. The idea suggested in the Pearson Report[9] that developing countries be prepared to grant tax favors to foreign companies in order to attract them, is moreover dangerous and inequitable. This starts the "auctioneering" process, by giving the multinational corporations the means to play one country off against another, thereby transfering the burden of taxation to that part of a country's population least able to bear it. It should be clear that such facilities for investment in developing countries should be given by the country of origin, that is, by the industrialized world itself.

Developed countries, particularly in Europe, are not justified in complaining about the competition of the United States giants. They have their own, which apparently enjoy a higher rate of growth than their counterparts in the United States. And rather than a new form of protectionism which instead of warding off the products from abroad, would tend to ward off the firms, a positive effort is in order. Suffice it to mention the necessity of creating a large unified capital market, and of reformulating research programs so that they are not a belated duplication of what has been achieved in the United States, but break new ground and are carried out in common and on an appropriate scale to avoid waste. It is certainly a strange situation that United States firms have much exploited the opening of a wide regional market economic space better than the European firms, and that European companies tend more to associate themselves with United States firms rather than with European partners. The EEC is trying to counter this by granting special facilities, which are likely to be of a discriminatory character, to companies of so-called European interest. But legal and psychological obstacles cannot be overcome while there is no agreement on a European company law, and no possibility of direct incorporation with the European authorities. Any European joint venture still must be pursued under the law of one of the member countries, and no important across-the-border mergers may be expected so long as one of the partners feels, of necessity, that he is less familiar with the rules and that he suffers a loss of prestige.

---

9. Pearson, op. cit.

In the case of developing countries, more factors and difficulties have to be taken into account. For a long time firms from the industrialized countries invested mostly in raw materials in order to obtain their essential supplies. This led to a rudimentary division of labor in which primary products were exchanged for manufactured goods which remained the monopoly of the advanced countries. Such investments were supplemented by the financing of infrastructure, mainly in transportation to allow movements of those goods. Then foreign investments took part in import substitution, and often demanded the same protection on each national market which local industry could claim. It is now essential that multinational corporations should contribute to the building up of competitive and export-oriented industries and they thus favor integration between existing narrow national markets. The drain on the balance of payments of host countries when profit remittances exceed the original inflow of capital must be considered. The stifling of local savings, entrepreneurship and managerial ability is another risk. Last but not least is the risk of political friction between powerful foreign companies and comparatively weak governments; this leads either to rash reactions or exploitation.

A new model of multinational undertakings seems to provide an answer to considerations such as these. The organization of The Atlantic Development Group for Latin America (ADELA) followed by the Private Investment Corporation for Asia (PICA) and a projected organization for Africa could provide a new type of relationship. Such organizations are truly multinational. Corporations from several countries subscribe the shares and the subscription of each is limited to a certain amount to avoid any one corporation acquiring a dominant position. They engage in joint ventures with local partners in several countries at the same time. This tends to encourage saving and to train management on the spot. It also creates an interest in integrated rather than protected markets. The financial standing of the member corporations makes not only venture capital, but also loan capital easily obtainable. A gradual increase of the share of the local partners in any venture through a process of resale and divestment, which by the same token releases the funds to be used in other ventures is a key idea. In other words this kind of multinational investment acts as a prime mover and avoids, as far as possible, negative effects on the developing countries' growth and balance of payments.

This model of multinational investment has been devised by

enlightened entrepreneurs from the industrialized countries. Developing countries could adopt this procedure by announcing clearly that this is the most welcome form of direct foreign investment. If it could become the standard in relation to developing countries, it would remove most of the negative effects, and more important still, most sources of conflict. The root of many troubles in the Third World is the feeling of dependence which creates resentment and provides an alibi for inaction by allowing the blame to be put on others, that is, on the industrialized countries. Potential investors would have to take this type of joint investment seriously instead of regarding it just as a token of goodwill and a contribution to a favorable image.

More generally, let us be frank. The call by businessmen to the social conscience of business is a *confusion des genres*. Only those firms which enjoy monopoly profits can afford to cater to their image and engage spontaneously in welfare and environmental activities. The only tools which are of general effectiveness are competition and public regulation. Competition may work both ways, according to the level of employment. It may set a limit to wages and other benefits, or raise them by attracting labor away from less attractive to better conditions. It is not for corporations to create the general framework of economic activity, but to work within it and adapt to it. Thus it is largely out of place to speak of the responsibilities of multinational corporations. The more multinational they are, the more the governments have to coordinate their actions, and be aware of their international repercussions.

Comment

Fred Bergsten

I want to make three basic points. The first is to push a bit further Pierre Uri's point that any perpetration of evil-doing by multinational corporations is basically the fault of the governments, which have a responsibility to regulate the climate in which the firms operate and which are shirking that responsibility in both the industrialized and in the developing countries. The second is to draw from that some implications for what might be appropriate policies for developing countries to achieve the kind of gains that they can and should be getting from the activities of multinational corporations, but are not always getting. The third is to point out, however, that precisely those policy responses by the developing countries will make the calculation of costs and benefits for home countries more unfavorable and thereby add to the likelihood that those home countries will themselves increasingly restrict the outflows of investment to the developing (as well as other) countries.

Pierre Uri's paper makes it clear, in a number of places, that it is up to governments to regulate the activities of multinational corporations so that those activities will conform to the competitive, free market model from which we can feel relatively safe in concluding that real economic benefits will flow. For example, he points out quite rightly that traditional theory would posit that multinational firms would bring capital with them, not borrow it in the country in which they are investing; that they would train local citizens on the basis of assumptions about factory immobility; that they would avoid market sharing arrangements which stifle competition. I think he is quite right that it is up to the host country government to assure that the multinational firm does bring with it these and other alleged benefits.

But I would go even further than Pierre Uri in listing some of the responsibilities of governments in regulating the activities of multinational firms. He points to the problem of intracorporate pricing, and how it can distort the economic effects of foreign investment by multinational firms, but was pessimistic that governments could do very much about that. I reject that notion. It is preposterous for a host country not to insist upon full disclosure of the activities of a multinational firm. By so doing, it would have a handle on the intracorporate pricing practices and could tax profits— as they should be taxed—on the basis of real earnings in the country in which the investment takes place. Even if a country cannot get that kind of full disclosure, however, it can simply construct shadow prices and demand higher tax payments if it feels it is being bilked. Multinational firms would doubtlessly discover a new interest in new international rules and codes to govern international investment relations if a number of host countries began to tax them on the basis of such shadow prices. Indeed, the oil countries have done that for a long time. I am not sure I want to replicate the oil results in all respects, but I would be more optimistic than Pierre Uri about the possibilities for dealing with the problem of intracorporate pricing by the action of national governments.

Governments must, of course, adopt national macroeconomic policies which will prevent international flows of investment from causing new distortions. For example, they must have the right exchange rate. If they undervalue the exchange rate, they can expect foreign companies to buy up assets that look cheap to them, with resulting effects that may not be beneficial to the host country. A host country has to assure that competition prevails, rather than an environment in which the multinational firm can pursue—as it usually wants to—oligopolistic practices, which also carry distortions that may rebound unfavorably to the host country.

Indeed, at the international level, governments have a responsibility to set up rules which will not permit the multinational corporations to take unfair advantage of any individual country. The international monetary system is a clear case in point. Pierre Uri referred quite rightly to the activities of multinational corporations speculating in the exchange markets. That speculation may often be equilibrating and therefore in both the international interest and the national interest of most countries. But it is quite clear that one reason the corporations have been able to speculate successfully is the nature of the monetary system, with its faulty exchange rate regime of excessively narrow margins around parities and infrequent changes in parities. It has thus been "duck soup" for any multinational treasurer to speculate against a given exchange rate. Therefore, governments have a responsibility to keep the international monetary system in the kind of shape that will not permit multinational corporations to take "unfair advantage" of it, as in speculating against an exchange rate. I would also agree with Pierre Uri about the need at the international level for coordination of tax laws and antitrust policies.

Turning to my second point, I think we can see quite clearly a number of actions that developing countries would try to take if they wanted to maximize their gains from multinational investment in their countries.[10] with their increased concern about unemployment, one thing they will clearly want is labor-intensive investment by these firms. In some cases, the multinational corporations will on

---

10. In passing, I caution about a correlation between the level of private investment in a developing country and the level of development of that country, implying that there was a causal relation which ran from the private investment to the development of the country. I think it is equally plausible, from what we know about the motivations of multinational corporations, to hypothesize that they invest heavily in countries that are already developing. Obviously there are feedbacks between the two sides, but I caution against the kind of implication there.

their own initiative invest in labor-intensive practices, even if that is not the model they follow in their home country, but it is quite logical to expect developing countries to promote actively such investment. But that would in truth exacerbate concern about the export of jobs in the home country that is exporting the capital. Labor-intensive investment abroad would not necessarily mean an export of jobs greater than capital-intensive investment to produce the same output, but it would certainly exacerbate home-country concern.

The developing countries might also want the highest degree of technology available in the multinational corporation (in different circumstances than those in which they wanted labor-intensive production, for the most part). In some cases they might even go beyond what the market might indicate, as in the case of job creation, by requiring on-the-spot research or the transfer of technology that might not even be particularly relevent to their internal situations. That too exacerbates the concern expressed in a number of home countries about the export of their highest technology, again making more difficult the home country decision as to whether to permit the export of capital carrying with it the highest technology in that country.

A third result that the developing countries will want from the multinational enterprise is exports. Pierre Uri pointed out that it is logical for a developing country to require multinational enterprises investing therein to export some significant part of their output to ease the country's balance of payments constraints. This may well go beyond preventing the multinational firm from not exporting at all, as a result of market-sharing arrangements. Exports may be pushed beyond what market indications would suggest, into some agreed quota of output. Such an arrangement also runs counter to the balance of payments and mercantilist trade concerns of the home country, whose firm is exporting the capital and then suddenly exporting from the developing country in which it has invested (including to the home country market itself), undercutting the balance of trade and the balance of payments position of the home country. So the cost-benefit calculation from the standpoint of the home country interest is again rendered negative to some extent, reciprocating the positive gain to the host country.

Still in the balance of payment context, the host country will generally also want the multinational firm to reinvest a large share or *all* of its earnings and limit its repatriation of capital. This again may run directly counter to the desire of the home country for a high level of repatriated income, to offset at least in part the ongoing stream of capital outflow which is, least in the short-run, hurting its balance of payments position.

There are a number of policy responses by developing countries to the activities of multinational firms, which added together also turn the cost-benefit calculations for the home country in a less favorable direction and thereby tilt it in the direction of putting controls on the very kind of investment which the host country is attempting to maximize. It has traditionally been recognized that the host country must be careful not to insist on conditions so tough that the firm will be dissuaded from investing there in the first place (assuming of course that the country wants the investment on terms that are acceptable to the firm). In the present environment where host countries (at least the United States) are increasingly questioning the wisdom of foreign direct investment from the standpoint of *their* national interests, the host country could also turn off the investment by tilting the balance of benefits too far against the home country even in cases where the firm itself was not significantly hampered.

It is not true that all policies toward foreign investment undertaken by developing countries would be regarded as negative by home countries. Indeed, some of the responses one might expect from host countries might allay some of the problems perceived by home countries. One example is the possibility of global cartelization by these firms, which is not yet a first-order concern on the part of most home countries but may increasingly be one—witness the inclusion of international considerations in the recent United States antitrust actions. The objective of avoiding global cartelization would be promoted by proper host country competition policies. So would some of the concerns on the part of home countries about the activities of their multinational firms which intervene in their foreign policy.

There are ways other than capital controls in which the home country can respond to problems that are generated for it by host country actions: they include full employment policies, effective adjustment assistance programs to deal with all sorts of structural changes in the economy and proper exchange rate policies which take care of the balance of payments.

There may also be a need for a new range of policies by home countries to deal with the activities of multinational firms based in their own countries. In trade policies, we have traditionally had safeguards which operate on a case-by-case basis when there are clear abuses to internal economic welfare in a country which is faced by a sudden flow of imports. It is curious that there are no such policies in the investment area, especially now that it rivals pure trade flows in quantitative importance, and there may be room for analogous safeguards in home countries to deal with abuses caused by particular capital outflows. One can imagine direct analogies with the escape clause, for example, under which a particular foreign investment which suddenly disrupts a particular industry internally might be subjected to certain restaints. One can imagine analogies to countervailing duties, where a tax is applied in the home country to a foreign investment which is promoted uneconomically by subsidies in host countries and causes injury in the home country. There are many kinds of conceptual problems in how to go about defining such cases and it is a challenging area for research; it may well be the direction in which national policy in capital-exporting countries should develop to maximize the welfare effects of international investment. Such policy may have to be evolved if the kinds of pressures that are now being brought to bear against foreign investment as a whole, including pressures from developing countries quite logically pursuing their own interests, are not to lead to a very restrictive seizing-up of international flows of capital across the board.

Comment

Gerry Helleiner

The breadth of coverage in the contributions by Pierre Uri and Fred Bergsten is so thorough that it is difficult to know where to begin. Let me do so by defining what it is we really are or should be talking about in this discussion of manufactured exports and multinational corporations. (I do so because Pierre Uri and others have expressed some doubts on this matter.) I believe the focus of our attention must be intrafirm international trade. What we are concerned with are those instances where trade takes place across international borders but remains under the control, and usually the ownership, of a particular private firm. Whether this is "multinational" in some ultimate sense does not really matter; for our purposes, the key point is that the control is exerted by foreigners to the developing world.

I believe a bit of confusion may have crept into some of the previous discussion; a foreign firm need not be an *investor* (either of its own or locally borrowed funds) to be a very important *actor* in the world. Many instances exist wherein the activity of the multinational firm is based on what Raymond Vernon calls "global scanning capacity." The major wholesalers who "source" labor-intensive consumer goods in low-wage countries (Sears & Roebuck, Macy's and the Japanese trading firms), for instance, have typically had only limited amounts of working capital tied up in their activities in the Third World. It is the capacity to organize—with or without capital transfers—together with detailed knowledge of and access to markets which is in such cases their crucial contribution.

For the purposes of organizing discussion on the subject of multinational firms and manufactured export prospects I believe it is useful to classify. First, one must distinguish between those foreign firms already operating in the developing countries and those only now moving operations there for one reason or another. Those already there are typically of two kinds: those engaged in primary production (mines and estates) and those engaged in import-substituting manufacturing. Both kinds may develop manufacturing activities for export based on their original plant overseas. Mining and agricultural enterprises may engage in further processing of primary products. Import-substituting manufacturers, who originally invested there for defensive reasons in order to protect their overseas markets in the face of tariff and other protective devices imposed by host governments, may switch a part of their production into export activity.

Foreign firms engaged in the latter switching to exports can move in two directions: they can export to other developing countries or they can sell to the industrial countries. Their manufactured exports to other developing countries are themselves classifiable into two categories: those geared to the peculiar characteristics of the markets in the Third World (perhaps catering to new tastes which may be developed through a strategy of the type advocated by Mahbub Haq and those arising from the rationalization within or between forms of existing overseas manufacturing enterprises when individual national market barriers within the Third World fall. Multinational firms already active in the developing world are likely to possess a comparative advantage in the supply of products of the former type catering exclusively to that market. The export potential or, more accurately, the rationalization possibilities of the latter sort make multinational enterprises firm advocates and prime beneficiaries of economic integration arrangements in the Third World; their behavior and success in this sphere must be understood not so much in the context of prospects for "competition," as in that of the potential for "planning complementarities" within large private firms or oligopolistic industries.

It is, however, with the foreign firms only now shifting their interests to the developing world for the first time that there seems at present to be the most concern. (Certainly it is the new entrants to Third World activity which most occupy the attention of the AFL-CIO.) These new multinational entrants are themselves again of two types: the wholesalers—who have no production facilities to speak of, either in high-wage or low-wage countries, and who are concerned merely with "sourcing" their product more efficiently— and the owners of the "runaway plant"—the large international manufacturing firm that relocates highly labor-intensive operations which were formerly undertaken at home in low-wage countries.

In the latter type of multinational firm activity, involving the manufacture or assembly of components overseas, it seems to me that there exists a real possibility for "adjustment" to take place *within* the large firm. Many of the firms engaging in this form of Third World manufacturing activity are in high growth industries, notably electronics. The potential for rearranging their own activities at home in such a way as to guarantee the employment of those whose jobs are immediately threatened by "runaways" is clearly considerably greater in such industries than is the potential for such intrafirm adjustment in response to job losses in stagnant industries, such as textiles. Apart from the limited growth prospects of labor-intensive final product industries, the owners of capital in these industries typically have few overseas interests and consequently, unlike their counterparts in the industries in which "runaways" are found, are allied in their clamor for protection with the trade union movement in the rich country. It should also be evident that large firms relocating assembly of component manufacturing activities overseas have an interest, particularly when prodded by labor's representatives, in arranging suitable reemployment for workers whose jobs are "exported." Their concern is greater than that of the wholesalers who, of course, have no interest whatsoever in the ramifications of their overseas sourcing for domestic employment. The oligopolistic character and resulting profitability of many of the industries in which "runaways" are found provide further ground for optimism concerning the potential for internal readjustment *within* firms in consequence of the development of Third World manufacturing activity for export.

For a number of reasons, I believe that manufacturing for export from the Third World is likely to develop fastest in the next decade or two through acceleration in the "runaway plant" and "overseas sourcing" phenomena. In 1970, of its total manufactured imports from developing countries the United States acquired over 15 percent under the provisions of its tariff-schedule items 806.30 and 807.00, the items permitting the application of import duties only to overseas value added. This was quite apart from those imports to which these provisions could not be applied, but which nevertheless were also the result of "overseas sourcing" or the overseas transfer of labor-intensive activities within multinational manufacturing and marketing concerns.

How multinational mining, manufacturing or wholesaling concerns behave depends, of course, upon the structure of tax and other incentives which set the rules of the game they play. Their roles in the development of manufactured exports from the Third World therefore depend upon policies with respect to incentives both in the importing and potential exporting countries. Value added tariffs in the industrially developed countries (such as are applied under the provisions of items 806.30 and 807.00 in the United States tariff) increase the profitability to them of overseas component manufacturing or assembly. It is therefore in the interest of the Third World that such provisions be introduced where they do not now exist and liberalized where they do.

The application of import duties to value added rather than gross value follows logically from the conventional argument for free trade. As usual, however, the application of free trade arguments in a second-best world may produce distortions which are not wholly desirable. If Third World exporters are blocked, through protection, in the fields of textiles, cutlery, footwear, mineral processing and so on, and if they cannot be expected to possess a comparative advantage in the production of those final products they now produce for domestic markets, then manufactured exports of the "runaway plant" type may be the only avenue open. The introduction or liberalization of value added tariffs, which will be championed by the multinational firms, will then push the developing countries *further* along a path which would not have been chosen in the absence of the distorted tariff structure in the markets to which they sell. While this avenue is no doubt preferable to no avenue at all the bargaining strength of the host Third World country is likely to be peculiarly low in this form of manufacturing for export; it can therefore be expected to try to develop alternative industrial export activities as quickly as possible.

The classification system for analyzing the role of multinational firms in the development of manufactured exports from developing countries is obviously only the beginning of the story. To put some flesh upon the "skeleton" it will be necessary not only to forecast general development in each "box," but also, for each country, to consider the likely domestic impact of expansion, the most suitable institutional arrangements and bargaining strategies for Third World countries, and, the potential for "easy adjustment" in the importing countries. Suitable policies for both developing countries and advanced potential importers can only be constructed if the types of manufacturing activity one seeks to promote for export are known, and if the types of multinational actors likely to be involved can be identified.

Lastly, I cannot resist responding to Fred Bergsten's point that it is simply "up to the governments" of developing countries to make required changes in policies for the effective management of multinational firms. This strikes me as very superficial and even naive. He neglects to consider the underlying explanations as to *why* such governments frequently have not the will (or the capacity, or both) to introduce such policies. In the bargaining which takes place between the host government and a foreign firm the former is much influenced by the presence of a variety of interest groups. Why is it that we continue to attribute irrational political behavior on the part of the United States to the activities of particular interest groups and yet attribute analogous failures of governments in developing countries to their own inherent "unwillingness"? Among the groups typically seeking to influence host governments in the developing world are powerful representatives or allies of the foreign firms themselves.

I do agree, however, that the basic issue *is* that of the bargain to be struck between the host country and the foreign firm. I would add that the object of the host country is to establish the range within which the bargain *can* be struck and then to do the best it can within that range. Since in the field of manufacturing for export the major contributions from foreign firms are in organization, marketing and technology, one ought to ask whether there may not be ways of acquiring these contributions which are superior to the importation of foreign-owned establishments. Can "arms length" purchases of marketing services and technology from foreign firms be undertaken by the governments or private investors of developing countries? Here in the IBRD as elsewhere there appears to be a great deal of interest in the development of more labor-intensive technologies in the field of manufacturing. Because the development of labor-intensive technology is itself a highly *skill-intensive* activity, these new technologies are likely to be developed by foreign firms rather than by indigenous research establishments. There is obviously therefore a continuing need to strengthen the bargaining power of Third World host countries through assistance and information, and to develop means for them to acquire technology and marketing services from foreign firms at minimum cost.

4

Employment in the Industrialized Countries

Caroline Miles

This paper is about the adverse consequences for advanced countries of an increasing flow of imports of manufactures from developing countries. It examines some of the problems of structural change and adaptation to which these imports may give rise, and considers the range of policy measures that governments might bring into play as alternatives to additional protection. Inevitably, by concentrating on the hurtful aspects of economic change, the paper presents a rather gloomy picture, though it will be argued that the potential size of the problem over the next decade is not very large and should be readily manageable.

In order to see adjustment problems in their proper perspective, it is important to bear in mind the short-term nature of these problems, which are essentially problems of transition, and the long-term benefits of freer trade, including gains in real incomes and a better distribution of world industrial production. The experience of the advanced countries over the past twenty years or so suggests that liberal trade and payments policies play an important role in bringing about this better distribution, when allied to appropriate national and international development policies. Growth among the advanced countries has been uneven, with some of them adapting their structures more readily than others, but even where adaptation has been slow and reluctant, as in the United Kingdom for instance, major structural changes have taken place without mass unemployment.

The basic question the advanced countries now have to tackle is how to engineer further changes in their economic structures, so as to allow the developing countries to realize their inherent comparative advantages and supply an increasing proportion of the world's growing demand for labor-intensive manufactured goods, while at the same time maintaining acceptable rates of growth and levels of employment. There are those who argue that the advanced countries are already so rich that they have no need to grow much more. But a policy for structural changes, involving job losses in uncompetitive industries, that does not create attractive and varied new employment opportunities is unlikely to win acceptance in a democratic state, and economic expansion is the best way of providing them. This does not mean that the new jobs will necessarily be in manufacturing industry; both governments and working people are going to have to become more flexible in their thinking on what constitutes acceptable employment.

The paper has three main sections. The first is concerned with the economic aspects of the adjustment process from the point of view of the importing country. It emphasizes the extent to which nonreciprocal liberalization of trade in favor of developing countries gives rise to different problems and policy questions from multilateral liberalization of trade among countries at a roughly similar stage of development, as in the creation of the EEC.

The second section considers the potential scale of the problem over the next decade. It does not attempt to assess the possible impact of the multinationals, but it should be emphasized that this could be significant if the growing tendency of advanced country corporations to shift their labor-intensive manufacturing and assembly operations to low labor-cost developing countries proceeds unhindered.

The third section examines the concept of adjustment assistance, drawing on the approaches embodied in the various measures that different countries have adopted in recent years. An attempt is made to outline the content of a policy appropriate to the practical case of trade liberalization in favor of developing countries. None of the existing programs contain measures specifically linked to developing country imports.

Finally, the main conclusions of the paper are summarized, and some suggestions put forward as to areas on which further research seems necessary.

I. ECONOMIC ASPECTS OF THE ADJUSTMENT PROCESS IN THE CONTEXT OF INCREASING TRADE WITH DEVELOPING COUNTRIES

All imports that compete with domestic production have some impact on the economic structure of the importing country, unless—which is highly unlikely—they are exactly matched by an equivalent volume of identical exports. As a rule, however, the impact does not give rise to specific and identifiable adjustment problems, being but one, and not usually a very important one, of the many forces of change in a dynamic and mobile economy. Among the most significant of these are shifts in the pattern of demand, including the emergence of new products, and technological developments, which usually alter production functions and may also result in making established manufacturing processes obsolete. The governments of nearly all advanced countries are preoccupied in greater or less degree with the problems of aiding the adaptation of their industrial structures, but most national industrial, regional and labor policies are not directly linked to the impact of imports. The main exceptions to this generalization appear in the third section.

The first question that has to be raised about the impact of imports of manufactures from developing countries is whether it is in some way different from the impact of imports from other advanced countries; whether it gives rise to different problems of adjustment and adaptation that call for special measures. In theory the answer must be no. The source of imports of a commodity is irrelevant to their impact on domestic production of that commodity. However, the advanced countries' acceptance of the principle of nonreciprocal preferences in favor of developing countries at the 1968 UNCTAD conference, and the subsequent implementation by many of them of a variety of schemes, means that in practice they are prepared to distinguish between trade among "competing" countries—that is, those with broadly similar economic structures and per capita income levels—and trade with developing countries. Where trade among themselves is concerned, they at least pay lip service to the importance of reciprocity and fair conditions of competition, though it remains to be seen how far they are prepared to continue the drive to make these conditions a reality. But they have recognized that developing countries need help if they are to win a

larger and more diversified share of world markets for manufactured goods, and that as a temporary and transitional measure they
should be prepared to grant freer access to their own markets for
products from developing countries without seeking reciprocal
concessions.

It follows from this that imports from developing countries may
result in adjustment problems of a rather different kind from those
caused by imports from other advanced countries, requiring
different policy measures. While it may be reasonable to argue that
if the objective of a program of structural adaptation is to enable a
country to compete with its peers, then temporary financial
assistance to ailing industries to help them restore their competitive
position is justified, it is not logical to seek to prop up industries
suffering under the impact of imports from developing countries. In
these circumstances, adjustment assistance policy's aim must be to
speed up the contraction of the affected industries, and encourage
the movement of resources into other areas of economic activity.[1]

An industry may be quite narrowly defined. To take an obvious
example, the application of a type of adjustment assistance policy
designed to help developing countries expand their textile exports
would not have to aim at the total elimination of the importing
country's textile industry. There are many areas of textile production in which the special skills required, the high level of capital intensity, the need to be near final markets, or some combination of
these factors can be expected to confer significant comparative advantages on advanced country producers for some time to come.
There are however other more labor-intensive sectors, such as the
production of simple cotton and man-made fiber spun yarns and
fabrics, where developing countries possess the necessary technical
competence and tend to have a comparative advantage. A sensible
adjustment assistance policy for an advanced country should encourage contraction in these sectors, perhaps along the lines of the
1959 United Kingdom cotton industry scheme,[2] but should restrict
investment subsidies, if any, to diversification schemes.

1. The case for holding that improved access to markets in advanced countries for the
developing countries' exports of manufactures will promote economic development is not
considered in this paper. It is assumed that developing countries will benefit from the opportunity to increase their exports, especially exports of labor-intensive manufactures. Nor does
the paper discuss alternative ways of granting improved access.
2. For a description of the scheme, see Caroline Miles, *Lancashire Textiles, A Case Study
of Industrial Change,* NIESR Occasional Paper no. XXIII (London: The Syndics of the
Cambridge University Press, 1968), pp. 46-65.

Two further points about the nature of imports of manufactures from developing countries require mention here.

The first concerns the confusion that tends to arise between imports from low-wage countries and so-called low-cost imports. Although the developing countries are, almost by definition, low-wage countries, most of them are high-cost producers of most manufactured goods.[3] The main exceptions, leaving aside the manufacturing operations of multinational companies, discussed below, are a group of relatively low-technology, labor-intensive industries, often based on indigenous raw materials, including cotton textiles and other simple textile products, footwear and clothing, sports goods, furniture, some light engineering products and processed foods. Even in these industries, levels of efficiency vary greatly from country to country, as might be expected, and only a handful of developing countries are at present competitive on world markets in a reasonably broad range of manufactures. It is a mistake, therefore, to suppose that there is a vast quantity of frustrated exports of manufactured goods in developing countries, only awaiting removal of barriers to trade so that they can be poured on to advanced country markets. Furthermore, the limited concessions extended by the various countries that have so far introduced non-reciprocal preference schemes in conformity with the UNCTAD decision cannot be expected to alter the picture significantly.

The second point concerns the growing tendency of manufacturing firms based in advanced countries to shift their labor-intensive production and assembly operations to developing countries, where they are carried on by subsidiaries or by local private or public management under licens?. The point is not developed here. But it is evident that manufacturing enterprises employing advanced country technology and management expertise, and low-cost labor and operating at efficiencies equal or near to their advanced country counterparts, constitute a bigger potential competitive threat than do most firms owned and run by developing country nationals.[4]

We now turn to a consideration of the economic impact of an increasing flow of imports on industry and employment in the importing country. The question of how rapid the increase has to be

---

3. For a discussion of industrial problems and policies in developing countries, see Ian M.D. Little, Tibor Scitovsky and Maurice Scott, *Industry and Trade in Some Developing Countries* (Oxford: The University Press, 1970).

4. There are, of course, instances of very high levels of entrepreneurial efficiency in the poorer areas of the world, notably in Hong Kong. But Hong Kong cannot really be regarded as a developing country in the normal sense of the phrase.

before the adverse effects are sufficiently marked to require specific government action is not discussed in this paper: it will vary from industry to industry, depending on the rate of increase of domestic and export demand for the products concerned, including availability and price of substitutes. Nor is the concept of "market disruption" examined. For the purposes of the analysis contained in the following paragraphs, it is simply assumed that there are circumstances in which an increase in imports results in industrial contraction and job losses of sufficient importance, either because of their scale and/or their geographic concentration, to suggest a possible need for remedial action by the government.

The immediate impact of increased imports on a domestic industry, assuming that demand for its products is not expanding fast enough to absorb the additional supplies while leaving its output unchanged, is on the profit margins and cash flow of the affected firm or plant, some time before the point of actual factory closures and displacement of resources is reached. As profit margins decline, the competitive position of the firm worsens, because it lacks the means to modernize its plant. Wages also tend to decline relative to wages in the economy as a whole, as employees in stagnant and contracting industries, usually in a poor bargaining position, are reluctant to push costs to the point at which their jobs will be at risk.

It may seem surprising that managements let things slide in this way, failing to diversify into new lines of production where profit margins are less subject to erosion. Successful managements—and indeed many young, mobile and perhaps better educated employees—do these things, of course. What we are concerned with, however, in analyzing the problems of structural adjustment, are the less successful, the firms and workers who for one reason or another lack the ability or the opportunity to move away from their existing industries and occupations.

Sooner or later, these less successful firms will be forced into closure, though it is remarkable how long some of them manage to hang on, particularly the small, privately owned concerns. Whether or not the closures lead to unemployment on a large enough scale to require special policy measures depends on two main factors, the overall level of activity in the economy as a whole, and the degree of regional concentration of the affected industry. In slump conditions, additional factory closures merely exacerbate an already difficult industrial situation, and special measures to deal with them will probably be subsumed in a general recovery policy. But when the overall level of activity and thus the demand for labor is high, there may still be a need for an active labor market policy to assist workers to move quickly and easily into new occupations where there is a high degree of regional concentration. If there is no lack of demand in the economy in general, there may also be a need for measures to encourage the establishment of new enterprises in the region.

II. THE SCALE OF THE PROBLEM IN THE 1970S

Starting with Salant and Vaccara's pioneering work, *Import Liberalization and Employment,* published in 1961,[5] a number of attempts have been made at quantifying the employment effects of increased imports. The most recent of these is the calculations made by the UNCTAD Secretariat, published in a report on adjustment assistance measures prepared for the third session of UNCTAD in 1972.[6] Unlike the earlier studies, the UNCTAD estimates are based on a continuing increase in imports over a five-year period rather than assuming a once and for all rise, and moreover give some indication of the offsetting effects of a rise in the importing countries' domestic consumption of the product groups considered.

In principle, the methodology of the UNCTAD study (described in detail in a technical annex to the report) is to assume that imports will rise twice as fast over the period 1969-73 as they did over the period 1965-69, and that a 1:1 substitution relationship exists — that is, that a $1 million rise in imports will lead to a $1 million cutback in domestic production. It is acknowledged that this is a maximum assumption and that in reality the cutback in domestic production is likely to be less than the rise in imports. A simple average labor productivity ratio is used to calculate the displacement effect.

The main conclusion of the study, which is confined to three advanced importing countries — the Federal Republic of Germany, the United Kingdom and the United States — is that the overall displacement of labor that might follow a doubling of the rate of increase of imports of manufactures from developing countries in the product groups analyzed (twenty International Standard Industrial Classification groups) would be modest. The annual rate of displacement of labor is estimated to be 0.7 percent of total manufacturing

5. Walter S. Salant and Beatrice N. Vaccara, *Import Liberalization and Employment: The Effects of Unilateral Reductions in United States Import Barriers* (Washington, D.C.: The Brookings Institution, 1961).

6. UNCTAD, "Adjustment Assistance Measures," Document no. TD/121 (New York, December 1971) and Supplement 1 (New York, January 1972).

employment in 1969 in the most sensitive of the three countries studied, the United Kingdom; 0.5 percent of 1969 manufacturing employment in Western Germany; and 0.5 percent of 1967 manufacturing employment in the United States. These figures do not take into account the employment-creating effects of rising domestic consumption.

In some industries, however, the annual rate of labor displacement works out considerably higher, rising to 3.7 percent in the United Kingdom footwear and clothing industry and to nearly 6 percent in the German leather and leather goods industry. An indication of the extent to which unemployment problems are likely to be concentrated in a few industries is given by calculating the annual average labor displacement in industries estimated to lose more than one percent of their employees each year as a percentage of total labor displacement in the twenty industry groups analyzed. The figure is 70 percent for the Federal Republic of Germany and the United States and 85 percent for the United Kingdom.

Even the level of disaggregation employed in the UNCTAD study may not be high enough to identify all the problem areas. The textile industry, for example, is taken as a single entity, and the result for the United Kingdom shows an average annual displacement of 116 employees, a negligible number, completely dwarfed by the same study's estimate of the number displaced by rising productivity, 23,000. But the import displacement effects are not spread over the whole industry. They are concentrated in the sector producing spun and woven cotton and man-made fiber textiles, which account for only about 14 percent of total United Kingdom textile industry employment. The UNCTAD study assumes that resources are completely mobile within each industry, but this assumption is not valid in practice for textiles, nor, probably, for many of the other industries considered in the study. Neither capital—in the form of fixed assets and managerial know-how—nor labor is likely to move easily even into other areas of the textile industry without some kind of assistance and retraining.

Despite these criticisms, the basic methodology of the UNCTAD study could be a valuable tool for identifying potential crisis points. Its assumptions need to be refined; no single substitution ratio of imports for domestic production, for example, is likely to hold good across a range of industries. But if the data inputs can be improved, and a higher level of disaggregation employed, the technique could be used by governments to pick out industries facing potentially serious adjustment problems, where special assistance might be made available to individual enterprises and employees.

III. ADJUSTMENT ASSISTANCE MEASURES

Structural maladjustments, especially where they are associated with significant variations in prosperity and income levels among different regions of a single country, have concerned economic policy-makers for many years. Governments have tried, with more or less success, to secure a more uniform distribution of economic activity and employment by means of a wide range of incentives and benefits to capital and labor. But in implementing these industrial and labor policies they have not, on the whole, paid overmuch attention to causes, except in a rather general way, and have not sought to limit assistance to firms or employees displaced for specific and identifiable reasons. The exceptions are the handful of schemes to aid industries hit by import competition, including the United States Trade Expansion Act of 1962, the Canadian General Adjustment Assistance Program introduced in 1968, assistance to the textile and shipbuilding industries in the United Kingdom, and the adjustment provisions of the European Coal and Steel Community and European Economic Community treaties.

In what follows, adjustment assistance measures are defined as measures specifically intended to help firms and workers affected by import competition. Obviously, the effectiveness of such measures, or indeed the need for them in any particular case, cannot be judged in isolation from the general industrial and labor market policies of the country or economic group in which they may be applied. All these policies are concerned with structural adaptation, and all are forms of adjustment assistance. They provide many lessons as to the kinds of measures that are effective in various circumstances and societies. Even among advanced countries the variations in industrial and trade union structures, and in national attitudes towards the roles and functions of the state and the individual, are so great that there is no reason to suppose that measures that work in one country will necessarily work in another, at least not without substantial modification.

A review of adjustment assistance policy seen in the context of broad industrial and labor market policy is obviously beyond the scope of this paper. Nor will the details of existing adjustment assistance programs linked to imports be described; some of them are examined in later papers. Instead, the rest of the paper will look at three major issues that have to be resolved by adjustment assistance policy-makers, and will put forward some preliminary suggestions on how they might be dealt with. The three issues are: the definition of eligibility—the problem of making sure that those who need and are entitled to assistance get it, without also aiding too many undeserving cases; diversification versus restoring competitiveness—finding the right balance; and aid to displaced labor—problems and policies.

IV. THE DEFINITION OF ELIGIBILITY

The main question to be considered under this heading is how to define and measure the injury done to a domestic industry by an increasing flow of imports from developing countries. In practical terms, the problem is to develop a definition and a yardstick that will insure that assistance is available to those who are being displaced by rising imports, without opening the doors to all firms and workers facing change. If assistance is too freely available its economic and political impact on the specific situation it is intended to deal with will be diffuse and less effective, quite apart from budgetary cost considerations, while if eligibility criteria are too tightly drawn the measures may fail to make the desired impact.

The way in which the adjustment assistance provisions of the United States Trade Expansion Act have worked in practice illustrates the point.[7] Originally, a firm or group of workers applying for assistance had first to demonstrate to the Tariff Commission that tariff cuts were the main reason for the increase in harmful imports and, secondly, that these increased imports were the major cause of injury to the domestic industry, or to individual firms and workers. In practice, the Tariff Commission interpreted the major cause as meaning the single most important cause, rather than the majority cause, but even so the criterion was hard to fulfill, and not one of the twenty-six petitions presented between 1962 and October 1969 was granted. In November 1969 the second criterion was modified, requiring appellants to demonstrate that imports were a

---

7. Some authoritative comments on the working of the Trade Expansion Act adjustment assistance provision appear in Stanley D. Metzger, "Injury and Market Disruption from Imports," in *United States International Economic Policy in an Interdependent World*, vol. 1 (Washington, D.C.: U.S. Government Printing Office, 1971), pp. 319-42. A description of the operation of the measures is given by Marvin M. Fooks, "Trade Adjustment Assistance," ibid., pp. 343-66.

substantial cause of injury, rather than the major cause, and since then a larger number of petitions has been filed (eighty up to March 1971), and about a quarter of them have been granted. Even so, Fooks concludes that the program has not achieved its goals—it has failed to neutralize resistance to a liberal trade policy, and the goal of economic adjustment has not been attained.

The Trade Expansion Act program was, of course, part of a package designed to persuade Congress to give President Kennedy the authority to negotiate tariff reductions primarily with Europe, and was not related to developing country imports. Nor was assistance limited to specific industries or firms and workers in them. By contrast, the only other significant import-linked country programs (apart from the Canadian measures, which follow the same approach as the Trade Expansion Act), namely, the shipbuilding and cotton textile industry schemes in the United Kingdom, were confined to particular industries. The cotton textile measures, moreover, were—admittedly rather loosely—associated with imports from developing countries. The White Paper giving the background to the 1959 Cotton Industry Act described its aim as being "to bring about a reorganized and reequipped industry which could compete with success in the markets of the world with the types of cloth that are wanted wherever living standards are high." This implies that the policy did not envisage the elimination of imports from developing countries (mainly Hong Kong, India and Pakistan), an interpretation which has been borne out by subsequent policy statements, and which is accepted by the United Kingdom industry.

If programs are limited to specific industries it becomes less necessary to establish elaborate rules for determining the eligibility of individuals. In legislative terms, it may be possible to undertake to provide assistance to all firms and workers who need it in certain industries, without entering into a more or less unlimited financial commitment. In the 1959 United Kingdom cotton textile scheme, which cost the government about $70 million, all firms in the industry were automatically eligible for cash grants if they scrapped plant, and all employees losing their jobs as a result were automatically eligible for special redundancy payments. (Grants towards the cost of reequipment were subject to individual scrutiny and approval.)

Looking beyond this single case, to circumstances in which developing countries will be trying to sell a growing range of manufactures on world markets, the problem becomes one of identifying the industries. It is here that the UNCTAD approach could be of use. If governments were prepared to draw up a general guideline for eligibility for adjustment assistance, such as, for example, that the projected annual rate of labor displacement in an industry was more than 2 percent, or whatever figure seemed appropriate, then the UNCTAD method could be used to identify industries at risk. By looking at projected displacement, rather than historical displacement, it would be possible to bring adjustment assistance measures into operation when they are needed most, before injury has become widespread and protectionist lobbies have gathered strength. A number of practical questions would have to be resolved, including the important issue of the appropriate level of industrial disaggregation.

V. DIVERSIFICATION VERSUS RESTORING COMPETITIVENESS

In Section I it was argued that if the overall objective of an advanced country's adjustment assistance policy is to give developing countries the opportunity to capture growing shares of markets for labor-intensive products, it must aim at reducing rather than rebuilding the affected domestic industries. This implies that incentives to firms should take the form of compensation for displaced assets rather than aid for reequipment in the same industry. It is possible, in principle, to limit reequipment finance to diversification projects, but it is doubtful whether small companies that have lacked the entrepreneurship to diversify successfully on their own initiative will suddenly display it when offered finance on concessionary terms. And it is very doubtful whether big, multiplant, multiproduct companies should be considered eligible for import-linked reequipment finance, though on equity grounds they should be entitled to compensation on the same terms as small firms if they are forced to close plants because of import competition.

A proposal to compensate the owners of fixed assets might be objected to on accounting grounds—an asset that is not capable of yielding a stream of earnings is rightly regarded as worthless by corporate financial analysts. In theory, the firm could use its accumulated depreciation to acquire new, earnings-yielding assets. However in reality this is often not possible, partly because the assets may not be fully depreciated at the point in time at which they are economically displaced, and more importantly because, as has been indicated earlier, the marginal firm that gets itself into a position where it needs adjustment assistance probably does not have enough reserves or an adequate cash flow to finance purchases of new equipment. In theory, such firms would quickly be driven to close down, but in practice, again, many of them struggle on for surprisingly long periods—and become keen members of protectionist lobbies. The proposal to buy them out is therefore based on practical considerations.

VI. AID TO DISPLACED LABOR

Two separate issues arise in considering the kinds of assistance and incentives that might be effective in persuading labor to accept the need for structural change. The most important questions concern the problems of providing the financial and institutional facilities, including training schemes, that will enable labor to seek out and qualify for new employment opportunities. But there is also a question as to whether labor should be compensated for displaced skills, which can be regarded as assets yielding a stream of earnings for the man who possesses them, analogous to the fixed assets employed by owners of capital.

This principle would appear to have been applied, though the arguments are not fully developed, in the United Kingdom textile industry scheme of 1959, and more recently in the British docks. In both instances, it should be observed, the special payments to displaced employees were or are being made by employers, not by the state, and are distinct from official unemployment benefits. The main argument for compensatory payments of this kind is precisely that they are supplementary, that they do take into account the particular circumstances in which labor is being displaced. Because the industries affected tend to be, at best, slow-growing, employing a high proportion of elderly workers, the additional compensation payments may help to meet a real transitional need for the worker nearing retirement age, who is not yet eligible for a state old-age pension but who is unlikely to get another job.

Turning now to the problems of aiding labor's transition to new employment, these fall into two groups: the problems of providing an adequate income during the transitional period, including funds for traveling to seek work, assistance in moving house and so on, and the problems of creating new jobs and providing the necessary training facilities.

National redundancy and unemployment pay arrangements vary so much from country to country that it is not possible to make any useful generalizations about them. Whether or not labor displaced by competition from imports should receive additional unemployment pay, as a supplement to the standard benefits, would appear to be a question that needs to be considered country by country. There would not seem to be any strong arguments for special unemployment pay where national levels are adequate, but even in these circumstances it may be desirable to offer displaced workers extra allowances during retraining—for an extended period if necessary—and subsidies for traveling to look for work and where necessary for moving house.

The most effective way of creating new employment opportunities is to keep the economy buoyant and growing—a prescription that looks less simple in the 1970s than it did in the 1960s. A discussion of this problem lies outside the scope of this paper, however, as does an examination of the problems of generating increased economic activity and employment in depressed regions. One question about general industrial policy measures that is relevant in the present context, though, is whether they have approached labor market problems in the right way. In a recent comparative study of Swedish and United Kingdom labor market systems, Santosh Mukherjee has argued strongly that Sweden's commitment to the full use of its labor force, with a strong emphasis on training, amounts to a totally different attitude toward labor market problems from that shown by the United Kingdom, which is more nearly typical of the advanced countries in general. He points out that, whereas in Britain unemployment is regarded as something to be endured until it ceases, and the policy emphasis is on improving financial support for the unemployed, in Sweden unemployment is seen primarily as a wastage of resources, to be eliminated by putting the unemployed to work, and unemployment benefit is a last resort.[8]

These comments have a direct bearing on the subject under discussion. They draw attention, once again, to the need to view adjustment assistance measures in the context of industrial and labor market policy as a whole. If the object of adjustment assistance measures linked to increasing imports from developing countries is to eliminate competing manufacturing activities in the importing country, then their principal objective must be to induce labor—and indeed other productive resources—to move into new areas of activity. However, it is unlikely that a program pushing from behind

8. Santosh Mukherjee, *Making Labour Markets Work—A Comparison of the U.K. and Swedish Systems*, PEP Broadsheet no. 532 (London: George Berridge and Co., Ltd., 1972).

as it were, operating on the resources threatened with injury or displacement, can achieve this objective for itself. It must be integrated with a broad program for maximizing the use made of all resources available to the nation or community. Adjustment assistance measures can compensate for lost assets, which may be physical items of plant or their acquired skills, and can provide extra support to firms and individuals confronting transitional problems. By themselves, however, they cannot deal with all the problems of structural change and maldistribution of resources that the advanced countries face.

VII. CONCLUSIONS AND SUGGESTIONS FOR FURTHER RESEARCH

This paper has taken for granted the case for enabling the developing countries to increase their exports of manufactures to the advanced countries, and the case for holding that the actual or potential harm done to competing industries in the importing countries is better dealt with by adjustment assistance measures than by imposing quotas or other forms of protection. During the next decade the problem of labor displacement should be of manageable proportions, and will be modest in relation to structural changes stemming from other causes, notably technological advance. This does not mean, however, that reabsorption of labor in similar manufacturing jobs will always be possible.

The UNCTAD generalized preference scheme is designed to give developing countries a chance to capture an increasing share of markets in products where they have a comparative advantage, and to encourage increased specialization in world industrial production. It is therefore important that adjustment assistance measures introduced by advanced countries should aim at reducing the size of competing domestic industries, and perhaps ultimately eliminating them, rather than endeavoring to raise their levels of efficiency and rebuilding them.

A successful adjustment assistance policy is one which makes change seem more attractive than the continuance of existing activities, with or without protection. It seems reasonable in equity and as a practical matter that owners of assets displaced by imports — whether these are in the form of physical plant or technical skills — should be compensated for their losses. Beyond this, policies for increasing the utilization of resources throughout the economy must be worked out nationally and internationally, though adjustment assistance measures may have a part to play in providing additional support and incentives to those workers displaced by import competition.

A number of areas in which further research is needed have emerged in the course of this short paper. One, mentioned in Section II, is the exploration of methods for identifying in advance the industries most vulnerable to resource displacement, and for quantifying the size of the problem. Research into the closely related topic of the scale of displacement that might be caused by advanced country operations shifting their more labor-intensive manufacturing and assembly operations to plants in developing countries should also be mentioned here.

It would also seem useful to make a comparative analysis of existing and proposed adjustment assistance programs, concentrating attention on the different approaches adopted in the various programs, their effectiveness and their appropriateness to the particular circumstances of adaptation to an increasing flow of imports from developing countries.

But the biggest area in which more work is needed is the exploration of the relationship between adjustment assistance measures and broad national and international industrial development and labor market policies. Consideration of adjustment assistance problems and policies in isolation from these larger questions of economic policy is unlikely to prove very rewarding, either in terms of illuminating the basic features of the economics of advanced industrial societies, or as a guide to effective action.

Finally, the proposal for an international Adjustment Assistance Code[9] requires mention, if only to plead for further clarification of the objectives of such a code before embarking on detailed research. It is an attractive idea, but the force of such a code, in circumstances where its signatories still held to their present widely differing viewpoints on issues of structural adjustment, would be very doubtful.

---

9. See Gerard Curzon and Victoria Curzon, *Global Assault on Nontariff Trade Barriers,* Trade Policy Research Centre Thames Essays, no. 3 (London: Ditchling Press Ltd., 1972), pp. 32-33.

Comment

Nat Goldfinger

These comments are based on the perceptions and analysis of developments in international trade and investment from the viewpoint of the American labor movement.

I agree with Caroline Miles when she says that "all imports that compete with domestic production have some impact on the economic structure of the importing country ..." [p. 103]. I agree too that the source of imports of the commodity is irrelevant to their impact on the importing country's production of that commodity. For that reason, it is not possible to isolate the impacts of imports from developing countries from the other impacts of international trade and investment, as if each were a separate development, either from the viewpoint of analysis or, more particularly, from the viewpoint of policy. Nor is it realistic or sensible to attempt to leave aside the manufacturing operations of multinational companies in analyzing the impacts of international trade and investment.

As Caroline Miles pointed out briefly in her paper, it is obvious enough that manufacturing enterprises that employ advanced-country technology in the developing countries—and use their large labor supplies, low wages and so forth—can have significant impacts on employment and the economic structure of the developed country. Moreover, in terms of the realities of the 1970s, preferences for manufactured goods from developing countries would largely mean preferences, not for the developing countries but for the large multinational companies. While the degree would vary from one developing country to another, the preferences would be largely for the multinational corporations based in the developed countries. So we are not dealing simply with a one-way shift of benefits, but with a complicated shift the benefits of which would largely flow—in terms of income distribution, for example—to the big multinational corporations of the developed countries, unless a lot of other things were done, such as comprehensive regulation.

The problem of adverse impacts on employment and economic structure cannot easily and neatly be compartmentalized, as I see it. The causes of such adverse impacts are interrelated, and so are their impacts and problems. For example, the issue is *not* imports from this specific source or that source only, and it is not even imports from one specific industry or another. In that regard, I do not believe that Caroline Miles is altogether correct when she says "an industry may be quite narrowly defined." Perhaps an economist or statistician can so define an industry, but people who are directly related with real problems and with policy issues cannot do so—certainly not with ease, if at all.

In the 1970s, for example, what are the specific confines of the textile industry as distinct from the confines of the chemical industry, and how does one distinguish, in terms of employment and structural impacts of imports of man-made fibers and textiles, between the so-called chemical company and the so-called textile company? It is not easy to isolate narrowly the impacts, either for analysis of real problems or, more particularly, for policy purposes.

Nor do I understand Caroline Miles when she speaks of the short-term nature of these adverse impacts. Perhaps twenty or thirty years is short-term, in terms of an analytic discussion, but to the overwhelming majority of people, twenty or thirty years are a large part of their working lives, approximately a generation. And the actual adverse impacts on employment and economic structures may well be of much longer duration, beyond thirty years.

The New England textile industry in the United States started to move South in the 1920s, and the New England shoe industry began its migration at about the same time. Yet today, large parts of New England are relatively depressed, and this certainly is not a short-term, easy kind of problem, even though it is internal, within the borders of the United States.

The point I am trying to make is that the adverse impacts of international trade and investment cannot be compartmentalized or isolated neatly as to the specific source or even as to a specific, narrowly defined industry. Nor are the problems typically of short-term duration, at least in the sense that I use *short-term*.

The issue is the actual and potential adverse impacts of international trade and investment generally, and the need is for policies and measures to deal with the current realities of international trade and development. Among these realities are the existence of managed national economies which manage their international economic relationships, the realities of technology transfers among subsidiaries and firms across national frontiers, the realities of international investment and operations of foreign subsidiaries, the realities of multinational companies. It is only within such a general framework that the issue of imports from the developing countries can be confronted.

I want to comment on adjustment assistance because that seems to be the current fad and also the focus of much of the discussion. In the first place, as Caroline Miles points out in her paper, in addition to the adverse impacts of international trade and investment, we live in a period of rapid technological change and in the United States technological change has been extremely fast. Furthermore, in the United States there has been a massive employment displacement in the past couple of decades out of agriculture, mining and the railroads. This displacement has been accompanied by serious problems in the structure, location and employment of many manufacturing industries. These are economic problems that have festered and have become social problems in the United States, such as recent and current urban problems, constituting what is sometimes called the "urban crisis."

The problems that emanate from the adverse impacts of international trade and investment are in addition to all other problems of rapid change which confront American workers and communities. The change in the volume and composition of imports and exports, in recent years, resulted in the net loss of about 900,000 job opportunities from 1966 to 1971, according to an AFL-CIO estimate.

I want to emphasize here that workers are people. They are not merely an economic resource or a statistic. They cannot be easily pushed around, and they are not pawns on a chess board. In a democracy, they vote and it is extremely important to keep that point in mind.

It is also essential to see the difference between labor and capital, in terms of adverse impacts. Capital is mobile and investments can be moved out of one business to another and they can be moved from one part of the country to another or to other countries. Workers are infinitely less mobile than capital, because labor is "people" and not an automatically interchangeable resource. And communities are not mobile at all.

In terms of the realities, a displaced shoe worker in Maine does not automatically become a clerical worker in New York or even in Portland, Maine. With good fortune, the son of a displaced electronics production worker in Chicago may become a computer programmer in San Francisco. But the displaced worker loses his seniority-related benefits when he loses his job. He probably will be unemployed for many months and, if he is lucky enough to find a job, he will possibly wind up with a job at lesser skill and lesser pay. These are some of the realities that are faced by workers and institutions in the United States. These are the realities with which we have to look at adjustment assistance.

Adjustment assistance, in the mid-1950s, I think could have made a lot of sense within the American context. In fact, the very early or perhaps even first appearance of the adjustment assistance idea, in relation to international trade, was presented in a footnote comment by an American trade union leader to the Randall Commission Report on international trade in 1954. In that period, the adverse impacts were relatively small in number and in scope; they were slow in speed and the problems would have been manageable, if a low level of unemployment, generally, had prevailed. It is estimated that about 30 percent to 40 percent of imports were comparable to goods produced in the United States at that time. Adjustment assistance could have been and should have been an important policy measure. However, it was not adopted then; we got it later in 1962, in a somewhat mutilated form. As Caroline Miles pointedly indicates, it did not work at all until late 1969 and then it became a cruel hoax.

Moreover, during the 1960s, the whole picture changed drastically. The adverse impacts on employment and the economic structure increased sharply in number and in scope—in terms of workers, industries, products and product-lines—and the adverse impacts accelerated. The volume of imports skyrocketed and the rise of exports lagged. In addition, by 1966, according to official estimates, about three-quarters of the volume of imports were comparable to United States-produced goods. Within a few years, the United States rapidly became a net importer of a great variety of products, displacing United States production. One does not have to be a Marxist dialectician to realize that such a change in quantity and speed means a change in the quality of the problem. The nature of the problem changed considerably. Under these changed conditions, adjustment assistance can be only a very small part of any kind of workable solution to the problem of the adverse impacts of international trade and investment.

In fact, some American trade unionists now refer to adjustment assistance, rather realistically, as burial insurance. It is a measure of temporary aid after the fact, after the worker is displaced. After displacement, the government would throw him some crumbs, in the form of extended unemployment insurance benefits for perhaps fifty-two weeks or a somewhat longer period. In an economy of high unemployment he is offered some retraining for a job that may not exist, or possibly for a job in a location to which he can hardly move without considerable financial loss. Moreover, the numbers of workers adversely affected have mushroomed to scores of thousands each year, in a wide and growing variety of industries and product-lines—all within the general context of high levels of unemployment.

I am not saying that adjustment assistance is utterly valueless. But in terms of any scale of reality, it is of very little value at this point. I would suggest that you people face up to the current reality that adjustment assistance just is not going to work as a significant policy solution to the adverse impacts of international trade and investment. You can sit around here for days, weeks and months and poke around this issue, back and forth, but you are not going to be able to convince any large numbers of American workers that it is workable as a significant solution to their problems in the 1970s. The size, scope and rapidity of adverse impacts require basic solutions, rather than an emphasis on adjustment assistance.

So, I return to the point that there is a need to develop realistic measures and policies to handle realities. One must cope with the fact that national economies are managed, there are vast technology transfers, many manufacturing companies operate foreign subsidiaries and we live in a world of multinational companies.

We are calling for a workable solution to the general problem that is posed in the real world, and not as it was frequently posed here. As trade unionists, we in the American labor movement have to deal with reality. The specific problem for us is not merely imports from the developing countries or imports of one or two products, but a complex of problems that are related to recent developments in international trade and investment in general. For example, there is much discussion about textiles. Textiles are a small part of the American problem. An indication of the American problem in the past number of years was noted by Göran Ohlin. The whole scope of the problem rapidly widened during the 1960s into many economic areas, including sophisticated product lines and components. For example, the United States is now confronted by serious problems in the broad area of electrical manufacturing and electronics.

Whole branches of American industries have been wiped out rapidly, within the past decade, by rapidly rising imports. All of this happened, not over a long period of time, in which some adjustments would have been at least manageable, but rapidly, within a period of two, three or five years. The Electronics Industry Association, for example, reports that, in the five years from 1965 to 1970, 122,500 jobs were directly displaced, in radio, television and electronic component production. The United States now hardly produces any radios anymore. I do not want to present an entire list of displaced production at this point, but scores of thousands of jobs have been displaced each year, in a wide variety of industries, as a result of the rapid displacement of United States production.

An example of the problem is that within a period of about a decade, imports of manufactured goods—and that is where the problem lies—rose from a little less than $7 billion in 1960, to an annual rate of about $37 billion in 1972. Furthermore, in 1960, United States exports of manufactured goods were close to twice as great as manufactured imports; by 1972, the United States is importing a larger volume of manufactured products and components than it exports. If you tell me that that kind of very rapid change does not create problems, then I do not know what you mean by problems. Clearly, it is not simply a textile problem, or a problem located in this specific town or another, and it is not a problem of isolated geographical or industrial pockets. It is a problem that is across the board in the United States, in most industries, in most products, and a very serious problem in some industries and product lines.

We were told that New England is in good shape, because the region shifted from textiles to electronics, but they are moving out of electronics, and unemployment is still a serious problem in New England. The area around Boston Route 128, which was posed as *the* great solution—with electronics industries and electronic research development—is now largely depressed. The problem shifts from one economic activity to another, and unfortunately, it shifts much faster than economists realize. But the people, who are affected, know that it is there, and it becomes a political problem. The issue, in a democracy, cannot be avoided, even though you may like to do so.

We have been given quite a number of lessons on elementary economics—that, for example, increases in imports would also mean increases in exports. Well, let me tell you something about some of the increases in exports. The United States increased its exports to Mexico—component exports for the assembly of products in Mexico by subsidiaries of United States firms, at low wages, for reexport, required by Mexican law, back to the United States at a preferential duty, under American law, so that the combination results in troubles for American workers. For that reason we are not simply interested in series of economic statistics, in themselves, because we want to know the meaning of the statistics. In the case I just cited, an increase in exports of components comes back in the form of job-destroying imports of finished products. All this is a process that starts on a small scale and builds up. What was a minor problem along the Mexican side of the border a few years ago quickly becomes a large problem. It is merely one other example of the rapid and complex process of adverse impacts, in the United States, due to developments in international trade and investment.

Paul Streeten asked, what kinds of ideas do we have for adjustment? First, I do not believe that it is a matter simply of temporary compensation and retraining, as I indicated earlier. The major goal at this point, is to slow down substantially the whole rapid process of disruption, of dislocating industries and communities, of displacing production and employment.

I think the Swedish experience is very enlightening in a number of ways, because Sweden has done more than any other country in terms of manpower adjustment policies. Furthermore, the problem in the United States is far greater and much more complex than in Sweden. The United States is a vast continental country, with a huge and heterogeneous population and many regions; it runs almost 3,000 miles in one direction and close to 2,000 miles or thereabouts in another direction. It is infinitely harder—even with good active manpower policies—to get an approach to solving the American problems within the confines of a continental, diverse and heterogeneous country. Yet, even in a relatively small and homogeneous country—with a much-advertised active manpower policy—the problem of adjustment in recent years has hardly been solved, according to Göran Ohlin's comments.

We are also told that we have to pay some attention to consumers. The American labor movement does pay attention to consumers. Workers are consumers. When workers lose their jobs, that means consumers have been hit. When large numbers of workers are displaced, one not only gets the direct displacement of workers who lose their jobs, with the loss of payrolls, one also gets an adverse impact on the community, on the local merchants, on the tax base of the community, and, thereby, on services in the community. The shutdown in recent years of radio plants, television plants, electronics components production and so forth has caused widespread unemployment, not only among unskilled and frequently black workers and moderately paid workers, but also among highly skilled and technical employees. Such shutdowns have had adverse impacts on those consumers and on their communities.

Furthermore, we are told that profits on imports are typically the same as on domestic production. As far as I know, in the United States, markups on imports are typically greater than on American production, and that is why the American Retail Federation, as well as American importers and multinationals are so much interested in imports. Typically, the consumer gets little, if any, price benefit, although it varies from one product to another.

The solution we seek may not be acceptable to many of you, but it is our proposed solution. And we will keep working at it. In the long run, international regulation of trade and investment and the multinationals will probably take care of a large part of the problem. But at present, we do not even have the institutions, let alone the policies, to move forward in the international area. Since we are dealing with people, we cannot wait for one or two generations to develop international solutions. So we are proposing United States government action, now.

We are proposing the Burke-Hartke Bill, which many of you have heard about, probably in a distorted form. The Burke-Hartke Bill would provide regulation and restraints on the export of technology from the United States and on the export of capital. It would also set up a sliding-door quota system to limit imports, through which imports would be guaranteed a share of the United States market, and which would permit imports to grow, as United States production grows. If adopted, this bill would substantially slow down the whole process of adverse impacts, which have been narrowing and undermining America's industrial base, with devastating effects on many workers, industries and communities.

In our judgment, the Burke-Hartke bill represents a pragmatic, reasonable and moderate way of dealing with a serious economic and social problem. We are convinced that it is a practical alternative to senseless economic isolationism. It is geared to the need to strengthen the position of the American economy, at present, as an integral part of an expanding world economy.

Comment

Max Corden

I find Caroline Miles' arguments very convincing, especially in view of the fact that she has worked for many years on the adjustment problem in the United Kingdom, that she knows the problem in detail at the grassroots and is the author of a principal study of the adjustment of the United Kingdom's textile industry. I have no critical comments, but would like to focus briefly on one important aspect of this whole subject. My theme is that, while there are undoubtedly some real problems of adjustment, there are also problems of understanding—that is, *psychological* problems.

A lot of people seem to forget that more imports from developing countries must also be associated with more exports to them. There is no reason to expect the developing countries to accumulate reserves rather than spend the foreign exchange they earn. One must keep pointing out—as American economists pointed out in the nineteenth century—that if balance of payments equilibrium is being maintained the developing countries cannot be cheaper producers of everything. There seems no reason to expect that the developing countries will prefer balance of payments surpluses to adjusting their exchange rates and expenditure levels.

If in the first instance the adverse effects on employment and incomes of an inflow of manufactures from the developing countries are felt by the labor force in developed countries *across the board,* rather than being felt by a narrow sector—such as the textile industry—then when exchange rates have been adjusted there should not be great income redistribution effects. The sectional impacts would be minor. Of course, if the impact is mainly in a few industries, as it has been in past years—mainly in textiles and a few other industries—then there are genuine sectional income and employment effects with which to cope. But one of the arguments advanced here is that we can expect much more widespread effects from exports of manufactures by developing countries than in the past because the latter will export many different types of products. I find this argument quite convincing. So the effects would not be confined to a few industries. When one allows for appropriate balance of payments adjustment this effect must be regarded as a favorable prospect.

In any case, it seems necessary to stress that there are bound to be employment gains in the export industries to balance the unemployment effects in some import-competing industries. Indeed, sometimes the same industries will find sales of some products declining and sales of other products increasing.

It also needs to be stressed that the outflow of capital or the spread of know-how internationally by multinational corporations is unlikely to lead to an "export of jobs." Indeed this would be so only if there were fixed coefficients in the United States between capital and labor all round, or if a failure of balance of payments adjustment prevented the pursuit of normal full employment policies on Keynesian lines. There can, of course, be some fall in real wages in the United States or at least a failure of real wages to rise as much as they would have otherwise—as a result of such outflow. But this should be distinguished from employment effects, and furthermore, it is by no means certain that it would happen.

Since there may be as much a problem of *understanding* as a *real* problem associated with the effects on developed countries of increased imports of manufactures from the developing countries one may have to think about the public relations or educational aspects of the whole subject. Should UNCTAD or the major developing countries hire some public relations consultants in the major OECD capitals? The latter would have to stress, above all, the employment gains for exporters in the developed countries. There is, of course, the familiar difficulty that the export employment gains may be potential while the employment losses owing to import replacement will be losses in actual existing employment. On the other hand, the imposition of restrictions on imports from the developing countries could be shown to lead indirectly to reduction in present export employment. I am, of course, aware that some members of this seminar may have been concerned with this type of educational activity, and probably have not found it easy.

Another problem of understanding or psychological problem is the following. Why is the threat of "cheap labor imports" or "pauper labor" imports from developing countries often felt to be more severe than the threat of imports from other advanced countries, even though the magnitude of any actual effect of reducing trade barriers against imports from other advanced countries may be the same or even greater? In the United Kingdom there seems to be surprising equanimity about the threat of extra imports from EEC countries, though it must be admitted that the United

Kingdom has also been fairly liberal in accepting imports from the developing countries. If there is a fear of some vast potential threat—the traditional "pauper labor" fear—then perhaps there is a failure to distinguish between cheap labor and cheap goods. There is a failure to appreciate that there are productivity differences as well as wage rate differences, and that one may offset, or more than offset, the other. These productivity differences between the developing countries and the developed countries are the essential reason why the developing countries are less developed.

To sum up, then, there seem to be two problems. One seems to be how to convey some simple points that are normally discussed in elementary economic textbooks. The other is how to rally the potential gainers from trade expansion. These gainers are likely to be primarily those industries and workers producing products that would be exported in increased amounts to the developing countries if the latter are permitted to increase their international purchasing power, and secondarily those industries and workers exporting to *other developed* countries which obtain increased purchasing power owing to *their* extra exports to the developing countries.

5

Developing Country Alternatives

Mahbub Haq

Whatever else the developing countries may be suffering from, they certainly do not suffer from any lack of advice in the field of trade policy alternatives. These days they are being offered a liberal choice between outward-looking strategies, inward-looking strategies, regional and subregional cooperation and many shrewd combinations of all three alternatives.

I. OUTWARD-LOOKING STRATEGIES

Clearly, the front-runner is the outward-looking strategy. This is the favorite prescription of most economists from the academic community. They argue, with a good deal of righteousness, that the pursuit of an outward-looking strategy would be consistent with international comparative advantage and would insure an optimum allocation of resources. Academics dismiss, with a certain degree of irritation, some of the practical difficulties in persuading the international world to become more liberal in its actual trade practices, as they believe that the world should be more rationally organized along the lines of international division of labor—and if it is not so organized at present, it ought to be changed. On the whole, they represent the voice of economic liberalism and command considerable respect and support.

On the other hand, the policy-makers from the developing world generally throw up their hands in despair and frustration every time one mentions outward-looking strategies. Such practitioners typically come out with a handful of statistics and a long litany of terrible experiences they have had in gaining access to the markets of developed countries.

With considerable justification, these policy-makers point to agricultural protectionism in the developed countries. They contend that not only is the demand for their primary commodities growing slowly, but a further injury is suffered as the developed countries keep some of their primary exports out of their markets, through deliberate action to protect their own farm lobbies. For instance, the United States, Britain, Japan and the EEC spend about $21-$24 billion a year on direct and indirect support of importable primary commodities, which contrasts rather sadly with the $7.7 billion of net official development assistance.

In the field of manufactures, policy-makers from the developing countries are apt to raise an accusing finger at developed countries' high tariffs and restricted quotas for the import of manufactured goods from developing countries. With considerable anger, they point to the fact that the average tariff on imports of manufactures into industrialized countries is 6.5 percent for items from developed countries, but 11.8 percent for those from developing countries, despite the Kennedy Round cuts of early 1972. The differential exists because most of the manufactured exports of developing countries are concentrated in certain groups such as textiles, leather, footwear and other cheap consumer goods which are subject to heavier than average tariffs in the developed countries, in addition to restrictive quotas.

Many policy-makers in the developing countries would acknowledge that, despite all this, manufactured exports from developing countries to the developed world increased at a healthy rate of about 14 percent in the 1960s. But they are quick to point out that much of this increase was accounted for by only six countries—Hong Kong, Taiwan, Korea, Mexico, Yugoslavia and India. Obviously, it pays to be small if one is pursuing an aggressive export policy. If India or any other large country were to try to unload, on a per capita basis, the same quantity of manufactured goods as Taiwan and Korea presently do, world markets would surely become chaotic and severely test the economic liberalism of the most ardent advocates of outward-looking trade-policy strategies.

As if this is not a sufficient list of grievances, the developing country policy-makers keep pointing out, from any forum that they can get hold of, a number of other complaints which restrict their freedom of action in international competition. One of the favorite complaints is that the developing world faces unfair competition from tied aid from the developed countries, which often insures that high-priced imports available under the cover of aid from developed countries win over lower-priced imports available from developing countries without the benefit of the cover of suppliers credits. The developing countries are also likely to point to the strength of pressure lobbies and vested interests in developed countries which normally assure that protectionism triumphs over liberalism when the chips are down and actual policy decisions are taken.

It is difficult to decide between the liberal academics and the complaining policy-makers in this case. Basically, an outward-looking strategy, while attractive in principle, is still a very high-risk strategy. It assumes that developed countries are also likely to become outward-looking. But, in the international field as in any other walk of life, it takes two to tango. Since it is not quite under the control of the developing countries to make the developed world "tango," except of its own accord, the developing countries take a tremendous risk in basing their entire future development strategy on the assumption that—to pursue the metaphor—the developed world will definitely tango. If they are denied fair access to the markets of the developed countries, they are likely to be stuck with unwanted export capacity. On the other hand, import substitution strategy carries fewer risks for the harassed policy-makers; high-cost goods produced behind protective walls can still be shoved down the throats of the local populations by closing down any decent alternative. As far as the developing country policy-makers are concerned, particularly in the large countries, this high element of risk is fairly decisive in their attitude toward outward-looking strategies.

II. INWARD-LOOKING STRATEGIES

The other alternative strategy is what is described as inward-looking, though such a description is often resented by many of its advocates. This is generally the preferred operational strategy in many developing countries, even though it is attacked with considerable vehemence by the academic community. Its advocates use all possible arguments in its favor—from export pessimism to the infant industry argument, and from balance of payment crises to the need for the development of capital goods industries to sustain long-term development. If one looks around the developing world scene in the 1950s and 1960s, one would find that import substitution has generally been the basis for industrialization strategy, particularly in simple consumer goods. It is being argued by many developing countries that the 1970s should be a decade for import substitution in capital goods, as possibilities for easier consumer goods substitution are already being exhausted and as these developing countries are not likely to obtain the capital goods they require for their accelerated development through generous aid or expanding trade.

Import substitution strategies traditionally have been the favorite target of the academic community. Many fair-minded analysts concede that import substitution is a necessary stage in the industrialization process, but they accuse the developing countries of taking import substitution to an excess and managing it behind inefficiently high protective walls, resulting in serious misallocation of resources. Often the criticism here is directed to inefficient types of import substitution rather than to import substitution strategy as such, but too often the attack is carried so far as to lose this important distinction.

It is sometimes forgotten in this debate that in most industries some part is meant for import substitution and some part becomes available for export expansion. It is clearly wrong to characterize certain industries as import substituting or as export industries because, over a period of time, one characteristic can shade into the other. Far more important, most of the debate on import substitution has unfortunately concentrated on the industrial sector, while policy-makers in the developing countries view this strategy as a fairly broad-based one. For instance, considerable import substitution is possible and desirable in agriculture and in services. The unconscious identification of import substitution with industrialization has often meant that its critics have tended to overlook the possibilities of domestic agricultural development to replace food imports and manpower training to replace foreign consultants. However, I do not wish to say anything further about inward-looking strategies at this stage as I shall have a good deal more to say about this aspect later, in a different context.

III. REGIONAL AND SUBREGIONAL COOPERATION

Some people, who have felt increasingly disillusioned with the debate on outward- and inward-looking strategies, have turned to regional cooperation among the developing countries as a viable alternative or, at least, a supplement. These people argue that if the developed world is not being accommodating and not opening up its markets to the developing countries, then these countries can gang up together and form regional groupings wherein they can exchange their simple consumer goods and equipment with greater assurance and at better prices. The idealists in this field think in terms of grand designs for regional markets covering large areas. The realists, however, stick to the possibility of subregional groupings among a limited number of countries—particularly small countries—sharing similar problems and having some natural complementarities.

Unfortunately, the developing countries, which display considerable keenness in ganging up against the developed world, have shown conspicuous unwillingness in cooperating with one another. The experience of subregional groupings in the Central American Common Market, the East African Community or the Regional Cooperation for Development (RCD) among Turkey, Iran and Pakistan, has been fairly disappointing, quelling even some of the ardent supporters of the regional cooperation alternative. There is nothing wrong with the alternative as such, but it appears that the time for this idea has not yet arrived. It is possible that the developing countries may sink their political differences and turn to one another if they feel sufficiently disturbed about their poor bargaining position in the international world and about the unfair treatment that they are getting in the markets of the developed countries. But so far, at least, they have shown very little inclination to do so. It is my own belief that regional cooperation on any worthwhile scale is a matter still a decade or two away, not a practical possibility during the 1970s.

At the same time, I believe that it is possible for the developing countries to agree on one or two audacious actions which may protect their interests in the international world vis-à-vis the developed countries. One such action can be a major and uniform depreciation of the exchange rates in all developing countries, which could help insulate them as a group and set up a natural advantage for trading among themselves. For instance, I believe that the developing countries should explore among themselves the possibility of a large devaluation, say 50 percent to 100 percent, particularly for manufactured exports, which would leave their exchange rates vis-à-vis one another the same as before but would give them a major advantage in the markets of the developed countries. Such a bold action can succeed only if there is complete uniformity among developing countries and if the developed countries do not retaliate. At a time when the developing countries still cannot come to any agreement among themselves on a host of detailed measures which are necessary in forming regional markets, it is better to concentrate on some overall sweeping measure, preferably through the price system, which would give them a collective edge over the developed countries and an incentive to trade among themselves.

Other fields where some collective action might be possible on the part of developing countries are the negotiation of prices of agricultural commodities or minerals and the exploitation of common-property resources of mankind, such as seabed resources. Many analysts point out that the recent action by The Organization of Petroleum Exporting Countries in negotiating higher prices for petroleum cannot set a precedent for other natural resources or for other developing countries as it was a fairly specialized case. I do not believe that. I believe that a number of situations are likely to arise during the 1970s where collective action on specific commodities or on specific situations may become feasible. For instance, the imposition of a uniform or varying tax on consumption of nonrenewable resources in the developed countries and use of the proceeds for the benefit of the developing countries can become a serious possibility during the course of this decade. Again, the developing countries can argue, with considerable justification and probable success, that they should get a proportionate share from the exploitation of seabed resources by multinational corporations in the developed countries. I do not regard these entirely as areas of confrontation. Rather, these are areas where the natural interests of developing countries are likely to bring them together for collective action against developed countries better organized with a better bargaining power who would otherwise dictate the outcome of these negotiations unless the developing countries really get organized.

IV. PRIORITIES FOR POPULAR WELFARE

After having said all this, I must also say that whenever I read or review the heated debate on outward-looking or inward-looking strategies or possibilities of regional cooperation, I often wonder whether these are really the relevant policy alternatives in the developing world. All these alternatives assume, implicitly or explicitly, that trade is the main engine of growth or can be the leading sector of development in the developing countries. There seems to be a certain harking back here to the experience of the developed countries a century ago when expanding trade paced economic development. To my mind, however, such an approach to development strategy starts by asking the wrong question or—to repeat a trite phrase—puts the cart before the horse. I believe that these countries first should define a viable development strategy and regard trade merely as a derivative from such a strategy and not as a pace setter.

There is a growing consensus today that developing countries need a new development strategy, concentrating more on a direct attack on the problems of employment and mass poverty. It is increasingly apparent that it is not enough to rely on a rapid rate of growth in the gross national product and hope that it eventually will filter down to the masses. What is required is specific and direct attention to the poorest sections of society through programs, projects and public services which would reach these sections. If this strategy is taken to its logical conclusion, planners in these countries will have to start with the identification of the minimum basic human needs for survival and a production program geared to satisfying these basic needs in the fields of nutrition, clothing, shelter, education and health. This will require either a deliberate turning away from the signals given by the market, which are weighted by the current income distribution, or sweeping institutional reforms to get the income distribution right first, before defining the development strategy for the country.

Whichever way it comes out, such a development strategy would inevitably mean a greater emphasis on the production of essential commodities—such as food, clothing and housing—a much simpler second-best standard of living geared to the poverty of the country and an all-out effort to create some kind of employment for everyone participating in the labor force. An inward-looking strategy becomes, as such, part and parcel of a development strategy revamped along these lines. But this is not inward-looking in the same sense of the word as import substitution strategies so far. If there is substitution involved here, it is substitution for the life styles of the developed countries, which the developing countries cannot afford on a nationwide basis at the present stage of their development. The developing countries would have to define for themselves living standards or life styles that they can afford on a nationwide scale and that are consistent with their present state of overall poverty. It is inevitable that this would mean not only a much simpler standard of living, but also a much greater concentration on public services which can be distributed more equitably—public buses, public hospitals, public education, even communal housing. If developing countries really undertake such a sweeping change in their development strategies, the prestigious symbols of private ownership may also change—the familiar example being a bicycle economy instead of an automobile economy.

How important is trade in the context of such a new strategy of development? Frankly, I cannot think of many consumer goods from the developed countries which would still be imported by the developing countries if they were to accept and manage such a comprehensive change in their economic and social systems. Probably they could import some essential medicines or books but, beyond that, consumer goods from the developed countries would only end up catering to the needs of the privileged few and not to the majority of the population. Again, I can think of few, practical illustrations of intermediate technology which could become available to the developing countries from the Western world. While machinery and raw materials would still figure prominently in the import budgets of developing countries embracing the new developing strategy, such imports would naturally be more limited when these countries increase domestic improvisation and use whatever local resources and talent they have to look after their own problems. A "poverty curtain" would descend across the developing world, isolating its development and trade from the traditional pattern.

So where do I come out after this rather rushed and sweeping survey of developing country alternatives? Let me recapitulate briefly, for I do not wish to be misunderstood.

First, I believe that we should deliberately reverse the presumed relationship between trade and development. Trade should not be regarded as a pace setter in any relevant development strategy for the developing world, but merely as a derivative. Developing countries should first define a viable strategy for attacking their problems of unemployment and mass poverty. Trade possibilities should be geared to meeting the objectives of such a strategy.

Second, I am convinced that, if this approach is followed, trade sectors will change in character in most developing countries. The privileged minorities, which are often one of the largest consumers of imported goods, will lose their foothold. These systems will also turn to a good deal of improvisation with domestic raw materials, local skills and indigenous technology. Probably, some new trade possibilities may emerge—in pots and pans, bicycles or simple consumer goods—among developing countries themselves as these countries evolve a new and indigenous life-style more consistent with their poverty.

Third, the developing countries should attempt to build a viable trading bloc by fashioning a new institutional framework for promoting trade among themselves. Most of the present institutional framework—shipping, banking, suppliers credits, exchange rates et cetera—is geared to stimulating trade between developing countries and the developed world. The UNCTAD can play a constructive role here by concentrating its energies on the evolution of an entirely different pattern of institutions which are more suited to the promotion of intra-developing-countries trade. It is in this perspective that the proposal for a uniform devaluation on manufactured exports, or .the recent Bank of Israel proposal regarding export refinancing for capital goods, or the demands for a review of current pattern of shipping rates should be viewed. All of these measures will help establish the "poverty curtain" which is needed to encourage the adoption of a relevant development strategy and a sensible trading pattern in the developing world.

Finally, while I strongly believe that any trade strategy should be clearly subordinated to a new development strategy, I am also convinced that the developing countries should take advantage of the trade sector in meeting their genuine needs and not turn towards autarky. It is in this context that the current debate over outward, inward and regional strategies in the field of trade policy is both helpful and necessary. Such a debate illuminates the areas of efficient international resource allocation, brings out the legitimate grievances of the developing countries in gaining access to the markets of the developed world and points out some genuine possibilities for regional cooperation and collective action. The debate also keeps a pressure on the developed world not to turn increasingly protectionist and on the developing world not to become completely autarkic. But it should also be frankly acknowledged that such a debate barely touches a fringe of the policy alternatives that developing countries must consider in fashioning their development strategy, primarily because it is traditionally conceived in a framework of accelerated growth and resource efficiency rather than within a broader framework embracing employment and mass poverty. It is necessary—indeed inescapable—that the present debate on development strategies should also be used to redefine the framework for the debate on trade policy alternatives.

Comment

Edmar Bacha

I am basically in agreement with the general philosophy that Mahbub Haq proposes. I did not expect such broad perspectives to be put forward in a "practical" seminar like this, but since Mahbub Haq started along this line, maybe I should also put forward my own ideas on this subject.

I shall be talking in terms of developing countries in general, but in fact my observations apply more naturally to the more advanced Latin American countries. Needless to say, the propositions I will be making are of a preliminary and hypothetical character. The only reason I put them forward is to stimulate empirical research which will shed light on the validity of my assertions.

The basic idea I would like to propose is that the so-called outward-looking strategy of the 1970s is the logical sequel to the import substitution stage, in the same way that the latter developed from the primary product export-led growth model before the 1930s. In other words, the productive system of a typical Latin American country, which is developing within the capitalist system, seems to go through successive historical growth stages. From one stage to the next, the economy experiences qualitative changes in its internal structure; within each stage, there is quantitative change, which can be measured by gross national product distribution of labor force among economic activities, and so on. However, there is one characteristic that remains constant throughout, namely, that the driving force of the economy comes from outside the national unit of analysis. In the primary product export stage, the driving force is the growth of demand for agricultural and mineral products in industrial countries. In the import substitution stage, the dynamic factor is the rate of investment of foreign firms in import substituting sectors. In the outward-looking industrialization stage, it is both the rate of investment of foreign firms and the rate of growth of foreign demand for the products fabricated by these firms—which are characterized by their labor intensity, their raw material intensity, or their pollution intensity or all three—that determine the rate of expansion of the economy as a whole.

Each of the stages of this growth model is, thus, commanded from the outside of the economy. It is in this sense that Latin American social scientists refer to their economies as *dependent*. In particular, the dynamics of the last two stages depend on the rate of growth of the subsidiaries of multinational corporations. Note that this is a qualitative characteristic of a stage, and cannot be dismissed by quantitative figures which show that the share of gross national product appropriated by foreign firms is relatively small. To use Marris's terminology, in developing countries foreign corporations are the "transcendent" firms. Through the research and development expenditure of the parent company, and the sales expenditure of its own, the subsidiary has the power to shift its demand curve and so create a market for its services. On the other hand, domestic enterprises are "immanent" firms, they typically do not undertake development expenditure and, thus, grow at a rate no faster than the average autonomous growth, if any, in the markets they have been content to enter. In other words, foreign firms are like "autonomous investment" in the simple Keynesian model, and domestic firms behave like "induced consumption." In the same way that autonomous investment can determine the level of short-run economic activity, although it represents only a small proportion of gross national product, foreign firms can control the rate of growth of the economy, even when, in quantitative terms, they are less important than domestic firms.

In this growth model, the economy expands, excluding most of the population from the industrial markets. Such expansion is due to the introduction of continuously more advanced technology, which does not generate significant employment growth. The industrial reserve army is never absorbed and the basic wage rate remains constant. Thus, growth excludes and marginalizes, in the terminology of Latin American structuralists. This means that, as the economy evolves, Baran's economic surplus tends to increase continuously. This is why the development of a domestic market for luxury goods (consumer durables) is so important for these economies. Also, the role of government, appropriating part of the economic surplus and generating new types of "sophisticated" demand, is much more important here than in industrial countries, where the basic wage rate tends to accompany the growth of labor productivity. In order to maintain high growth rates, however, government demand plus domestic luxury goods demand may not be enough, basically because the share of government in gross national product has to be kept within limits in order to preserve the basic traits of a capitalist economy. This means that as the expansion of domestic demand for luxuries falters, foreign firms have to develop export markets in order to maintain their growth—as a consequence the growth of the overall economy—at high rates.

From a purely technocratic standpoint, the outward-looking strategy commanded by multinational corporations is not the only growth strategy for countries emerging from the crisis of the last phases of the import substitution stage. Below is a summary view of the three basic development alternatives, their "growth agents" and the associated political structure:

Alternative Growth Strategies
after the Import Substitution Stage

Economic Strategy	Growth Agents	Form of the State
Capital goods import substitution	Indigenous capitalist firms (under the command of state enterprises)	State Capitalism
Expansion of mass consumption market	Collective enterprises	Socialism
Outward-looking industrialization	Multinational corporations	Dependent capitalism

I have not the time to elaborate on the three alternatives. Let me point out, however, that the first two "strategies" are not in the interest of the multinational corporations. Capital goods import substitution is much less attractive for them than developing a new "international division of labor," in which their subsidiaries in developing countries manufacture labor-intensive and natural resource-intensive components, and in which the basic research and development and capital goods production activities remain in the industrialized countries.

On the other hand, multinational corporations have a comparative advantage in attending demand patterns generated by high- and medium-income markets. Thus, they have no interest whatsoever in mass consumption markets with average per capita incomes of the order of $250 per year. This is about the average income of that 80 percent to 90 percent of the population in Latin American countries which have not yet been incorporated in the industrial market.

In order to proceed with growth under dependent capitalism, then, the only possibility is an outward-looking strategy, which is congruent with the interests of the multinational corporation.

My final thought is that we should not really be considering "alternatives" for the less developed countries, because there is only one: dependent capitalism or "outward-looking industrialization." The type of strategy that Mahbub Haq outlined, to permit the incorporation of the 80 percent to 90 percent of the population into the industrial market, would require massive institutional changes. Though he does not say this explicitly, he is suggesting a Chinese strategy, and I do not see why we should be discussing this possibility here, in this type of forum.

Maybe we should go back to our previous discussions, which consist of finding ways to ease the transition from import substitution to outward-looking industrialization. This requires basically that we devise ways to bribe labor unions in industrial countries to accept the new international division of labor between industrial and less developed countries. If my analysis is correct, the results of our efforts will be unfortunate, as far as the majority of the people in developing countries is concerned. At least, once we devise the new schemes, we will make it possible for other developing countries to replicate the so-called Brazilian miracle which, in essence, consists of finding new ways to preserve an island of Belgian prosperity in a sea of Indian poverty.

Comment
Ojetunji Aboyade

The theme of the seminar I find very apt and timely, especially for the developing countries now trying to sort out their own development strategies and trade policies, having regard among other things to their own past failures—failures which have been well documented, for example, by Little, Scitovsky and Scott.[1] Many of the developing countries are facing general difficulties in their overall social development; the President of the IBRD has regularly

---

1. See Ian M.D. Little, Tibor Scitovsky and Maurice Scott, *Industry and Trade in Some Developing Countries* (Oxford: The University Press, 1970).

in recent years invited our attention to their policy predicaments and dilemma. It is amidst all these difficulties that the present crisis in international payment arrangements has descended to compound their problems. The timeliness and significance of the seminar are further reflected in a similar conference recently held in Cambridge, over which Paul Streeten presided.[2] The atmosphere here at the Bank should provide another refreshing angle to the problem different from the cloisters of Cambridge Colleges. The IBRD, after all, is in the serious business of fostering development in the developing countries, even if it does not always succeed in doing so. We also have here a good mixture of academics and practitioners. One only needs to look to the hard-hitting, sometimes disheartening interventions of Nat Goldfinger. I think his approach should set the tone for very blunt and frank comments from participants from the developing countries who actually live with the problems.

As I have done on past occasions, I find myself in general agreement with much that Mahbub Haq has to say. I can claim to be one of his growing band of fans. In a way though, I think that he is far luckier than many of us. He has participated actively in the development game at the high level of national policy formation. But he was able to get out while the going was good—that is, before the sociopolitical blackout that was later to engulf Pakistan. Some of us are still very much in it without really being part of it, lacking both the continuous deep involvement and the detached position for objective appraisal. This means that we get all the blame and none of the compliments.

What I wish to do is consider Mr. Haq's present paper in the context of his other writings over the past three years. What runs through all is the same brilliant handling of complex subjects, incisive professional comment and a total commitment to a sense of social purpose. Some three years ago, Mahbub Haq was advocating that we throw away the gross domestic product and replace it with some index of quality of life. He has emphasized at various points the supremacy of employment, distributive equity and social welfare objectives. He has questioned the adequacy, even sometimes the relevance, of conventional economic analysis for grappling with the perennial problem of mass underdevelopment. It is difficult to fault his advocating (almost with evangelical fervor) that a meaningful attack on the problem must be directed at its roots.

---

2. Paul Streeten, *Trade Policies for Development* (forthcoming).

Similarly in this paper, and in what appears to be an iconoclastic kind of way, Mahbub Haq seems to be urging us all—and especially the developing countries—to have another close look at international trade as a vehicle of the developing process, and to dethrone it. He has not, of course, put it in so many words, but the message virtually amounts to that, reading between the lines. If I understand him correctly and this is what he really seems to be saying, I could not possibly agree with him more. I think it is a good and worthy point to make.

I remain, however, agnostic about being able to dethrone international trade. The failure—even the need—to dethrone the gross domestic product strengthens my skepticism in this regard. Dethroning is probably too large a task. What is probably needed is a restructuring of our development theories, such that look for an alternative set of growth prime movers. The fact that the sorry experience of twentieth-century international trade has launched many developing countries on a growth path that is slow, that is uneven and that is antiegalitarian compels us to doubt the operational validity of neoclassical trade theory. I am also impressed by Mahbub Haq's focus on the net rather than the gross benefits of international trade; I am particularly struck by his figures that show that the developed countries as a group spend three times their amount of net official development assistance in indirect support of importable primary commodities. It is not improbable, for instance, that in the Nigerian case the amount of real resource transfer out of the country by one major American oil company alone in a recent year would be greater than what the United States Agency for International Development had been able to make available to Nigeria over the last decade. I do fully accept Mr. Haq's point that trade is, and should be seen as, an integral part of development; but the relationship between the two should be reversed such that international trade no longer becomes the pace setter for domestic growth. Only a few weeks ago I was trying to make (perhaps less successfully) a similar point at the Cambridge Conference, that is, that the tail of external trade should not wag the dog of national development.

In agreeing with the general line of Mahbub Haq's argument, I would indeed like to extend what I consider the central issue for analysis and policy. In reconsidering the relationship between external trade and the development process, I would wish to contend that findings like those of Little, Scitovsky and Scott are not really an indictment of import substitution as such; at least I do not think that that is what they meant. It cannot be an indictment of import substitution in general, but only a criticism of certain types of import substitution. In any case, the real policy choice—as ten days of debate in Cambridge recently have shown—is not one between an inward-looking and an outward-looking strategy, or between import substitution and export promotion per se. The choice is in reality more complex; it varies from country to country and from one period to another even in the same country.

An inward-looking strategy does not mean autarky. So I do not think that Mahbub Haq needs to be apologetic that he might be misunderstood for advocating autarky. An inward-looking strategy involves far more than import substitution in the sense, for example, that it takes into account nontraded commodities, domestic agriculture and public works. Goods and services which do not enter the stream of international trade may be as important to the development process of the developing countries, especially in such resource-endowed regions as tropical Africa.

I would also like to argue that on the grounds of risk avoidance, interdependencies and externalities, one dollar saved by an underdeveloped country is to be preferred to one dollar earned by it. The two dollars are only nominally equal in an arithmetic sense, but they clearly have different implications for the development process. Developing one's domestic economy substantially on one's domestic steam has the added political and administrative-control advantage that foreigners cannot be blamed for domestic failures. Policy-makers would be denied a ready alibi. Essentially, what an inward-looking strategy means is that a given country is trying to extend its national economic capacity to make autonomous decisions and to accept the responsibility for the successes, for the mistakes or for the failures of those decisions.

Most of the international trading and payments arrangements in the developing countries are a product of a colonial and neocolonial process that still makes them the economic backyard of the world or, in less respectable terms, the enclaves—satellites of the metropolitan economies. With respect to resources, many developing countries (and certainly many of those in tropical Africa) approximate the early stage of the classical—especially that of Ricardo—transformation process. In contrast to the prediction of the classical growth model, the main reason for their weak growth performance lies precisely in the fact of their neocolonial structure of economic organization, which prevents a high rate of profit from being translated in high wages and a high capital accumulation rate.

Having said all this, I would, however, like to disagree with Mahbub Haq on a number of points. In the light of his own argument and our own additional points, it is difficult to see how or why he suggests that the front-runner in the renewed debate on development strategy among academics is the outward-looking strategy. It may well be that this is just a question of style or of semantics rather than of substance. At least among the academics from developing countries, I would seriously doubt the front-runner is the outward-looking strategy. Mahbub Haq does not in any case suggest that it is the same front-runner with the policy-makers. My limited experience is that the familiar gap between the points of view of academics and practitioners on development strategy is not as wide in the developing countries as in the advanced industrial capitalist countries of North America and Western Europe. At least in the tropical African case, and with respect to the role of foreign trade in the development process, the academics and policy-makers are shifting in the direction of an inward-looking strategy.

In Mahbub Haq's paper, developing countries are enjoined to take one policy action or the other. This has set me thinking about the process of decision-making. Who, in these developing countries, are supposed really to make these decisions? Is it the government (central, state or whatever), groups, individuals, enterprises? Or are the decisions made for the country vicariously, in spite of itself? It is indeed a fallacy to think that if Country A is supposed to have experienced event X, then that event is a result of decisions consciously made by the "policy-makers" in A. Many of the observed results in international trade and payments are in fact policy-action-neutral in the developing countries.

It follows, therefore, that any appraisal of the industrialization effort in a given country should be conducted or conceived in three analytically distinct, though overlapping, phases. There is first the very passive phase when normal exogenous shifts in comparative costs advantage lead to the establishment of manufacturing industries in developing countries. There is second the intermediate state when protective tariffs designed mainly as revenue-earning devices by government lead to the establishment of import-substituting industries. Then there is, thirdly, the real active phase when strong fiscal incentives within an integrated inward-looking strategy stimulate the growth of resource-based industries for an expanding domestic market. Policy formation has different meaning for each phase, but this has not been fully reflected in Mahbub Haq's paper.

One strong point of departure I have with Mahbub Haq is his suggestion for massive and uniform devaluation by the developing countries. Is this a politically practical proposition for the 1970s? It is at best arguable. It is certainly not immediately evident to me what massive, equitable and sustained benefits the countries of tropical Africa will derive if they join with their Asian and Latin American counterparts to devalue uniformly by a margin of between 50 percent and 100 percent. Indeed, I think that there are a number of a priori arguments why it might not be a real alternative policy strategy for the developing countries.

First (but perhaps this is not an insurmountable obstacle), the present rules of the game established by the International Monetary Fund would have to be changed in order to avoid a labyrinthine multiplicity of exchange rate systems. Second, the resulting effect of a high import content of both consumption and investment expenditure in the present circumstances of the developing countries cannot be ignored, in relation to inflationary pressures and social stability. Third, the budgetary burden of the servicing of public external debt is likely to be still greater and, as the IBRD has been saying in the last few months, this is already frighteningly high for some developing countries. Fourth, even if the low price elasticity of demand for most of the developing countries' exports is dismissed as unimportant, we would still be faced with the short-term problem of supply inelasticity of many primary producers, leading to a rapid evaporation of any potential price advantage which the massive devaluation might initially offer. There is, fifth, the importance of nonprice barriers to imports from the developing countries on the part of the advanced industrial countries. This problem was discussed at length both at the Cambridge Conference and already at this seminar, so evidently it cannot be ignored. To the extent that the barriers are there, it is clear that they can and will frustrate Mr. Haq's proposal. Indeed, the existence of the barrier makes the opposite of his proposal arguable — that the developing countries should devalue vis-à-vis each other, while substantially maintaining their existing exchange rates with the developed countries. This might even further encourage the flow of South–South trade and regional integration among the developing countries about which we have now heard so much. Finally, suppose Nigeria, Brazil and the Ivory Coast had joined Ghana in 1971 in massively devaluing their currencies — it is very doubtful how far this could have been beneficial to their cocoa export. But perhaps Mahbub Haq would reply by saying that his target of export promotion is not the primary commodities but manufactured products. Well, industrial exports are not now much in evidence, except for Brazil, and the time it would take to expand capacity for them is so long that the potential benefits of devaluation would have been wiped out.

The alternative proposal by Mahbub Haq, of seeking international agreement on the export of agricultural commodities from the developing countries, is easier said than done. Our experience of the last two decades is distinguished by frustrations at the lack of positive action. The lesson of this for policy is that a workable program is likely to come only from a concerted effort by the developing countries to cut back production by reordering the allocation of their domestic resources. This might, of course, create an adjustment process problem probably bigger and more serious in intensity than that Caroline Miles discussed for the developed countries in relation to the declining or aging consumer industries of Sweden and the United States.

I am all the way with Mahbub Haq on his treatment of the exploitation of the seabed and of other common resources of mankind. It sounds good and should be pursued relentlessly. But, as an alternative solution, it promises little impact for the developing countries in the short and medium runs. It is difficult to see what significant results it can yield for them in the 1970s.

Again, to get on first and fast with income distribution or redistribution, before "defining"—I am not sure whether Mr. Haq really meant defining—a country's development strategy, sounds like an attractive proposition. We are all for holiness and against sin. There must be few academics left, at any rate in the developing countries, who can be said to be against income redistribution. But simply reaffirming the noble objective does not carry policy formation far. Mahbub Haq seems to be assuming a viable structure of economic organization and institutions for social mobilization already in existence. For most of the tropical African countries (except perhaps Tanzania, as Gerry Helleiner may well argue), such existence is more an assumption than ground reality. Mr. Haq also seems to be underestimating the dimension of the problem. Income distribution in the developing countries is not only with respect to classes; it is also with respect to skills, regions, states or areas, as well as activity sectors. In heterogeneous societies with various ethnic groups, the regional or spatial dimension of the problem may be even more important to many than the distribution of income by factor shares of social classes. The proposal also ignores the serious problem of the transition period; that is, the problem of what to do in the meantime while we are waiting for the noble cow of income redistribution to come home. In any case, it glosses over the issue of the real and complex nature of the class struggle in an under-developed country that is at once trying to decolonize, rapidly develop its resources and achieve some measures of social justice. As I illustrated at the Cambridge Conference, the policy-maker might be faced with the unpleasant dilemma of not wanting to set head-long against the country's middle class in such a period of great strain. He might reckon that the greater and the first battle is with the external force. In other words, successful decolonization may initially require the support of the very objectionable characters of nationals who have appropriated to themselves a dispropor-tionate share of the national income. The policy choices in such a circumstance are not at all easy.

My final reaction to Mahbub Haq's paper is that it is really difficult and probably unrealistic to prescribe policy reforms for the developing countries without first breaking them down into different development typologies in terms of resource endowment, in terms of status or level of development, in terms of economic organization and in terms of the nature of their social crisis. In my view, it is a mistake to assume that the developing countries are sufficiently similar for such policy prescriptions. Although we do often recognize this fact in our discussion, we tend readily to ignore it in our serious global analysis. It is particularly a mistake to pro-ceed as if the short- and medium-run interests of the developing countries are in fact the same. The truth is that they often diverge and indeed conflict. Being anxious to see them work together does not remove the fact that policy decisions are taken at the level of the nation state on the basis of real or imagined national interests.

Tropical Africa, for example, has been treated peripherally in development literature; not as cases in its own right but mainly in relation to external trade. The vehicle of growth is always assumed to reside in its external sector; and thus it could scarcely have autonomous development stimuli of its own. There are however some significant features of the economy of tropical Africa that make it structurally distinct from the classic cases of Asia and Latin America for analysis and policy.

Some of the more important of these features include the widening gap between the gross domestic product and gross national product, unstable growth arising from heavy primary export dependence, relatively small average size of the nation state, development process based on exhaustible comparative advantage (petroleum, solid minerals, timber), neocolonial structure of monetary-fiscal policies, absence of the critical minimum size of the public sector as a leverage for meaningful mobilization and directed development and an agonizing process of national political formation and social cohesiveness. In the light of all these, the critical policy problem for the developing countries becomes one of how to improve and extend the capability of their nationals to design *and* implement sound development plans. That is the Hobson's choice.

The only real alternative for the developing countries of tropical Africa is meaningful, realistic and vigorous planning. It must be the kind of planning which identifies and clearly articulates national interests, specifies both the strategy and tactics for achieving the declared social objectives, improves the bargaining skills of the country in negotiating with the outside world and especially with the developed countries and the multinational enterprises, develops jointly with others the kind of economic-political clout that the world has recently witnessed with respect to the Organization of Petroleum Exporting Countries activities and occupies a commanding position over the use of all resources in tropical Africa. The task of the economists in the developing countries, in this context, is to try and understand as well as strengthen the bureaucracy of their countries in this arduous task of playing a difficult game in a hostile international environment.

As I see it, the issue for policy is not whether or not to increase the trade involvement of the developing countries. Indeed, they are already overdependent on external trade. The issue is how to improve the terms of their participation through structural shifts of resources at home. It is one of effecting a neocolonial structural break, and of accommodating the short-term real costs (for example, temporary slowing of growth of gross domestic product) which it would probably entail. What the developing countries need from institutions like the IBRD is an understanding, and possibly also the acceptance, of the fact that the reading of their own problems and the setting of their own priorities are likely to diverge from most of the conventional wisdoms on which we have all been brought up in the development literature.

6

Policy Issues in Adjustment Assistance: The United States

Robert Baldwin and John H. Mutti

For many years economists have been demonstrating in static terms that, setting aside terms of trade effects, the elimination of tariffs and other trade distorting measures increases a country's potential real income. Yet, while significant progress toward reducing import duties among industrial countries has been made over the last forty years, many impediments to free trade, particularly of the nontariff variety, still remain among these countries. Moreover, periodically there are strong (and sometimes partly successful) pressures to impose additional controls over merchandise trade.

I. THE FAILURE TO ACHIEVE FREE TRADE

There are a number of possible explanations for the failure of the economists' points of view to prevail in the area of commercial policy. One may simply be that we have neglected to present the case for free trade in understandable terms and to a sufficiently wide audience. However, the fact that there has been a steady stream of pamphlets and books written by free traders since the time of the classical economists, that there have been many hours of public discussion and debate on the subject and that thousands of students have been taught the merits of free trade would seem to suggest that we cannot dismiss our lack of success so easily.

Another possible explanation may be that policy-makers are aware of the concept of optimum tariffs and have attempted to increase real income by using tariffs to exploit any monopoly power over the terms of trade. Although it may well be true that for some large countries reducing tariffs decreases real income because of an adverse movement in their terms of trade, there is little evidence to indicate that policy-makers have deliberately employed tariffs for this purpose.[1] Even if they had, there is no guarantee that a country's income level can be raised in this manner once the retaliatory actions of other trading countries are taken into account. The impact of tariffs in stifling the efficiency effects of international competition must also be assessed in estimating the net effect of import duties.

A third possible reason for the difficulty in persuading nations to adopt liberal trade policies may be that the free trade case has usually been presented in static rather than dynamic terms. Perhaps there are sound reasons for protection in dynamic terms and political leaders have wisely viewed policy decisions in these terms rather than within the typical static framework of the economist. Although political leaders in developing countries have quite clearly been influenced by "infant" industry and "infant" economy arguments, even though there may be good reasons for questioning their validity, few people have tried to justify protection in industrial countries (with which this paper deals) on these grounds.

An important reason at the macro level for frequent pressures in the developed countries to apply broad protectionist or export promoting measures is to assist in attaining improved balance of payments and aggregate-employment conditions. In the United States, for example, the Domestic International Sales Corporation (DISC) proposal, which went into effect in late 1971, was designed to help the United States balance of payments by increasing exports. The tightening of the "Buy American" provisions and the increasing extent to which United States aid has been tied to United States purchases have also been aimed at alleviating pressures on our balance of payments. The temporary 10 percent surcharge imposed on imports in August 1971 is, of course, another classic example of using a trade-distorting measure for balance of payments.

What is very much needed in order to eliminate or at least

---

1. Georgio Basevi, "The Restrictive Effect of the U.S. Tariff and Its Welfare Value," *American Economic Review* LVIII, no. 4 (September 1968): 840-52.

mitigate the use of tariffs and other trade-distorting measures for balance of payments purposes is greater flexibility in exchange rates. Exchange rate changes must become an important adjustment tool in helping to cope with the type of basic structural changes in international markets with which this seminar is concerned. A disappointing feature of the Smithsonian Agreement of December 1971 was that a reduction of several nontariff barriers with significant balance of payments consequences did not accompany the currency realignments. It is most important that future international monetary agreements contain provisions that require countries to take into account trade-distorting policies with macro effects in the determination of appropriate exchange rate changes.

Even if a system of flexible exchange rates prevailed, there would, however, still be adjustment problems for particular industries and pressures to maintain or raise the degree of protection or export subsidization in these industries. The main factor that makes it difficult to eliminate the various measures that protect these industries is the effect of this action on the distribution of income. When a tariff is lowered, consumers benefit but factors involved in producing domestic substitutes usually are made worse off. Although it may be possible for the gainers to compensate the losers and still end up as gainers, full compensation is in fact almost never provided to those who actually lose by the change. Governments generally find it much easier politically to assist a particular income group by protecting the product they produce from import competition than by directly providing the group with an income level equivalent to what they had been earning through increased taxation of the general public. The tariff has the additional advantage that it yields tax revenue, which may in some cases make a major contribution to total government revenue. Although consumers dislike paying higher prices for the product, often the proportion of their income spent on any one taxed product (or even all imports) is relatively small, with the result that there is no effective counterpressure from consumers. Only when the import item is regarded as an essential consumer or producer good is there likely to be strong political pressure against import duties from consumers. On the other hand, the loss to producers tends to be concentrated within a smaller group of individuals and thus to generate strong political pressures for protection from the group. A partial counter political force from that exerted by import-competing sectors is the expansion of certain export lines, since tariff-cutting is now generally achieved through a multilateral negotiation in which all parties reduce tariffs. Usually the export industries affected are already quite profitable and there is likely to be little pressure from these firms for even higher profits. Furthermore, the additional workers who would be hired as exports increased are not organized into any effective political group.

An even more important aspect of the redistributional effects of a reduction in trade distortions is the loss of real income, both to individuals in the affected industry and to the nation as a whole during the period when productive factors are being transferred from the domestic industry whose output declines as a result of the tariff cut to other domestic industries. Traditional tariff analysis tends to ignore this income loss by assuming that the reallocation period is negligible. Figure 6-1 can be used to present the standard analysis of tariff changes in partial equilibrium, static terms and to indicate the effect of taking into account the income loss during the transitional period. For simplicity it is assumed that the import supply curve facing the country is infinitely elastic. The curve DD' represents the domestic demand curve, $S_dS'_d$ the domestic supply curve of the imported commodity and PS_f the foreign supply curve for imports. If an import tax of PT/PO is imposed, imports are equal to HJ and domestic production to OH. The tax revenue accruing to the government is $ABEF$.[2]

FIGURE 6-1

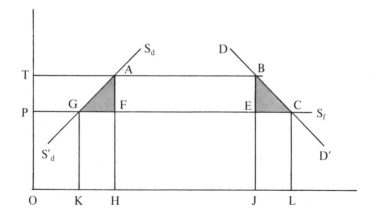

2. The demand curve DD' is drawn under the assumption that government revenues are held constant by using an income tax to supplement the value of import duties collected.

If this duty is eliminated, the domestic price falls from *OT* to *OP* and imports expand to *KL*. Domestic production declines to *OK*. The consumer surplus gained by this price decline equals the area *BCPT*. On the other hand, producers' surplus declines by *AGPT* and government tax revenue by *ABEF*. Thus, the net consumer gain for the country equals the two shaded triangles *AFG* and *BEC*.[3] The value of the released resources involved in domestic production, namely *AHKG,* is assumed to be absorbed into alternative productive lines sufficiently rapidly that any temporary adjustment problem faced by these resources can be ignored.[4] If in fact all or part of the resources involved in production are not immediately absorbed into other industries at earnings rates equal to their marginal productivity, then the relevant part of the area *AHKG* must be deduced from the two shaded areas *AFG* and *BEC* during the time period when these resources are idle. More specifically, the net direct gain or loss in welfare from reducing the tariff is the present value of the shaded areas—determined by discounting the sum over some appropriate time period and at some appropriate interest rate—minus the present value of the loss of productive output during the transitional period.

There also will be temporary unfavorable secondary effects associated with the tariff reduction because of the reduced spending on other products by the resources made idle by the tariff cut. This cut in expenditure can be particularly severe for producers who provide goods and services to workers in the industry and who are located near the plants that are shut down completely or that significantly reduce their levels of operations. Moreover, the increase in spending on imports by consumers will tend to reduce income and employment in other sectors still more.[5]

II. FACTORS AFFECTING THE DURATION OF UNEMPLOYMENT

The possibility that in the short-run the income-reducing forces involved in cutting tariffs may offset their income-raising effects

3. In this analysis, a given sum of money spent or received is regarded in welfare terms as equivalent to any other equal sum, no matter which income group spends or receives the funds.

4. It is assumed that there are no other distortions in other productive lines.

5. For simplicity, we ignore the feedback effects from foreigners because of the increased spending on imports as the tariff is lifted. Furthermore, the effects of any exchange rates changes in order to eliminate the deficit-creating effect of the tariff cut are not taken into account. This would seem to be a reasonable position for short-run analysis in a system of fixed exchange rates. On this point, see Basevi, op. cit.

may lead political leaders with short-time horizons to justify their lack of action in cutting duties on both efficiency and equity grounds. It is important, therefore, that we attempt to understand better the various factors influencing the duration of the adjustment period, the actual magnitude of the income-reducing effects in various industries, and the ways by which these effects can be reduced. Unfortunately, very little work has been undertaken by trade economists on these issues. Instead, in urging more liberal trade policies, economists have stressed the long-run benefits of freer trade and, on the basis of very little information, have minimized the adjustment problem.

There is, however, a body of literature in labor economics that would seem to be applicable to the adjustment assistance problem in the trade field. One aspect of this literature consists of case studies dealing with how rapidly workers become reemployed after losing their jobs because of such factors as automation, shifts of production to lower wage areas and shifts in demand. Another part of the labor literature in this field attempts to ascertain the effects of training programs, relocation allowances, lump-sum severance payments et cetera, in assisting the displaced workers to find new positions. At this point we shall discuss their findings with regard to the ability of various types of workers to find new jobs. In the last part of the paper, dealing with policy recommendations, some of the results obtained by labor economists as to the effectiveness of various adjustment assistance programs will be summarized.

As labor economists have themselves pointed out, there is a pressing need for detailed studies of the problems of reemployment within a reasonably comparable framework. As it is now, the many case studies cover varying time periods, focus on different variables and usually make no attempt to isolate the effect of any particular factor from other closely related variables—for example, labor skills from years of education. However, on the basis of the various studies it does seem possible to make some rough generalizations as to the different factors determining the length of unemployment after a plant has been closed.

As for the various factors that influence the length of unemployment, age seems to be the one single factor having the greatest effect on reemployment opportunities.[6] Older workers have a more difficult time in finding a new position than younger workers. There

---

6. William Haber, Louis H. Ferman and Harriet Hudson, *The Impact of Technological Change* (Kalamazoo, Mich.: Upjohn Institute for Employment Research, 1963), p. 21.

are several reasons for this. Employers regard workers in their forties and fifties as possessing less physical capabilities than young workers and as being more difficult to train. Furthermore, they are more costly to employ since they will start drawing pensions much sooner than young workers. Finally, since they have seniority at their former jobs, they may leave their new jobs and return to their old ones if given the opportunity.

Level of education is a second important factor influencing reemployment possibilities. Since many skills are not transferable to new jobs, a certain level of verbal attainment which is only gained through formal education is often needed to acquire the skills involved in the position. Skill levels themselves are another characteristic affecting the length of time involved in obtaining a new job. Work involving simple, repetitive tasks has been increasingly mechanized with the result that displaced, unskilled workers find it difficult to obtain new jobs. However, certain tasks performed by highly skilled workers—for example, photoengravers in newspaper work—have also been mechanized so that one cannot make an unqualified generalization about the influence of skills.

Two other individual characteristics affecting reemployment opportunities are sex and race. It has been well documented that women and those in minority racial groups are discriminated against even though they possess educational and skill levels comparable to those of white males.

A final condition having a very significant effect on reemployment opportunities is the level of unemployment within the region where the displaced workers live as well as in the economy generally. When unemployment rates are high, even young, highly educated, skilled workers tend to find it difficult to obtain a new job.

III. QUANTITATIVE EFFECTS

We now move from a theoretical description of the gains and losses of tariff removal to an empirical implementation of those ideas. We shall explain and attempt to justify the various data and parameters used in this analysis, but always with the recognition that at present there are severe limitations on what we know about labor market adjustments, industry supply responses, and so on. Therefore, this exercise points toward a method of approaching the problem and a possible guide for further research, and does not claim to arrive at absolute answers.

The Gains from Tariff Removal

With respect to measuring the welfare gains (ΔW) from tariff removal subject to all the necessary conditions listed previously, we use the formula: $\Delta W = \frac{1}{2}(\frac{t}{t+1})^2 \cdot e_m \cdot P_o M_o$, where t is the tariff rate, e_m is the price elasticity of demand for imports and $P_o M_o$ is the initial domestic market value of imports.[7] Since we are no longer considering the question of tariff removal in the abstract, we shall use data for 1969, a year recent enough to imply an institutional setting similar to the present. Regarding the level of aggregation, we shall use industry definitions from the United States input-output tables, and focus our analysis on five industries: (16) Broad and Narrow Fabrics, Yarn and Thread mills; (27) Chemicals and Selected Chemical Products; (37) Primary Iron and Steel Manufacturing; (56) Radio, Television and Communications Equipment; and (59) Motor Vehicles and Equipment. Our analysis is based on the assumption that tariff protection is unilaterally eliminated in one step for each industry while tariffs in the other four industries remain at their initial levels. No explicit account is taken of the secondary repercussions mentioned in the last paragraph of Part I nor of the effects mentioned in footnote 5.

Import data are readily available in f.o.b. terms, and can be adjusted to approximate their domestic market value by using the input-output spread ratios for foreign trade. Implicit tariff rates are calculated from collected duties, which requires us to assume that the composition of that industry's trade would not change greatly when tariffs are removed.[8] Of course, adjustment problems would accompany the removal of other nontariff barriers, and this level of disaggregation would be well suited to allowing for those factors, if a thorough, policy-oriented evaluation were called for.

Import demand elasticities are reported as a range of values, and calculations made for each figure. Although no elasticities to our knowledge have been estimated for those specific industries, several recent works have produced estimates for one-digit Standard Industrial Trade Classification, two-digit International Standard Industrial Classification, one-digit end-use, commodity-class categories and so on, from which we selected a range to represent plausible

---

7. Harry G. Johnson, "The Cost of Protection and the Scientific Tariff," *Journal of Political Economy* LXVIII, no. 4 (August 1960): 331-32.

8. Bureau of the Census, *U.S. Commodity Export and Imports as Related to Output, 1968/69*, Series ES2, no. 12 (Washington, D.C.: Department of Commerce, 1972).

elasticities for our five industries listed above.[9] Therefore, we did not use the same spread of values for each industry, since we had prior information on what would be reasonable elasticities. The majority of these estimates came from models using annual data, but if several estimates of long-term elasticities had been available, such as those from a partial adjustment model used by Houthakker and Magee, perhaps they would have been more appropriate. This short-run orientation particularly may bias downward our estimated benefits, because import demand is a residual from domestic supply and demand conditions, and a priori we expect supply to be more elastic over time.

The gains calculated from our formula apply to a single year, and this stream over time must be discounted to give us a present value figure of gains to be compared with costs. We shall avoid the explicit choice of a single proper interest rate. Instead a range of three interest rates is used: 5 percent, 10 percent and 15 percent. These three rates would seem to cover the plausible limits for such a rate and also enable us to check the sensitivity of our results to changes in the discount rate used. Given adequate information, these discount rates could be adjusted to allow for growth of income, and consequently demand, over time. Such an adjustment would require that we know the income elasticity of demand for the good and a projection of the average growth rate for the time horizon chosen. We ignore this factor here and merely observe that our estimates unambiguously will be biased downward if we are dealing with normal goods and some positive growth rate.

With respect to the relevant time horizon, we must consider the stability of our estimated relationships. Given the changes in tastes and technology which occur over time, discounting over an infinite time period seems unwarranted. We arbitrarily choose ten years as the proper duration of time, and also present calculations for a five-year horizon which might be more realistic for politicians who face frequent elections.

---

9. For instance, see Mordechai Elihav Kreinin, "Price Elasticities in International Trade," *Review of Economics and Statistics* XLIX, no. 4 (November 1967): 510-15; J. David Richardson, "The Response of Imports and Domestic Demand to Price, Tariff and Exchange Rate Changes: A Structural Estimation Study for Selected U.S. Manufactures," prepared under the auspices of the U.S. Department of State, Bureau of Economic Affairs, Contract SCC-1005-08817-70 (Washington, D.C., March 1972); William H. Branson, "A Disaggregated Model of the U.S. Balance of Trade," Board of Governors of the Federal Reserve System Staff Economic Studies no. 44 (Washington, D.C., February 1968); and Hendrick S. Houthakker and Stephen P. Magee, "Income and Price Elasticities in World Trade," *Review of Economics and Statistics* LI, no. 2 (May 1969): 111-25.

The Costs of Tariff Removal

From our partial equilibrium diagram, we see the fall in domestic production that occurs following tariff removal. We want to know how much unemployment this reduction in output will cause, and to arrive at a numerical answer we would multiply the change in production by a labor-output coefficient: $\Delta L = \Delta Q \cdot \frac{L}{Q}$, where the coefficient L/Q is assumed to be constant so that its average and marginal values are identical. Since the relevant information is available only in value terms, we instead deal with the formula: $\Delta L = P_o \Delta Q \cdot \frac{L}{P_o Q_o}$. To determine $P_o \Delta Q$, we use the following formula: $P_o \Delta Q = e_s(\frac{t}{t+1})$ $(P_o \cdot Q_o)$, where e_s is the price elasticity of domestic supply and $P_o Q_o$ is the initial value of domestic production.[10]

The value of manufacturers' shipments is a readily available figure, but since it also includes exports it is not the proper measure unless we are willing to assume exports are negligible. In fact, the whole simplistic model which regards domestic production and imports as identical products can be brought into question, since we cannot explain why a particular good will be both exported and imported. Hopefully, in a more disaggregated level of analysis this problem will not be as serious.

Estimates for the elasticity of supply at any level are practically nonexistent. We have chosen a range of supply elasticities based on several considerations. Previous articles by Robert Stern[11] and Bela Balassa[12] assume supply elasticities which vary from 0 to 1. Also, estimates made for those industries believed to be more competitive fell in this range. Since we have ignored the theoretical question of imperfect markets, we did not try to develop price reaction functions for noncompetitive industries.

In general one might argue that economic theory claims industry supply curves will be infinitely elastic in the long run, and therefore the range chosen is too small. However, we are dealing with unemployment, a short-run phenomenon attributable to market rigidities which are not immutable over time, and therefore, with respect to calculating costs, we do want short-run supply elasticities. Further-

---

10. For this formula to be used directly, we must add the constraint that $e_s \frac{(t)}{t+1} = 1$.

11. Robert Stern, "The U.S. Tariff and the Efficiency of the U.S. Economy," American Economic Association *Papers and Proceedings* LIV, no. 3 (May 1964): 459-70.

12. Bela Balassa, "Tariff Protection in Industrial Countries," *Journal of Political Economy* LXXIII, no. 6 (December 1965): 573-94.

more, given our perfect-substitutability model, we know that the following relationship holds between the elasticity of import demand (e_m), the elasticity of total demand (e_d) and the elasticity of domestic supply (e_s) where all elasticities are defined positively: $e_m = (1 + \frac{O_s}{O_m}) e_d + (\frac{O_s}{O_m}) e_s$, where O_s is domestic production, and O_m is imports. For all of the industries chosen, imports as a share of domestic production are less than 10 percent, so that O_s/O_m is greater than 10. If $e_m = 10$, then the maximum value e_s can take on is unity, given that e_d will never be negative. If we believe e_s should take on larger values, such as 10, then e_m must rise approximately by the same proportion unless e_d either falls or increases by a smaller proportion, at any rate the minimum value of e_m in such a case would be 100, which we might regard with skepticism. If all the elasticities are increased proportionately, the absolute size of the difference between gain and loss from tariff removal also will increase in the same proportion even though the ratio of the two remains the same, and therefore the choice of elasticities is not inconsequential.

From this calculation of $P_o \Delta Q$ we then determine how many workers will be laid off because of this fall in output, using direct labor/output coefficients for the various industries. We use the direct coefficients because we are less certain of the flexibility of suppliers of intermediate goods and services to this given industry; we assume either that intermediate inputs are immediately used elsewhere, or that those effects could be picked up through the multiplier referred to in the first section of the paper. After determining the number of workers laid off in each industry, we multiply this number by the average duration of unemployment in weeks in 1969 and by the average weekly wage in that industry in 1969. That product gives us the total loss to labor in the industry.[13] By using the average duration of unemployment as reported by the Department of Labor, we imply that the labor market is quite large, so that the closing of a given plant will not appreciably alter the average duration of unemployment. That assumption is rather optimistic and might be considered a lower bound on our estimate of costs. Dislocation studies, such as those on the Armour Meatpacking closings,[14] indicate that even at

13. Bureau of Labor Statistics, *Employment and Earnings, United States 1909-71,* Bulletin 13128 (Washington D.C.: Department of Labor, 1972); U.S. Department of Commerce, Office of Business Economics, *Survey of Current Business* (Washington, D.C.: U.S. Government Printing Office, 1970).

14. George P. Schultz and Arnold R. Weber, *Strategies for the Displaced Worker* (New York: Harper and Row, 1966).

the end of one year, over 30 percent of the workers may be unemployed. Therefore, we have reported costs based on the alternative assumption that the average duration of unemployment is twenty-four weeks instead of eleven, which reflects the fact that labor markets are often local and small, and that unemployment may be higher than the average 1969 figure.

Next we adjust this cost factor by personal characteristics of workers in the given industries. We might question whether a further adjustment is called for since we already have calculated the losses according to the wage in each industry. If wages reflect marginal productivity, then our value calculation already has allowed for varying age, education and so forth, in each industry because those factors help determine marginal productivity. However, the time dimension of unemployment costs also is likely to depend on these same factors. In other words, the means by which we want to quantify how sex, race, education and age affect an individual's duration of unemployment.

Such data are not available, and unfortunately very few labor studies do control on all these factors. We have relied heavily on a recently published study by Einar Hardin and Michael E. Borus which analyzes retraining programs in Michigan over the years 1962-64.[15] They report a multiple regression explaining the gain in earnings over a one-year period for a sample of 784 trainees and eligible non-trainees. Briefly, they control on labor market characteristics (occupation, percentage growth in local unemployment) and personal characteristics (age, education) and allow for the effect of training through interaction terms. We are interested in the noninteraction terms, and use their coefficients by asking that if the workers in a particular industry are the same in all respects as the average from the sample, except that they have one more year of education, then how will that affect their earnings over the year?

The interpretation we place on these coefficients is not explored by the authors of the study, and accordingly our use of them may not give very precise results. Claiming that the difference in earnings' gain attributable to education or age arises because the person with more education will be unemployed for a shorter period over the year may be overstating the case, but some adjustment does seem necessary. With respect to the calculations we make, Borus and Hardin's published results do not report the average values for

15. Einar Hardin and Michael E. Borus, *The Economic Benefits and Costs of Retraining* (Lexington, Mass.: D.C. Heath, 1971). See appendix for further elaboration of their results.

these factors, and we have approximated them by median age and education data in 1960. Furthermore, the estimates of the importance of age and education are not specific to any industry, and we assume for simplicity that they are identical across all industries. Since the study sample is not confined to workers in manufacturing industries, our use of their coefficients may be even less justified, and this step in our estimates clearly is more suggestive of what should be allowed for if data are available.

The calculations for each step in estimating the quantitative effects of eliminating tariffs are reported in the appendix. We present here only the final results in comparing benefits from removing tariffs[16] for the indicated elasticities and at a 10 percent discount rate over a ten-year period with two sets of cost—one based on an eleven-week period of unemployment and the other for a twenty-four week period. As can be seen from Table 6-1, the benefits gained by removing tariffs exceed both the low and high estimates of cost for Textiles, Chemicals, Radio, Television and Communications Equipment and Primary Iron and Steel. However, the market for Motor Vehicles gives a mixed result based on whether the period of unemployment for workers is eleven weeks or twenty-four weeks.

TABLE 6-1

BENEFIT AND COST ESTIMATES OF REMOVING TARIFFS[17]

Industry	e_m	e_s	Benefits (Mns. US$)	Costs (Mns. US$) 11-Week Unemployment	Costs (Mns. US$) 24-Week Unemployment
Textiles..............	6.0	.38	$617.6	57.9	135.6
Chemicals	2.0	.09	$ 39.6	6.2	17.0
Primary Iron and Steel ..	10.0	.75	$218.4	108.7	204.3
Radio, T.V., and Communications	7.0	.68	$225.3	78.5	158.6
Motor Vehicles.........	6.0	.59	$ 45.3	32.2	62.0

We again wish to emphasize that our estimates of the gains and losses in these industries are set forth more as illustrations of a methodology for calculating such magnitudes rather than as the ac-

16. No attempt has been made to include various nontariff barriers that protect domestic producers.

17. The supply elasticities and cost estimates reported here have been adjusted from those in the conference version of this paper to avoid the inconsistencies between the projected increase in imports and decrease in domestic output pointed out by Maurice Scott.

tual net gains or losses when tariffs are removed in these industries. We are urgently in need of studies that not only give us more accurate domestic-supply and import-demand elasticities, but also coefficients that relate the time involved in obtaining a new job to such variables as age, level of education, skills, sex, race and unemployment levels.

IV. ADJUSTMENT ASSISTANCE IN THE UNITED STATES

In the United States the legislative provisions for dealing with the problem of adjusting to increased imports are contained in the Trade Expansion Act of 1962. Under this Act there are two routes by which firms and groups of workers may receive adjustment assistance. One route permits a firm or group of workers to apply directly to the Tariff Commission for certification of eligibility to apply for adjustment assistance. The second enables a trade association, firm or group of workers to petition the Tariff Commission for a finding of injury to the entire industry. If an affirmative finding is made in the latter case, the President may either increase the import duty on the industry's product by as much as 50 percent more than the rate existing in 1934, or authorize firms and groups of workers within the industry to apply, respectively, to the Department of Commerce or the Department of Labor for certification of eligibility to apply for adjustment assistance. He can also take any combination of these two actions.

If the first route to obtaining assistance is followed, the Tariff Commission must issue its findings within sixty days. If these findings are affirmative, the firms or workers then apply to the Commerce or Labor Department for adjustment assistance. If firms or workers apply for industry-wide assistance, the Tariff Commission is given six months to conduct an investigation into whether the industry has been injured. When an affirmative finding is made in this case and the President authorizes firms and workers to request the Commerce and Labor Departments for certifications of eligibility to apply for adjustment assistance, these two departments are given sixty days to determine whether the individual firms or worker groups have suffered injury within the context of the Act. Between 1962 and the end of March 1972, only one case certified as eligible to apply for adjustment assistance was denied such assistance by the Commerce or Labor Department.

The criteria for judging whether an industry, firm or group of workers are eligible to apply for adjustment assistance are identical.

They are: (1) articles like or directly competitive with those produced domestically are being imported in increased quantities; (2) increased imports are occurring as a result in major part of concessions granted in trade agreements on an article; (3) the industry or firm is suffering or threatened with serious injury and workers are unemployed or threatened with unemployment; and (4) the increased imports must be the major factor causing or threatening to cause serious injury, unemployment or underemployment.

Clearly these are highly restrictive criteria, if literally interpreted. The Tariff Commission did in fact interpret these requirements in a very strict manner for several years after the passage of the Trade Expansion Act. Specifically, from October 1962 to November 1969 all 26 petitions submitted to the Commission by industries, firms and workers were denied. Between November 1969 and March 1972, however, out of the 108 workers adjustment assistance cases heard by the Tariff Commission, 16 were decided in favor of the workers while the commissioners were evenly divided on another 28. In case of a tied vote, the President makes the decision as to whether to accept or reject the petition. Invariably, he decides in favor of the petitioners. The number of cases involving firms heard by the Tariff Commission during this time period has been 23, of which 15 were either decided in favor of the firm or on which the vote was evenly divided. Ten cases for adjustment assistance on an industry-wide basis were also heard by the Commission. Of these, 7 were decided in favor of the industry or else were reported to the President with an evenly divided vote.

The main reason for the increase in affirmative decisions since late 1969 has been a more liberal interpretation of the second requirement listed above for eligibility to obtain adjustment. This requirement has been the one single condition that has been the basis of the largest number of negative findings. Those favoring a strict interpretation of the law argue that the major factor in any series of factors influencing imports must be the one that not only exerts the greatest influence, but one that dominates the overall results. Furthermore, the strict constructionists insist that there must be a strong causal connection between the concessions and the greater imports. For example, one of the commissioners holding this view decided in the negative in a case where, although a major concession was given in 1951, the cut since then amounted to only one percent, yet imports' increased significantly between 1965 and 1969. As he remarked, "To say that the increase in imports was caused in major part by duty reductions that took place at least 15 years ago taxes one's credulity too much."[18]

An increasing number of commissioners have abandoned this strict interpretation of the second criteria in favor of the "but for" criterion. Commissioners employing this criterion simply ask whether imports would be substantially at their present levels "but for" all the concessions granted since 1930. If imports would be much lower but for these concessions, then increased imports have resulted "in major part" from these concessions. Those adopting this position maintain that the phrase "in major part" must be interpreted in light of the whole statute and the intent of Congress.

Another one of the four criteria for obtaining adjustment assistance that has kept the number of successful petitions relatively small is the requirement that increased imports must be the major factor causing serious injury. The Commission considers all the factors that affect an industry's or firm's profitability and permits the industry or firm to apply for adjustment assistance only when increased imports are clearly the major factor causing serious injury. In many cases the commissioners have found such factors as greater competition from a domestic substitute, changes in private tastes, shifts in military demand and technical changes to be the major cause of injury to an industry rather than tariffs. On a firm level the Commission has cited such conditions as industrial disputes, poor business judgment and actions of domestic competitors as more significant than greater imports. In particular, if a firm claims serious injury from imports in an industry where other firms are successful, the Commission considers this as prima facie evidence that the injury was not caused in major part by greater imports.

Forms of Adjustment Assistance

Under the Trade Expansion Act, workers who qualify for assistance receive a Trade Adjustment Allowance equal to 65 percent of the individual's weekly wage, but it cannot exceed 65 percent of the average manufacturing wage. Those under 60 years of age who are not participating in a training program receive the allowance for fifty-two weeks, whereas workers involved in a training program receive up to twenty-six additional weeks of Trade Ad-

18. U.S. Tariff Commission, "Transmission Towers and Parts; Certain Workers of the Shiffler Plant, Pittsburgh, Pa., and of the Maywood Plant, Los Angeles, Calif., of the American Bridge Division, United States Steel Corporation," nos. TEA-W-9 and TEA-W-10, Tariff Commission publication no. 298 (Washington, D.C., November 1969).

justment allowances. Workers over 60 years of age may receive payments for thirteen more weeks beyond the basic fifty-two week period. In order to be eligible for this aid, an individual worker must have been employed in the adversely affected firm for at least half of the fifty-two weeks prior to layoff. Furthermore, he must have been gainfully employed for at least half of the three years prior to his unemployment.

Workers qualifying for assistance are also eligible to receive training, testing and counseling services available under any federal law. Relocation allowances are also available under the Trade Expansion Act. If there is a suitable job in another geographic area, the individual receives payment for the moving expenses of himself and his family plus a cash amount equal to two and a half times the average manufacturing wage.

Firms receive three types of aid under the Act, namely, technical assistance, financial assistance and tax relief. The technical assistance involves such aid as managerial advice, market analyses and development of new markets and products. Loans by the government or guarantees of private loans constitute the financial aid to qualifying firms. The loans may have a maturity of no more than twenty-five years and the interest charge cannot be lower than 4 percent. Tax assistance is in the form of a net operating loss carryback over a five-year period rather than the normal three years.

There is widespread agreement that the present adjustment assistance program is in need of significant changes. As Stanley Metzger, a former chairman of the Tariff Commission, has pointed out, the requirements that trade agreement concessions be the major cause of increased imports and that such increased imports be the major cause of injury to workers or firms greatly restricts the applicability of adjustment assistance under the Trade Expansion Act.[19] Apparently, concern about the costs of the program was the major factor causing the Congress and Administration to impose such severe requirements for obtaining adjustment assistance. Unlike increasing the tariff level on a product, one does not in practice have to be concerned about foreign retaliation when workers and firms are directly assisted with income supplements. Critics of the present law often point to the more liberal adjustment assistance

19. Stanley D. Metzger, "Adjustment Assistance," in *United States International Economic Policy in an Interdependent World,* Report to the President submitted by the Commission on International Trade and Investment (Washington, D.C.: U.S. Government Printing Office, 1971), pp. 319-42.

provisions under the United States-Canadian Auto Agreement of 1965 as providing for more sensible criteria for adjustment assistance. Under this Act a direct relationship between dislocation and the operation of the agreement is presumed to exist if output of automobiles declines and an adverse change in the flow of trade with Canada takes place.

As a result of the difficulties encountered by firms, workers and industries in satisfying the two criteria that there be a strong causal connection between larger imports and past trade concessions and that the increased imports be the major factor in causing injury, both the 1969 report to the President by the Special Representative on Future United States Foreign Policy (the Roth Report)[20] and the 1971 Report to the President by the Commission on International Trade and Investment Policy (the Williams Commission)[21] recommended substantial changes in these criteria. First, as far as assistance to workers is concerned, both reports recommend that the requirement linking increased imports to past tariff concession be eliminated. Secondly, they recommend that the Trade Expansion Act be amended to require only that increased imports are a substantial cause (rather than the major cause) of unemployment or underemployment. With regard to industry-wide aid, both reports also recommend elimination of the causal relationship between imports and past trade concessions. The Roth Report urges that increased imports should only be *the primary cause* rather than *the major cause* of increased unemployment. In other words, increased imports need not be the cause of injury that is greater than all other causes combined. On the other hand, the Williams Commission recommends retention of the requirement that increased imports be *the major cause* of injury where assistance on an industry-wide basis is sought. The Administration's trade bills of 1969 and 1970 eliminated the requirement that increased imports be caused by previous trade agreements and substituted the phrase that increased imports *contribute substantially* to injury rather than be the *major cause of injury*. Neither of these bills was passed in the Congress.

Two other frequently expressed objections to the present law are that the level of benefits to workers is too low and that the length of time between initiating a petition for assistance and actually receiv-

---

20. William M. Roth, *Future United States Foreign Trade Policy,* Report to the President submitted by the Special Representative for Trade Negotiations (Washington, D.C.: U.S. Government Printing Office, January 1969).
21. *United States International Economic Policy in an Interdependent World,* ut sup.

ing the assistance is too long. When the Trade Expansion Act was passed in 1962, the eligibility requirements were made more severe than those for state unemployment compensation benefits because payments under the Act were higher than those under state unemployment insurance law. However, since the Act was passed, many states have increased their unemployment insurance benefits, and in a few states these benefits can now exceed the maximum readjustment allowances. In part because of this, the Ways and Means Committee recommended in the 1970 trade bill that the level of benefits be raised from 65 percent of the worker's average weekly wage to 75 percent of this figure. The trade bill proposed in 1970 also reduced the time between filing a petition and the delivery of benefits. Under the 1970 bill, the period would have taken between 95 and 135 days as compared with three to eight months under the Trade Expansion Act. An important aspect of the proposed bill that reduced the time involved in obtaining benefits was that the Tariff Commission role would be limited to fact-finding and the Executive Branch would receive petitions and make the determinations whether firms and workers satisfied the stipulations of the new test for adjustment assistance.

V. THE NEED FOR FURTHER STUDIES
OF ADJUSTMENT ASSISTANCE PROGRAMS

While all the various proposed changes would undoubtedly help firms and workers to adjust better to the difficulties associated with sharp increases in imports, a basic problem associated with the program is its emphasis on increased imports in determining the need for adjustment assistance. A sharp rise in imports is only one of several factors that can lead to depressed conditions in a firm or industry. Even within the trade field, there seems to be no good reason for discriminating against firms producing for export as compared with import-competing firms. Such factors as greater competition from exporters located in other countries and changes in taste in export markets can cause workers in domestic export firms to lose their jobs just as increased imports can cause workers in domestic import-competing firms to lose their jobs. Furthermore, why are not workers and firms who lose their jobs as a result of such factors as technological changes, shifts in demands by private and public spenders and greater competition from firms located in other parts of the country rather than abroad just as deserving as firms in-

168 / *Robert Baldwin and John H. Mutti*

jured because of greater imports? The secondary repercussions on supporting firms and workers in communities within which the firms directly affected by such changes are located may also be severe, even if the government is pursuing a full employment policy with reasonable success. Ideally, we need more extensive adjustment assistance programs that cover all the causes of substantial dislocations for workers and firms. Yet before we proceed to a general program of adjustment assistance we need much better information as to the most effective way of reducing the time when a worker is laid off and when he obtains a new position and also the costs associated with various programs. Studies of retraining programs indicate that the social rate of return is at least 10 percent.[22] However, there has been little work done in comparing this method of handling the displacement problem with such other alternatives as migration allowances or a lump-sum severance payment. One recent study does show, however, that workers who received job training allowances and moved did not receive higher earnings than those who moved without first completing a training program.[23] Both groups, however, increased their earnings significantly compared to the nonmovers. On the other hand, in the group that did not migrate to another employment area, those who completed a training program fared better than those who did not. Thus, training served as partial compensation for the lack of labor mobility.[24] In both the mover and nonmover groups those who took training courses were able to obtain employment somewhat sooner than those who did not complete a training program.[25] These results as well as those of other case studies are interesting, but what we need are more comprehensive studies in which the data can be analyzed with more elaborate statistical techniques.

Suppose we make an arbitrary assumption that all of the displaced workers in the industries analyzed in Section II of this paper must be retrained in order to obtain new jobs. Einar Hardin and Michael E. Borus found in their Michigan study that the total government outlay per trainee was $1,119.[26] Applying this figure to

22. Einar Hardin, "Benefit-Cost Analyses of Occupational Training Programs: A Comparison of Recent Studies," in *Cost-Benefit Analysis of Manpower Policies,* ed. Gerald G. Somers and W.D. Woods (Kingston, Ont.: Queen's University Industrial Relations Centre, 1969), p. 114.
    23. Gerald G. Somers, *Labor Mobility: An Evaluation of Pilot Projects in Michigan and Wisconsin* (Madison: University of Wisconsin Press, 1972), p. 48.
    24. Ibid., p. 50.
    25. This relationship also holds in the study by Schultz and Weber, op. cit., pp. 160-61.
    26. Hardin and Borus, op. cit.

these five industries gives a cost of approximately $240 million. Since these industries account for roughly 25 percent of the manufacturing labor force, a comprehensive retraining program might require an expenditure of $1 billion. This estimate has no pretense to accuracy, but does provide an upper bound as to what might be required.

Even if the benefit-cost ratio for such a program was unfavorable when compared with other uses of these funds, this does not mean that a retraining program of this magnitude should not be carried out. Requiring the economic loss of the displaced workers to be shared by those who are employed is a perfectly acceptable socio-economic goal. Moreover, perhaps this form of compensation to those who lose by free trade policies is more acceptable politically than outright cash grants. Just how much efficiency is to be sacrificed in the transfer process as well as determination of the actual amount to be transferred are political decisions subject to considerable debate.

TABLE 6-2

CALCULATION OF BENEFITS FROM TARIFF REMOVAL, SINGLE YEAR

$$\Delta W = \frac{1}{2}\left[\left(\frac{t}{t+1}\right)^2 \cdot e_m \cdot P_o M_o\right]$$

Good	Price Import Elasticity of Demand		Tariff Factor	Domestic Value of Imports (Mns. US$)	Calculated Benefit (Mns. US$)
(16) Textiles............	(a)	.35	0.0414	786.643	5.6638
	(b)	2.00			32.5670
	(c)	6.00			97.7010
(27) Chemicals...........	(a)	1.40	0.0069	908.970	4.3630
	(b)	2.00			6.2718
	(c)	5.00			15.6797
(37) Iron and Steel........	(a)	2.00	0.0030	2,303.176	6.9095
	(b)	5.00			17.2738
	(c)	10.00			34.5476
(56) Radio, T.V. and Communications ...	(a)	2.00	0.0068	1,506.064	10.2412
	(b)	6.00			30.7236
	(c)	7.00			35.6393
(59) Motor Vehicles........	(a)	2.00	0.0005	4,782.024	2.3910
	(b)	6.00			7.1730
	(c)	7.00			8.7869

TABLE 6-3

Good			5%	10%	15%
(16) Textiles	(a)	5 years	25.057	22.285	19.923
		10 years	44.571	35.802	29.333
	(b)	5 years	144.076	128.141	114.558
		10 years	256.283	205.862	168.668
	(c)	5 years	432.229	384.424	343.673
		10 years	768.848	617.588	506.003
(27) Chemicals	(a)	5 years	19.302	17.167	15.347
		10 years	34.334	27.579	22.596
	(b)	5 years	27.746	24.678	22.062
		10 Years	49.355	39.645	32.482
	(c)	5 years	69.367	61.695	55.155
		10 years	123.390	99.115	81.208
(37) Iron & Steel	(a)	5 years	30.577	27.187	24.305
		10 years	54.374	43.676	35.785
	(b)	5 years	76.419	67.967	60.762
		10 years	135.934	109.191	89.463
	(c)	5 years	152.838	135.934	121.525
		10 years	271.869	218.382	178.925
(56) Radio, T.V. and Communications	(a)	5 years	45.307	40.296	36.024
		10 years	80.992	64.736	53.040
	(b)	5 years	135.921	120.888	108.073
		10 years	241.776	194.210	159.121
	(c)	5 years	157.668	140.230	125.365
		10 years	280.460	225.283	184.579
(59) Motor Vehicles	(a)	5 years	10.578	9.408	8.411
		10 years	18.816	15.114	12.383
	(b)	5 years	31.733	28.224	25.232
		10 years	56.447	45.342	37.150
	(c)	5 years	38.873	34.574	30.909
		10 years	69.148	55.544	45.508

27. Benefit streams were discounted over continuous, as contrasted to discrete time.

TABLE 6-4
NUMBER OF WORKERS DISPLACED DIRECTLY FROM TARIFF REMOVAL

$$\Delta L = e_s \left(P_o Q_o \right) \left(\frac{t}{t+1} \right) \cdot a_{oi}^{28}$$

Good	Elasticity of Supply[29]		Value of Domestic Production (Mns. US$)	$\frac{t}{t+1}$	$P_o \Delta Q$ (Mns. US$)	Direct Labor Coefficient/ Mns. $ Output	Displaced Labor
(16) Textiles............	(d)	1.00	12,604.7	.2084	2,626.8	55.943	146,952
	(e)	.38			998.2		54,984
	(f)	.25			656.7		36,738
(27) Chemicals	(d)	1.00	19,864.0	.0836	1,660.6	33.287	55,277
	(e)	.20			332.1		11,055
	(f)	.09			149.5		4,975
(37) Iron & Steel.......	(d)	1.00	30,816.0	.0627	1,932.2	43.680	84,397
	(e)	.75			1,449.2		63,298
	(f)	.25			483.0		21,099
(56) Radio, T.V. and Communications ...	(d)	1.00	15,575.3	.0825	1,285.0	66.127	84,971
	(e)	.68			873.8		57,780
	(f)	.25			321.3		21,243
(59) Motor Vehicles.......	(d)	1.00	48,514.7	.0232	1,125.5	25.736	28,967
	(e)	.59			664.0		17,091
	(f)	.25			281.4		7,242

28. The direct labor coefficient is represented by a_{oi}.

29. These elasticities of supply are calculated from the formula in the text, $e_m = \left(1 + \frac{\partial s}{\partial m}\right) e_d + \frac{\partial s}{\partial m} \cdot e_s$, where we have followed Salant and Vaccara in assuming that $e_d = 0$ so that the value of increased imports is equal to the value of reduced domestic production. See Walter S. Salant and Beatrice N. Vaccara, Import Liberalization and Employment: The Effects of Unilateral Reductions in United States Import Barriers (Washington, D.C.: The Brookings Institution, 1961). That this condition does not hold precisely in our numerical examples is due to rounding error in reporting elasticities of supply to two decimal places only. Regarding the assumption $e_d = 0$, we recognize that estimate costs tend to be overrated as total demand is more price elastic.

TABLE 6-5

ECONOMIC LOSS FROM TARIFF REMOVAL

Good		Average Weekly Wage	Average Duration Unemployment, Weeks	Discounted Economic Loss from Unemployment[30] (Ths. US$)	Adjustment Factors, Education & Age[31] (Ths. US$)	Adjusted Economic Loss from Unemployment (Ths. US$)
(16) Textiles	(d)	97.76	9.0	128,198.3	27,423.0	155,600
	(e)	97.76	9.0	48,715.4	10,420.7	59,100
	(f)	97.76	9.0	32,049.6	6,855.7	38,900
	(d')	97.76	24.0	336,949.9	27,423.0	364,400
	(e')	97.76	24.0	128,041.0	10,420.7	138,500
	(f')	97.76	24.0	84,237.5	6,855.7	91,100
(27) Chemicals	(d)	153.50	9.0	75,718.3	−5,922.3	68,300
	(e)	153.50	9.0	15,143.7	−1,480.6	13,700
	(f)	153.50	9.0	6,814.6	−533.0	6,200
	(d')	153.50	24.0	199,014.8	−5,922.3	191,600
	(e')	153.50	24.0	39,802.8	−1,480.6	38,300
	(f')	153.50	24.0	17,911.3	−533.0	17,300
(37) Iron & Steel	(d)	159.18	12.2	161,980.0	11,968.6	174,000
	(e)	159.18	12.2	121,485.0	8,976.5	130,500
	(f)	159.18	12.2	40,495.0	2,992.1	43,500
	(d')	159.18	24.0	315,096.1	11,968.6	327,100
	(e')	159.18	24.0	236,322.1	8,976.5	245,300
	(f')	159.18	24.0	78,774.0	2,992.1	81,800
(56) Radio, T.V. & Communications	(d)	130.87	12.2	134,077.4	−9,978.0	124,100
	(e)	130.87	12.2	91,172.6	−6,785.0	84,400
	(f)	130.87	12.2	33,519.4	−2,494.5	31,000
	(d')	130.87	24.0	260,817.9	−9,978.0	250,800
	(e')	130.87	24.0	177,356.2	−6,785.0	170,500
	(f')	130.87	24.0	65,204.5	−2,494.5	62,700
(59) Motor Vehicles	(d)	163.62	12.2	57,145.9	1,376.3	58,500
	(e)	163.62	12.2	33,716.1	812.0	34,500
	(f)	163.62	12.2	14,286.5	344.1	14,600
	(d')	163.62	24.0	111,164.6	1,376.3	112,500
	(e')	163.62	24.0	65,587.1	812.0	66,400
	(f')	163.62	24.0	27,791.1	344.1	28,100

30. This cost estimate is discounted continuously at an annual rate of 10 percent.

31. The calculation of education and age adjustments was made by applying Borus and Hardin's coefficients to the relevant industry data and the values for total manufacturing.

$$ADJ = \$ \left[(E_i - \overline{E})\, 109.40 + 62.5 A_i - A_i^2 - 62.5 \overline{A} + \overline{A}^2 \right]$$

where E_i is the average number of years of education in the ith industry,

$\overline{E}$ is the average number of years of education in manufacturing,

A_i is the average age in the ith industry, and

$\overline{A}$ is the average age in manufacturing.

The data by industry for 1960 are:

	E_i	$\overline{E}$	A_i	$\overline{A}$
16 Textiles	8.5	10.29	41.9	40.35
27 Chemicals	11.3		39.9	
37 Iron and Steel	9.4		43.0	
56 Television, Radio and Communications	11.1		37.7	
59 Motor Vehicles	10.0		41.8	

APPENDIX

A reader may be dissatisfied with the number of points covered in our general discussion for which no allowance is made in our calculations of costs and benefits of tariff removal. Such a procedure was followed because of the greater uncertainty involved in quantifying factors such as multipliers, terms of trade losses, growth, changing elasticities over time and so on, relative to the effects which economists have more carefully studied and estimated. It may be wishful thinking to claim that all such effects fall in the category of second-order smalls or that they all net out, and therefore we present in this appendix a rough indication of how our calculations are modified by relaxing the two assumptions of no growth and infinite foreign elasticity of supply. Again, neither the original nor modified estimates of gains or losses form a basis for policy decisions, but rather illustrate an approach to the problem.

The first modification we make is to allow for growth. If we assume the average yearly growth rate for the United States over the relevant time horizon is 2 percent, and that the income elasticity of demand for all goods is 2.5 percent, then we can conveniently use the discounted stream of benefits reported in Table 6-3 for a 5 percent discount rate in contrast to 10 percent. To the extent that the United States growth rate is higher and that income elasticities are higher, we still will underestimate the benefit stream, but to avoid a whole new set of computations based on "guesstimated" numbers, we shall use those already available.

In relaxing the small country assumption, we will not take as broad an outlook as Giorgio Basevi,[32] instead, we ignore balance of payments problems caused by tariff removal, since we are working on a disaggregated level, and therefore we do not allow for an exchange rate depreciation. Given an upward sloping foreign supply curve, tariff removal will alter costs and benefits in two ways: (1) the increase in imports, and consequent reduction in domestic output, will be smaller; and (2) the United States will suffer a terms of trade loss on its initial imports. We can relate the change in

FIGURE 6-2

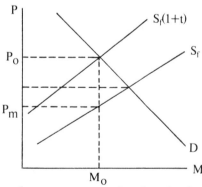

---

32. Basevi, op. cit.

imports to our previous estimate as follows:

$$dM = \gamma d[P_m(1 + t)] = \delta dP_m$$

where we have defined units such that $P_o = 1 = r$, and γ is the slope of the demand curve, and δ is the slope of the supply curve.

$$d[P_m(1 + t)] = (1 + t)dP_m + P_m dt = (1 + t)dP_m - P_m t$$

when tariffs are removed completely.

$$dP_m = \frac{\gamma t P_m}{\gamma(1 + t) - \delta} = \frac{e_m \cdot t \cdot P_m}{e_m(1 + t) + e_f} = \frac{e_m}{e_m(1 + t) + e_f} \cdot \frac{t}{1 + t}$$

$$\frac{dP}{P_o} = \frac{t}{1 + t} - \frac{dP_m}{P_o} = \frac{t}{1 + t} - \frac{e_m}{e_m(1 + t) + e_f}\left(\frac{t}{1 + t}\right) =$$

$$\left(\frac{t}{1 + t}\right)\left(1 - \frac{e_m}{e_m(1 + t) + e_f}\right)$$

Now our formula for the gain in consumer surplus is:

$$\Delta B = \tfrac{1}{2}e_m\left(\frac{t}{t + 1}\right)^2 \cdot P_o M_o$$

which now becomes:

$$\Delta B = \tfrac{1}{2}e_m\left[\left(\frac{t}{t + 1}\right)\left(1 - \frac{e_m}{e_m(1 + t) + e_f}\right)\right]^2 \cdot P_o M_o$$

In other words our benefits will be less by a factor of

$$\left(1 - \frac{e_m}{e_m(1 + t) + e_f}\right)^2.$$

With respect to the loss in home output, our formula

$$\Delta L = e_s\left(\frac{t}{1 + t}\right)D_o \cdot A_{io}$$

now becomes

$$\Delta L = e_s\left[\frac{t}{1 + t}\left(1 - \frac{e_m}{e_m(1 + t) + e_f}\right)\right]D_o \cdot A_{io}$$

and we see that our costs have been overstated by a factor of

$$\left(1 - \frac{e_m}{e_m(1 + t) + e_f}\right).$$

Alternatively, we could say that if

$$\frac{Benefits}{Costs} > \frac{1}{1 - \dfrac{e_m}{e_m(1+t)+e_f}}$$

then the categorization of our results from the original section will not be altered.

An additional overstatement of the gains comes from ignoring the terms of trade loss the United States suffers. We calculate this loss as a percentage of the initial value of imports and then add this figure to our above-adjusted costs.

$$\Delta \text{tot} = \frac{dP_m \cdot M_o}{P_o \cdot M_o} = \frac{dP_m}{P_o} = \frac{e_m}{e_m(1+t)+e_f}\left(\frac{t}{t+1}\right)$$

Two problems arise in using this methodology.[33] One is that we have few estimates of disaggregated elasticities of supply. Stephen P. Magee[34] reports estimates for total exports and manufactured goods from the United States which William H. Branson[35] apparently applies to United States imports. We shall take $e_f = 10.0$ for our calculations with the reservation that for individual goods the elasticities may be higher or lower. More important is the question of how productivity changes over time will affect these estimated elasticities, to which we have no clear answers.

Another difficulty with the above approach is that we have regarded the terms of trade loss as a one-period effect, when in reality it is a flow which should be discounted over time. Yet, such a calculation without regard to how supply elasticities change over time does not give conclusive answers. If the terms of trade effect is calculated as above, but then discounted as a flow, tariff removal would not be warranted except in the case of textiles, and even in that case we might expect to find an optimal tariff level between the current level and zero. Alternatively we present the following table of calculations where the terms of trade loss is considered only for a single period.

Even under these very restrictive assumptions regarding United States market power, the case for tariff removal is considerably

---

33. Another less critical issue is the index number problem in measuring welfare or national income.

34. Stephen P. Magee, "A Theoretical and Empirical Examination of Supply and Demand Relationships in U.S. International Trade," mimeographed (a study for the Council of Economic Advisers, Washington, D.C., January 1971).

35. William H. Branson, *The Trade Effects of the 1971 Currency Realignments,* Brookings Papers on Economic Activity, no. 1 (Washington, D.C.: The Brookings Institution, 1972), pp. 15-69.

altered. The arguments offered by organized labor remain basically unchanged since the terms of trade loss is felt by consumers and not variable factors of production, but the government who is looking after the welfare of society would need to investigate more thoroughly these factors and consider the likelihood of retaliation if an across-the-board optimal tariff policy were pursued.

TABLE 6-6

SHORT-TERM BENEFITS AND COSTS OF TARIFF REMOVAL

	Benefits	Costs: Displacement and Terms of Trade Effects	
		11 wks. unemployment	24 wks. unemployment
(16) Textiles	332.6	107.3	175.9
(27) Chemicals	34.5	23.9	44.4
(37) Iron and Steel	72.4	159.6	238.6
(56) T.V., Radio and Communications	102.0	86.8	125.0
(59) Motor Vehicles	22.3	59.6	72.9

Comment

Deane Hinton

Robert Baldwin has presented an interesting expert paper which tends to confirm, with an analysis including mathematics, the personal prejudices of this operating political economist. John Mutti has indicated the limitations on the analysis, so we have it from both sides.

We do not need a discussion of optimum tariffs, income redistribution and so on to understand why free trade is not practiced by all concerned—it is politics. And when we come to the adjustment assistance mechanism, for which I think there is a convincing case—a case Robert Baldwin has strengthened in some respects, but not in others—it is not hard to understand why labor union leaders are against it. However good adjustment assistance may be for labor union members, of course, from a member's point of view, keeping the job he has got is much easier than being retrained and moved or pensioned off. This really becomes binding when we look at it from the level of the union leadership. If union members move, the leader does not have a union, he does not have a dues check-off, he does not have anything; this is one reason why I presume Nat Goldfinger talked about adjustment assistance as a burial program or some such phrase. The same thing goes when we get to the core of this problem, since we are talking about it in a development aspect. Those industries which are developed or efficient in developing countries are precisely those industries, according to the conventional wisdom, which in developed countries have large labor inputs, relatively low wages and what in the political sense is most important, wide geographic dispersion. In the United States, some industries have vanished rather rapidly, if not painlessly, like black-and-white television tubes. But when one comes to textiles and shoes, these industries are represented in hundreds of congressional districts and there are hundreds of congressmen that are subject to the pressures from these people and these interests.

I am not going to discuss the economic analysis—I think Bela Balassa will have something to say, and he will say it far better than I. Let me say that in moving ahead with the process of restructuring the world monetary and trade system, which the President of the United States believes he started on August 15, 1972, we sincerely hope to go on toward an open economic system. This was evident in his remarks to the IMF and the World Bank meeting, but there are some cautions in that speech, and it depends on which paragraph one reads, since Mr. Nixon is a political realist. He also talked about not condoning the loss of jobs in circumstances which involve unfair trade practices.

If the United States gets, as it may, a legislative proposal including a number of reforms in adjustment assistance moving before the Congress next year, it is dubious what will happen to it in a Congress which basically is highly protectionist. There has been a great deal of work done in the government toward this, and we are pretty far along.

Robert Baldwin has touched on some of the issues we faced, and I would like to add just a little about those and suggest a few others. There is a philosophical problem and his use of the word *compensation* bothers me. Is this a program that compensates labor that is displaced and capital that has been displaced, or is this a program to facilitate the adjustment of the economy? I think there is a difference here, and I think one gets different operational results depending on how one thinks about the problem. He asks elsewhere, and I quite agree, why is this done for plants and workers impacted by trade, and why is it not done on the export side? I would add, why not in some cases of plants shut down because the investment goes overseas? It may be a variant but I would be explicit: one should cover workers in such plants. But to be interested in the adjustment process, one must also be concerned about adjustment in the cities, in Appalachia, in defense industries. In fact, many adjustment programs in the United States do just this. However, we do not have an overall adjustment assistance concept, a manpower policy or really a comprehensive approach on either the labor or the capital side, but I think most of us are—certainly I am—convinced that is the direction we must take. The Union of Automobile Workers (UAW) is the one labor union in favor of adjustment assistance. UAW has a very advanced and ambitious concept going back to what was done on the railroads, where the featherbedding problem and the redundancy problem were attacked with some explicit adjustment assistance programs. UAW is proposing a form of adjustment assistance, but when that form of adjustment assistance is put in the political context of the United States in the 1970s, the budgetary amounts implied are far, far greater than even the top estimates. With a runaway budget and a political battle over spending ceilings, and whether or not taxes are to be raised, it is hard to see how the outcome will be for a very heavily funded across-the-board adjustment assistance program, even though the discussion continues. That leaves the alternatives of concentrating on how to improve and perhaps broaden somewhat the concepts on the Act. Everybody agrees that the 1962 Act is a disaster for the reasons Robert Baldwin has outlined, and that much can be done on redefining a criterion and the access mechanism. When we come to do this there is a major problem that bothers me intellectually and that is not covered by Robert Baldwin or in the comment, and that is the notion that since we are a capitalistic society, there are property rights involved in this process as well as people. We are all agreed that people are more important. People can move around; one has to take care of people, and I am sure that a new program will concentrate on facilitating the adjustment of human beings, as it should. What we also need is some serious work on the adjustment issues on the capital side. How does one use assets that are no longer being economically employed? How does one transfer those physical assets? We have reached some conclusions, I think, but to go the compensation route, with a firm that is failing, a program such as the 1962 Act, providing financial assistance to keep it floating, may be compensation, but it certainly does not promote adjustment—it does precisely the reverse. I believe some policy thinking and some research in the academic world on what would be a meaningful adjustment program on the capital side is needed. Strangely enough, we have tended to think that it is easier at the industry level than at the firm level, and having said that we are not quite sure what in the world we do next. But such thoughts open up all kinds of perspectives that go into the area of antitrust policy, that go into the area of research and development across the industry, that go to such interesting ideas as, how to make the bankruptcy process work better. These are nice questions and we have no answers.

Comment

Bela Balassa

We are indebted to Robert Baldwin and John Mutti for having tackled the problem of estimating the cost of dislocation resulting from tariff reductions, setting this against the benefits obtainable in the form of improved resource allocation. Theirs is indeed a pioneering effort of an important problem and should be followed by further research in the United States and elsewhere. It is hoped that my comments will prove to be useful for future work by the authors and by others who have an interest in the problem.

I will begin with some general considerations concerning the effects of unilateral as opposed to multilateral tariff reductions, the implications of eliminating tariffs on trade with developed and with developing countries and the time-frame of the analysis in the Baldwin-Mutti paper. I will further indicate the various biases in the authors' calculations of the gains and losses associated with tariff removal in selected industries.

In considering the case of trade liberalization undertaken unilaterally by the United States, Messrs. Baldwin and Mutti disregard the exchange rate changes that would be necessary to re-equilibrate the balance of payments following increases in imports brought about by tariff reductions. They submit that "this would seem to be a reasonable position for short-run analysis in a system of fixed exchange rates" [p.153, fn. 5]. Elsewhere they state, "we ignore balance of payments problems ... since we are working on a disaggregated level ..." [p.174]. Neither of these arguments can justify, however, the omission of balance of payments effects in the calculations.

From the point of view of the balance of payments impact of trade liberalization, it is irrelevant whether estimates are made on an aggregated or a disaggregated level. Nor can one argue that balance of payments effects may be neglected because they are small since in this event the gains from increased imports would also be small.[36] The balance of payments costs of trade liberalization should be set against the gains from increased imports, and the ratio of the two is not likely to be affected by the extent of trade liberalization.

It should further be emphasized that balance of payments costs will arise *pari passu* with increases in imports, irrespective of the length of the horizon.[37] Unless we assume that the United States is able and willing to continue financing its balance of payments deficit by increasing dollar liabilities to foreign holders, unilateral trade liberalization will lead to losses in reserves that entail a cost to the national economy. As reserves have alternative uses, they will have an opportunity cost even if reserve holdings exceed desired levels. And if reserve holdings were at desired levels, reserve losses would involve a cost in the form of the effects of deflationary measures necessary to replenish these holdings.

To avoid these consequences, governments may impose other types of restrictions, devalue the currency, or engage in multilateral tariff negotiations. There is no presumption that the welfare losses involved in imposing restrictions on other items of the balance of payments would be smaller than the gain from increased imports following unilateral tariff reductions. In turn, unless the prices of imports and exports expressed in foreign currency remain unchanged, devaluation will result in a term of trade loss.

It can hardly be assumed however that tariff reduction *cum* devaluation would leave the price of United States exports and imports unchanged. In fact, according to calculations made by Giorgio Basevi, in the United States the terms of trade loss due to the

---

36. At any rate, the industries under consideration account for 25 percent of the United States's manufacturing employment.
37. The question of the choice of the time horizon is taken up below.

elimination of all tariffs combined with the devaluation necessary to maintain balance of payments equilibrium would more than offset the welfare gain associated with increases in imports.[38] At the same time, unilateral as well as multilateral tariff reductions will have different implications depending on whether trade with developing or with developed countries is affected.

While unilateral reductions in tariffs on imports from the developing countries would lead to a deterioration of the United States balance of payments position, this may not occur if all developed countries take parallel action as in the case of generalized preference schemes. Since developing countries tend to spend the increments in their foreign exchange earnings rather than adding to their reserves, the outcome will depend on the so-called reflection ratios which indicate the pattern of the developing countries' spending increments in their foreign exchange receipts.[39]

Should, however, the elimination of tariffs be undertaken on an m.f.n. basis as is implicit in the calculations made by Robert Baldwin and John Mutti, imports from developed countries would also rise so that, barring a devaluation, offsetting increases in exports would require multilateral trade liberalization.[40] Multilateral trade liberalization is indeed the rule rather than the exception among the developed countries. In turn, the effects of multilateral tariff reductions on trade flows will depend on export supply and import demand elasticities in the trading countries.[41]

But, the conventional measurement of welfare gains and losses applied by Robert Baldwin and John Mutti will not be appropriate with regard to the expansion of trade in manufactured goods among the developed countries since this in large part involves intraindustry rather than interindustry specialization. Whereas in the event of interindustry specialization resources move from import-competing to export industries with corresponding changes in output and in employment, intraindustry specialization involves increased ex-

---

38. Basevi, op. cit.

39. Cf., Whitney Hicks, "Estimating the Foreign Exchange Costs of Untied Aid," *Southern Economic Journal* XXX, no. 2 (October 1963): 168-74.

40. In this connection, note that, in the industries considered by Robert Baldwin and John Mutti, 92 percent of imports come from the developed countries.

41. I have elsewhere suggested that, given the lower share of exports and imports in its national income, elasticities of import demand and export supply tend to be higher in the United States than in the other industrial countries. Taking account also of intercountry differences in tariff levels, I have reached the conclusion that multinational trade liberalization would not affect the balance of trade of the United States. See Bela Balassa, *Trade Liberalization among Industrial Countries: Objectives and Alternatives* (New York: McGraw Hill, 1967), Appendix tables 4.3 and 4.5.

change of consumer goods as well as increased specialization in narrower ranges of machinery and intermediate products. The exchange of consumer goods is compatible with unchanged output levels in the trading countries; in turn, in specializing in narrower ranges of commodities, firms may alter their product composition without necessarily affecting production volume and employment.

In a paper published a few years ago I showed that in the European Common Market much of the expansion of trade took the form of intraindustry specialization, so that the participating countries largely escaped the cost of adjustment in the form of losses in output and employment in particular industries.[42] Updated calculations for the period ending in 1970 show a continuation of this trend and, most importantly for the present discussion, similar results are shown for the United States.[43] Thus, multilateral reductions in tariffs among the developed countries have apparently led to increased intraindustry specialization that involves lower adjustment costs while its benefits are found in higher consumer welfare and in the application of large-scale production methods.

I come now to the time-frame of the analysis. In the statement cited above, Messrs Baldwin and Mutti consider this to be of a short-term character. They suggest that "given the changes in tastes and technology which occur over time, discounting [of benefits from increased imports] over an infinite time period seems unwarranted. We arbitrarily chose ten years as the proper duration of time, and also present calculations for a five-year time horizon which might be realistic for politicians who face frequent elections" [p. 157]. Changes in tastes and technology may however increase as well as reduce gains over time and consumers are likely to consider price reductions to be permanent rather than temporary. Correspondingly, the limitation of the time horizon to five or ten years does not appear to be warranted.

By limiting the time horizon of the estimates, Robert Baldwin and John Mutti tend to underestimate the potential benefits. A further source of underestimation is the use of short-term import demand and domestic supply elasticities; the domestic supply elasticities implicit in the import demand elasticities utilized in estimating the gain from increased imports are the same as those

---

42. Bela Balassa, "Tariff Reductions and Trade in Manufactures among the Industrialized Countries," *American Economic Review* LVI, no. 3 (June 1966): 466-73.
43. Bela Balassa, "More Evidence on Intraindustry Specialization," mimeographed.

employed in estimating the adjustment cost.[44] The benefit-cost ratio of tariff reductions is understated as a result, since short-term supply elasticities are appropriate for estimating the cost of adjustment but not the benefits of increased imports. This leads us to the question of the direction and the extent of the biases in the authors' estimates of gains and losses from tariff reductions. They will be taken up in turn.

The underestimation of the gains from increased imports calculated by using short-term import demand elasticities is apparent from the results of Hendrik S. Houthakker and Stephen Magee. Using quarterly data for the period 1947-66, these authors obtained long-term elasticities of United States import demand that were four times as high as the short-term elasticities.[45] These differences may be explained by demand as well as by supply factors. On the demand side, lags in information, reticence to change suppliers in the event of temporary price changes, as well as the need for repair facilities, lengthen the process of adjustment. On the supply side, competing domestic firms will continue production in the short run as long as their variable costs are covered while in the long run the price should also compensate for the fixed costs.

The estimated benefits of increased imports due to trade liberalization will rise further if we take a longer time horizon. Calculating with an interest rate of 10 percent, the discounted value of benefits in the industries in question will rise by 39 percent if we consider benefits obtainable in twenty rather than in ten years and by 63 percent if we take an infinite time horizon.

The use of short-term import demand elasticities as well as the limitation of the time horizon have thus entailed an underestimation of the benefits from increased imports in the Baldwin-Mutti study. In turn, unilateral tariff reductions will involve a cost to the national economy that has been disregarded by the authors, whereas the effects of multilateral tariff reductions will depend on the relevant domestic and foreign elasticities and the identity of the trading partners.

The identity of trading partners also affects the cost of adjust-

---

44. It is a different question that the assumption of perfect substitutability under which the relationship between import demand and domestic supply elasticities has been established [see section, The Costs of Tariff Removal, above] does not generally hold for manufactured goods. Rather, product differentiation as well as transportation costs will reduce the import demand elasticity corresponding to a given substitution elasticity. In turn, the assumption of zero demand elasticity represents a bias in the opposite direction. On these points, See Balassa, "Tariff Protection in Industrialized Countries," loc. cit.

45. Houthakker and Magee, op. cit.

ment. As noted above, multilateral tariff reductions on trade among developed countries may involve largely intraindustry specialization whose adjustment costs are small since large-scale resource shifts are avoided. Should we take instead the case of interindustry specialization, and thus meet Robert Baldwin and John Mutti on their own ground, various criticisms need to be made concerning their method of estimation.

First of all, the losses suffered by the industries that are directly affected by reductions in tariffs will be understated if we consider unemployed labor only. Rather, we should estimate the loss in value added that is occasioned by the contraction of domestic production associated with increases in import following tariff reductions.

Second, Robert Baldwin and John Mutti appear to underestimate the duration of unemployment in adversely affected industries. They start out with the average United States unemployment of eleven weeks and arbitrarily take twenty-four weeks as an alternative assumption. However, the fact that adjustment assistance is provided by law for fifty-two weeks and may even be extended to seventy-eight weeks indicates that the lawmakers expected unemployment in industries adversely affected by imports to be considerably longer than the national average. This is explained by the need to retrain and in some instances relocate labor.

Against these sources of underestimation of the cost of dislocation in adversely affected industries, one should set the gains due to the expansion of export industries that would follow under multilateral tariff reductions as well as in the event of unilateral reductions in tariffs accompanied by a devaluation. If labor does not move from import-competing to export industries, the latter will absorb the unemployed. Thus, assuming that the labor requirements of imports and exports are more-or-less the same,[46] the increase in unemployment in one industry would be matched by a reduction of unemployment elsewhere. Now, if we followed the authors in assuming that unemployment is the only cost of dislocation in a given industry, the cost of adjustment on the national economy level would be nil.

There are other factors, however, that Robert Baldwin and John Mutti leave out of account. These include the cost of moving defined in a general sense as well as income distributional considerations. As to the cost of moving, one can relatively easily quantify the expenses of relocation, retraining, and the loss of investment in

---

46. For such a result, see Salant and Vaccara, op. cit.

human capital. By contrast, the psychological cost of leaving an established location and job are more difficult to establish. Problems of quantification also arise with regard to the changes in regional and interindustry income distribution that follow the liberalization of trade.

These considerations indicate the sensitivity of the estimates of gains and losses from trade liberalization to the assumptions made. Further research would be necessary to reduce the uncertainties associated with the estimates; such research should preferably be oriented towards in-depth studies of particular industries. The paper by Robert Baldwin and John Mutti represents a step in this direction and, whatever the inadequacies of the method applied, they deserve our gratitude for a pioneering effort in an area that has considerable importance for policy-making.

7

The European Economic Community Approach to Adjustment

Ferdnand Braun

The European Economic Community's chief accomplishment has been the establishment of a customs union abolishing tariffs and quantitative restrictions between member states during a transitional period that lasted from 1958 to the middle of 1968. Tariff policy is a Community responsibility, and international negotiations touching on tariff matters can only be conducted by the Community institutions, with the Commission negotiating, and the Council of Ministers giving the necessary negotiating mandates and approving results. A common agricultural policy too well known to need description has also been defined. It should be stressed again that trade policy concerning agricultural products is an EEC matter and can only be decided by Community institutions.

Commercial defense measures are another matter of trade policy for which the EEC has taken over responsibility from its member states inasfar as such measures concern the application of tariffs. This means that for all practical purposes the EEC is to act as a single entity on matters of antidumping and applications for safeguarding measures under Article XIX of GATT. It is true, however, that until now, in exceptional cases of special urgency, member states could apply national safeguard measures by imposing quantitative restrictions.

The various preferential trading agreements that the EEC has concluded with a large number of countries, especially in Africa and around the Mediterranean basin, can be viewed as being within full EEC competence.

In the context of the seminar, it will be noted that the EEC has tried—and in my view managed—to define the first steps in establishing a coherent policy toward developing countries. The EEC first used the instrument that by definition was one of the few which it could use at an early stage of the transitional period, when a full Community competence was clearly established by the Rome Treaty. This instrument was the common external tariff. Thus, at a relatively early stage, even when member states were not yet fully applying the common external tariff, the EEC concluded (or is presently concluding) agreements for the establishment of customs unions or free trade areas with various developing countries, starting with eighteen formerly dependent countries of black Africa (1958), Greece (1961), Turkey (1963), Malta (1971) and Portugal (1972). Other agreements, less ambitious for the time being, complete the circle with Morocco, Tunisia, Egypt, Israel, Spain and so on. Most of the agreements in the Mediterranean basin are customs unions or free trade areas which are being established on a previously agreed timetable.

The Community however, at an early stage, also made use of an additional instrument in its relations with some developing countries; that is, economic and financial cooperation. The European Development Fund was created and then enlarged over the years. It is now financing projects in countries associated with the EEC under the Yaoundé Convention of the order of $200 million per year. The agreements with Greece and Turkey contain financial protocols which grant these countries access to the European Investment Bank, partly at preferential interest rates,[1] but within certain limitations.

The tendency to supplement preferential and even nonpreferential trading arrangements by clauses providing for financial and/or industrial and technical cooperation, is likely to continue. Thus, the Council of Ministers of the Community is just about to define a mandate of negotiations with the Maghreb countries providing for financial and technical cooperation. The nonpreferential trade agreement with Argentina also provides a possibility for the

---

1. The financial protocol has not been applied to Greece since 1967, when the armed services overthrew the civil government.

partners to take questions of economic cooperation into the framework of the agreement. Conferences between the Community and ECLA members periodically discuss all problems "existing in their economic and commercial relations." Such problems comprise the coordination of the technical and financial aid of the member states of the Community, scientific-technological cooperation, EEC technical aid concerning regional integration schemes in Latin America, the possibility of European Investment Bank loans and guarantees of EEC investments.

With a comprehensive network of special relations between the EEC and the less developed countries, one could have expected that the question of adjustment assistance would have been put on the agenda at an early stage. This has not been the case, the reason being that the EEC's partners were either not sufficiently developed or were pushing ahead with their development plans in a way which was not considered likely to create major problems necessitating adjustment assistance. However, in all preferential trade agreements the possibility of applying safeguard measures at short notice is built in. No situation has yet arisen when the EEC or its member states have felt compelled to take action.

With the maintenance of overall tariff protection against third countries and, since 1958, of a high level of employment, most EEC countries have been able to make industrial adjustments, insofar as their competitive strength vis-à-vis third countries was concerned, acceptable or tolerable to national governments without calling for major assistance. In fact, highly beneficial adjustments were forced upon several sectors in practically every member state by the sheer progressive creation of the customs union among the six countries. Adjustment help was sometimes provided through temporary application of safeguard measures during the transition period, but more often through state subsidies authorized by the EEC Commission. EEC financial instruments used in that context were the European Investment Bank, the Social Fund and, in the case of coal and steel, specific funds created by the European Coal and Steel Community Treaty as far back as 1952.

The question of adjustment assistance nevertheless did arise, if only marginally, in the context of the EEC's endeavors toward an *erga omnes* liberalization of trade, and at a relatively late stage of EEC's trade policy. The first case occurred during the Kennedy Round of tariff negotiations. The EEC institutions discussed the problems of adjustment assistance in connection with the concessions they were to make in the paper sector. At that time, however, that discussion did not lead to any positive results. More recently, adjustment assistance became a more acute subject in the context of discussions regarding the Generalized Preference Scheme, and also in the context of new trade negotiations to be undertaken on a large scale within the GATT framework.

This paper tries to outline some of the problems with which the EEC is confronted in the context of its general policy vis-à-vis less developed countries, and adjustment assistance. It is incomplete because the EEC's policy in this field is still incomplete, and thus only suggests general tendencies. I am convinced, however, that these tendencies make a good start, and they will have a favorable effect on developing countries. I do not claim to treat the problems concerned scientifically, but look at them rather from the practical experience of a civil servant who has worked for some fifteen years for European unification. I hence ask my learned colleagues participating in this seminar in advance for understanding and comprehension of such an unscientific approach.

I. THE EVOLUTION OF THE EEC'S GENERAL POLICY TOWARD DEVELOPING COUNTRIES ASSOCIATION UNDER PART IV OF THE TREATY OF ROME

Part IV of the Rome Treaty provides for the association of overseas countries and territories which had special relations with France, Belgium, Italy and Netherlands. The purpose of the association was defined to be the promotion of the economic and social development of these countries and territories and the establishment of close economic relations between them and the Community. The Treaty defined the special relationship envisaged. There was to be a free-trade area giving the developing countries the possibility of numerous contributions for the requirements of their industrialization and their fiscal needs. The principle of an EEC contribution to the investment required by the progressive development of the countries and territories concerned was also established.

The purpose of the association of these countries and territories was to place special relations existing between former colonial dependencies and their "mother" countries on a Community basis, thus transforming remnants of a colonial past into a new and voluntary relationship between a group of industrialized and developing countries. The form chosen was a flexible one as it was implemented by conventions; these were concluded for periods of five years, after which they were renegotiated and adapted to new situations which had emerged in the meantime. This scheme has worked to the satisfaction of the associates and of the EEC for fourteen years. The EEC has played a major role in developing the economic and social infrastructure of the associated states. In the framework of the second Yaoundé Convention it started to make a financial contribution toward their industrialization. However, in the trade field, even though the Yaoundé associates have free entry to the EEC for practically all their products, the results of association have not been positive. The Yaoundé associated states have lost ground and continue to lose ground in the EEC markets. This is probably because the advantages from which they profited in the markets of their former "mother" countries were more substantial than those offered by the EEC.

In 1962, after the first negotiations for British entry, the EEC offered to extend association to other developing countries having the same economic and social structure as the Yaoundé associated states. This led to the signature of an association agreement with Nigeria, but this was not subsequently ratified by the Nigerian Parliament due to the outbreak of civil war. Similar negotiations with some of the formerly British East African countries were most successful, although these countries did not wish the European Development Fund to extend its activities to their territories.

After enlargement of the EEC, about twenty Commonwealth countries and territories with a similar economic and social structure to that of the Yaoundé associated states will have the choice between joining the Yaoundé convention (in the renegotiation of which they can participate), obtaining an arrangement which is similar to the agreement with the East African countries, or opting for nonpreferential trade agreements.

Developing Countries in the Mediterranean Basin

As early as 1959 the EEC found itself confronted with demands from Greece and Turkey for associate membership. It was understood that such an associate membership would be an interim stage, permitting the countries concerned to become full members of the EEC once they had reached the degree of economic development necessary to fulfill all the obligations of the Rome Treaty.

An agreement with Greece was concluded in 1962 and with Turkey in 1964. Both Treaties provide for progressive achievement of customs unions, a certain amount of policy harmonization in such fields as restrictive practices and state aid. Financial protocols, again within certain limits, give these countries access to the European Investment Bank. There is also a provision for preferential interest rates on part of the Bank loans. Greece and Turkey profit from the free entry of manufactures, and substantial preferences for most of their agricultural products, into the EEC market. In return they will reduce tariffs on EEC exports over periods of twelve to twenty-two years. During this time Greece and Turkey will also adjust their tariffs against countries other than the EEC to bring them into line with the EEC's common external tariff at the end of the transitional period.

Similar agreements have been signed, or are under negotiation, with Malta and Cyprus.

Another category of agreements are those concluded or envisaged with the Maghreb countries. Algeria, still a part of France in 1958, was until independence part of the customs union of the six European Community states. For Morocco and Tunisia the Six had formulated a declaration of intent at the time of the conclusion of the Rome Treaty. They proposed to these countries negotiations with a view to concluding conventions for economic association with the Community. This declaration led to negotiations with Tunisia and Morocco in 1967, and the conclusion of association agreements in 1969, providing for the first stages of free trade areas. For Algeria various rounds of negotiations have taken place with a view to concluding an agreement which would be similar to the Tunisian agreement. Algeria, however, insisted on financial assistance, technical cooperation and measures in favor of Algerian workers in Europe before the conclusion on an agreement with the Community. After years of discussions, the Council of Ministers of the EEC is now about to give a mandate to the Commission to negotiate with Algeria, taking into account its wishes for financial and technical cooperation. It is understood that if such arrangements are concluded with Algeria, they will be extended to Morocco and Tunisia when the agreements with these countries are renegotiated following the enlargement of the Community.

A third category of countries around the Mediterranean basin with which the Community has concluded preferential agreements are developing countries that did not have special relations with member states of the Community and do not wish, at least as yet, to become full members of the Community at a later stage. These are

Spain and Israel (1970),[2] and negotiations are now being pursued with the United Arab Republic and Lebanon.

Special relations with these countries can be considered as the first step of the Community toward a common foreign policy. This policy is the expression of a profound conviction that it would be neither in Europe's interest, nor in the interest of Mediterranean countries, if the latter were to be exposed to the exclusive influences of the two great world powers, and that the EEC has a vocation to exercise a stabilizing influence in an area of the world situated at its door step.

EEC Relations with Other Developing Countries

While the first negotiations for British entry in 1961/62 were in progress, it was proposed that India and Pakistan should conclude comprehensive trade agreements with the Community to solve the problems that might arise for them from the EEC's enlargement. After the interruption of the negotiations, these countries expressed their interest in concluding trade agreements even if Britain did not become a member of the EEC. The Community, however, failed to respond to this demand as it was felt by some member governments that it would be too early to engage in a common policy toward that part of the world while the EEC itself was still in the midst of the process of achieving a customs union.

There was also fear that such agreements would be considered a precedent, provoking a multiplication of trade agreements before the completion of the transitional period of the EEC Treaty, with all the complications, and the necessary abandonment or dilution of bilateral relations involved. The Community thus decided to lower the tariffs on some products of interest to India and Pakistan, and to open substantial tariff-free quotas for handloom and handicraft products. Broader assistance was left subject to the evolution of the question of the EEC's enlargement, and the evolution of plans for worldwide generalized preferences favoring developing countries.

At a later stage, Latin American countries asked for trade negotiations with the EEC. Subsequently, trade talks have been carried out with Argentina and Uruguay, and a nonpreferential trading agreement with the former was concluded in November 1971, giving easier access to European markets for Argentina's meat exports.

2. It appears, however, that new negotiations which might take place with Spain and Israel would have to take into account their tremendous economic advances, which would not make it possible to consider them, in the long run, as developing countries.

The agreement with Argentina also provides for the possibility of enlarging the agreement by ventures of industrial and technological cooperation.

In general, more developing countries in Latin America and Asia are beginning to show increased interest in having special relationships with the EEC. These links are regarded as promising by the developing countries concerned not only for reasons of preferential tariff or quota treatment, but also because establishing special links would likely facilitate industrial, technological and perhaps even financial cooperation. So far the Community has taken only the first few steps in responding to such wishes. They were too preoccupied initially with their internal consolidation and, in the last two years, with enlargement. The problems of enlargement virtually overwhelmed the institutional structure, which was consequently not capable of dealing simultaneously with a large number of other important questions. A positive political response of most member states may nevertheless be discerned. The experience of UNCTAD III, moreover, clearly indicated to the Community that it had to act as an entity if it wanted to constitute an important partner for developing countries.

The Generalized Scheme of Preferences

The application of the generalized preference scheme in favor of developing countries has largely been a result of initiatives of the EEC, which has for several years pushed industrialized countries in OECD to go ahead with the abolition of tariffs against imports of manufactures from developing countries. The EEC's leadership in applying the generalized preference scheme is surely one of the most positive and most encouraging factors of its trade policy. The fact that the EEC has been able to define a scheme without exception, if not without limits, is an interesting demonstration of the relative inefficiency of the pressure of lobbies in a multinational context. It clearly shows the political engagement of member governments and the real ability of the EEC to apply liberal policies toward imports from developing countries to lead to a more reasonable division of labor, and of wealth, in the world.

II. IMPORTS OF MANUFACTURED GOODS
FROM DEVELOPING COUNTRIES INTO THE EEC

Developing countries' manufactures still provide a small percentage of total EEC imports, but there has been a remarkable increase from $300 million in 1963 to $1 billion in 1970. The trend has been particularly steep in the last few years; there was an 86 percent increase in imports of manufactures between 1968 and 1970. Imports of manufactures from developing countries are still remarkably concentrated on relatively few products: textiles, including jute and coir, leather products, iron and steel, wood manufactures, electronic products, shoes and machinery. The most spectacular increases in imports have taken place in clothing, machinery and transport materials, leather and leather goods and electric equipment. It is also to be noted that imports of manufactures come from a relatively few countries, with Yugoslavia, Hong Kong, India, Israel, Brazil and Mexico being by far the most important.

Problems Concerning Imports

Difficulties arise when a *problem area* created by imports has to be defined. The EEC has some experience in this area from its transition to a customs union. Article 226 of the Rome Treaty provides that, if in the course of the transitional period there are serious difficulties which are likely to persist in any sector of economic activity, or difficulties which may seriously impair the economic situation of any region, a member state may ask for authorization to take measures to safeguard or restore a given situation and adapt the sector concerned to the common market economy. It was the prerogative of the Commission of the European Communities to apply this article and to grant the necessary authorization to the member states. This only had to be done on rare occasions, but every time the Commission investigated the details of a case where disruption was supposed to have been caused by excessive imports from other member states, it found that it was difficult, or even impossible to disassociate the import element from other factors that were causing the difficulty. Thus the French durable consumer goods industry which supposedly encountered difficulties because of Italian competition was found to have run into structural problems which might have caused difficulties even if France had not been a member of the EEC. That is, France's problems were really independent of the abolition of tariff protection against Italian imports. It was also found that the French government would probably not have asked for safeguard measures if the industries concerned had not been located in regions where, at least in the medium run, no other employment was available.

Similar conditions applied in most other cases where the application of Article 226 was requested by member states.

In the EEC's trade relations with nonmember countries, it is often just as difficult to establish whether disruption has been caused by imports or by other factors such as declining consumption, substitution, internal competition, structural weakness or regional factors. Even if a relationship between imports and the disruption of a branch of industry could be established for one member state, it would at the present stage in many cases be impossible to establish it for the whole of the Communities as market conditions still vary in the various national markets of the member states. For some particularly sensitive products, some of the member states still apply quantitative restrictions against socialist countries, some developing countries, Japan or all three, whereas others do not.

Table 7-1 indicates quantitative restrictions still applied by member states for products exported by developing countries early in 1972. It clearly shows the diversity of import regimes in the various countries of the Communities.

The fact that quantitative restrictions are still being applied shows that the governments of the member states concerned consider imports likely to cause disruption in a completely free market. They appear convinced that, for most items on this list, the threat is caused by some developing countries which have developed a highly competitive export-oriented industry which can produce manufactures of good quality at prices far below those of their European competitors. In this context it could be argued, in fact, that many of the quantitative restrictions concerned are designed to *avoid* the necessity for adjustment assistance. In some cases they are presented as measures allowing industries concerned to convert to more competitive production lines over a longer period.

One may wonder why national quantitative restrictions are still applied by most of the EEC member states several years after the end of the transitional period and why, so far, the EEC has not succeeded in applying a common policy in this field. The explanation may be found in the following motives:

(1) In a market economy, governments refrain from direct intervention into the production process if they can find other ways to achieve similar effects. Quantitative restrictions are considered to be more or less objective instruments of trade policy, whereas adjustment assistance necessitates detailed intervention and control, so quantitative restrictions exist as long as there is no absolute necessi-

THE EEC APPROACH / 197

ty for their elimination. (2) The administrative infrastructure for the application of quantitative restrictions has existed for many years. Measures of adjustment assistance necessitate the creation of a new administrative apparatus for examining demands, collecting economic data, delivering available funds in the most effective manner, controlling the use of funds and so on. (3) National budgets are limited. Providing funds for adjustment assistance often means curtailing other kinds of expenditure. This implies conflicts among various short-term political priorities. In these conflicts adjustment assistance is often, for obvious reasons, the loser. (4) Sheer traditionalism is not a negligible force in any administration which is therefore likely to oppose radical innovations, such as adjustment assistance measures, as long as it can rely on other instruments.

EEC countries have, however, gone a long way toward reducing the list of quantitative restrictions and can be expected to work out a common commercial policy providing for a Community program of gradual elimination of the quantitative restrictions still applied against developing countries. Particular measures are being devised for geographical "problem areas," such as Hong Kong, Macao, Singapore, Korea and Taiwan.

This process should be helped by the growing consciousness that quantitative restrictions are a very inadequate remedy for difficulties caused by third country competition. Quantitative restrictions, like tariffs, are geared to insure or increase the profitability of whole industries, not of individual firms or groups of firms running into difficulties in particular regions. By this nonselective effect, quantitative restrictions can solve social problems in areas where no other means of employment are available. But at the same time they prevent the economically favorable flow of labor toward more productive activities within regions of industrial concentration, thus hampering optimal allocation of resources and growth.

When discussing problems caused by imports from developing countries, there is, however, one area where the EEC as a whole has been and is being affected. This area, of course, is textiles, undoubtedly the most spectacular, and politically the most important case. One easily understands why this is so if one bears in mind the following factors. (1) Textiles form a branch of relatively high importance in the production patterns of the EEC; its share of the total production of the industrial sector is over 12 percent in the EEC, compared with only 6 percent in the United States. (2) The textile industry is labor-intensive, employing over three million people in the

EEC. This corresponds to 12 percent of all workers employed in industry. (3) The bulk, 70 percent to 80 percent of the EEC textile industry, is located in a limited number of regions, where it employs up to 30 percent of the active population. These regions often have characteristics of mono-industrialization, or are relatively underdeveloped. The industry usually predominantly employs women, and the earnings of the female labor force are necessary in developing regions to support the family budget because men, being employed mostly in agriculture, are poorly paid. (4) Difficulties arising from competition from developing countries are combined with competition from Japan, which is still a low-cost industrialized country. Internal competition is also intense because of low growth rates. Sometimes consumption is even declining. The rapid substitution of man-made for natural fibers adds to competitiveness.

Issues for the Seventies

These difficulties are not new. They have existed for years, and they have been aggravated from time to time. Protests of employers and the labor unions have become particularly strong and outspoken after the Community's decision to include textiles in generalized preferences, when it was well known that this was not to be followed by other industrialized countries granting, or intending to grant generalized preferences, in favor of imports from developing countries. In their protests, employers and unions stress particularly the visible decline in the Community's textile industries. This decline is more pronounced than, for instance, in the United States; in the EEC, employment in the industry is being reduced by about 40,000 workers a year.

Lately and under stress of a worldwide textile crisis, the intensity of protests has increased. As in other countries, a unified front of employers and labor unions is creating political conditions with increasing dangers of old-fashioned protectionism.

It is this threat that explains steps which, at first hand, seem to contradict the move toward liberalization pursued by the Community. These have included active participation in a working group of GATT which is to study the worldwide problems of textile trade even though there is a substantial risk that such a study group will eventually result in a limitation of export facilities for, at least, some developing countries to the markets of industrialized countries. Whatever formula is worked out by the contracting parties of GATT, certain basic principles will have to be respected: (1) Any formula that might be elaborated in this context should provide guarantees for a gradual and orderly transition toward full liberalization of trade after a certain period of time. (2) Measures should be taken to protect developing countries, and particularly those least developed countries that do not yet have that "overindustrialization" of certain branches which results in overcompetitiveness, often at the expense of the least developed countries.

The experience of the Long Term Agreement for Cotton Textiles (LTA) shows that this is possible. It is interesting to note that the least developed country signatories to this agreement have consistently underlined their interest in maintaining it. They argue that the absence of quantitative cotton textile controls by the industrialized countries would mean that they would be pushed out of these markets by more developed, more efficient competitors, such as Hong Kong, Taiwan, Japan and South Korea. The ceilings negotiated with producer countries by the EEC have effectively taken account of the degree of development of the countries concerned, attributing considerably larger increases in the ceilings to the least developed countries than to the others.

This kind of arrangement granting developing countries a growing part of the market in mutual agreement has avoided problems for the Community as well as for the least developed countries. This seems to indicate that in some exceptional cases this kind of formula can be a positive contribution to development policy.

While textiles have been the one important problem area in the sixties, the seventies may well bring others, particularly if and when new tariff reduction agreements and the removal of other trade obstacles become effective. In most instances, as in textiles, the problems might result from the combination of intensive and aggressive competition in European or United States markets by Japan, and by several, though by no means all, competing developing countries. If, for the purpose of argument, one could consider Japan evolving rapidly to a more balanced industrial structure, with production costs rising to European levels, the difficulties would become in practically all cases more of a nuisance than of an adjustment problem. At any rate, the adjustment would be manageable, regionally, socially and from a technical point of view. However, if Japan does not fall in line, and if one considers cheap manpower and/or natural resources in several developing countries with sufficient planning capacity existing, the seventies may bring problems in, for example, shipbuilding, steel, zinc and lead, electronics, optical instruments, ceramics and shoes. For a different reason, namely the mounting desire of oil-producing countries to enter petrochemical production in the seventies, the chemical sector may also face considerable adjustment problems.

In most of these cases, the Communities, and each member state individually, will face several issues: (1) the level of supply security or of production capacity it considers necessary to maintain; (2) the level of industrialization in regions particularly affected; and (3) the ways and means of solving possible layoffs in manpower.

Most of these industries obviously cannot be phased out for the benefit of their competitors, although some may shrink and others grow at a less rapid pace than consumption. Commercial policy will have to make sure that the pace of change is adapted to the possibilities of political, economical and social change in the Community. Even so, adjustment problems are likely to grow markedly and require considerable budgetary resources. If the decline of industry results from measures such as EEC commercial policy, there will be a strong case for EEC financial intervention in the process of adjustment. Proposals submitted recently by the Commission to the Council concerning the inclusion of textile workers in adjustment programs of the European Social Fund are the first example. However, some member states may well have different objectives, and diverge considerably when it comes to allowing market forces to decide an industry's chances of survival, whether for strategic, economic or social reasons. Therefore, there will also be considerable scope for national adjustment assistance, above all by subsidies—under the control of the Commission—to benefit the injured industry, the injured region or both.

Summary

The EEC experience shows that the definition of "problem areas" in connection with imports from developing countries is largely empirical, and that criteria are not always the same when adjustment assistance measures are applied. In general, the following tendencies emerge from EEC experience. (1) The fact of a decline in the production of any branch, whether caused by increased imports or by other factors, is not as such regarded as a sufficient motive to grant adjustment assistance or to take other measures to save the industry concerned. (2) Redundancies arising from such shrinkage are not considered a serious problem if unemployed workers can find new jobs in the same geographical region. The state might, nevertheless, intervene to grant aid for retraining to avoid social hardship. (3) The state feels obliged to react when industries run into difficulties, and when redundancies arising therefrom occur in geographical regions where there is no or little possibility of reemploying redundant workers in other activities.

Such cases are, for obvious reasons, considered to constitute threats to law and order. Corrective measures taken tend to use all instruments at hand. As, however, instruments implying import restrictions are either in the Community's competence (tariffs) or subject to the limitations defined in international conventions, the measures applied are usually in the area of state intervention in the financial or fiscal field rather than trade measures.

Other problems which have arisen in the EEC in relation to products exported by developing countries have been caused not so much by the quantities of imports, but by the distortion of competition inherent in the export incentive programs of some less developed countries. These problems arise in cases where the raw material which constitutes a high percentage of the cost of the manufactured product is subject to some kind of equalization scheme, taxing or restraining the export of the raw materials and subsidizing local processing industries. Such cases have arisen for certain wool products as well as for castor oil, leather goods and lead oxide imported from Latin America, and for coir goods from India. In such cases it is generally admitted that the aspirations of the developing countries to process their raw material before export are legitimate, but it is difficult for any government, and even for EEC institutions, not to take some kind of compensatory action if the industries of the developed countries can prove that such practices artificially distort competition, and are being applied regardless of GATT rules.

IV. ADJUSTMENT ASSISTANCE

The previous section demonstrates the difficulty of evaluating adjustment measures in the EEC; it has been pointed out that it is particularly difficult to indicate areas where problems are likely to arise from developing country export competition. How much more difficult is it to analyze where measures of adjustment assistance have helped to permit the liberalization of imports from the developing countries.

Again I have to limit myself to some general considerations. Past experience clearly shows that problems of industrial and agricultural decline arose in various sectors and regions of the Community and assistance of various kinds has been granted in some cases in order to solve them. However, there is no hard evidence to indicate whether adjustment measures taken so far have, or have not, had an influence on trade with developing countries. It is, indeed, almost impossible to evaluate the motives for adjustment assistance measures where they have been accorded, as initially several factors were involved in decisions to grant assistance. UNCTAD has summarized the variety of adjustment assistance measures as follows:

> Adjustment assistance in the developed market economy countries is given to industry and/or labor either for their rehabilitation and modernization as productive factors within an industrial activity, or for their reallocation to different and presumably more productive activities. While national or local or regional governments within these countries are usually the source of such assistance, there are cases in which aid is provided principally by private industrial groups.

> Adjustment assistance measures to industry may include capital grants, low interest rate loans, loan guarantees, interest rebates or subsidies, various types of tax concessions, liberal depreciation allowances, engineering, marketing and management advice and provision of development sites and related infrastructure. Assistance to labor typically consists of one or more of the following: a supplement to, or an extension of, ordinary unemployment insurance payments; funding and provision of vocational retraining services; and assistance in relocating, including reimbursement for moving expenses.

> Governmental adjustment assistance measures in the developed market economy countries are typically available within the context of national programmes designed to help workers and firms adapt to economic dislocations whatever the proximate cause. Furthermore, adjustment assistance may occur within the framework of regional development programmes pursued by the national government, often in cooperation with local or regional development authorities. Adjustment assistance programmes geared specifically to economic dislocations caused by increased imports are the exception rather than the rule.[3]

3. UNCTAD, "Adjustment Assistance Measures," Document no. TD/121 (New York, December 1971).

Several points of this analysis are confirmed by the Community's experience. Germany's adjustment assistance[4] illustrates the multitude of measures administered by central, regional and local agencies typical for adjustment policy in many European countries: (1) Adjustment assistance measures are not specifically geared to compensate disruption caused by increased imports. (2) The central government grants unemployed workers financial assistance for retraining and resettlement; in Germany mine workers affected by the structural crisis of the coal and iron ore mine industries have been the chief beneficiaries. (3) Central government loans at preferential interest rates have been granted to orient production programs toward new products, and to help traditional, declining industries to convert their production toward growth sectors. (4) Central government investment incentives have been given to enterprises and workers to enable them to adapt to structural changes. (5) Regional authorities have granted credits at preferential rates to assist small- and medium-sized enterprises to make structural adjustments.

It may be added that in many European countries even local authorities grant various kinds of investment incentives to attract new industries where traditional industries have been closing down. Governments also have subsidized or "sponsored" the restructuring of industries running into trouble by offering incentives, or pushing them into mergers to create more efficient and productive entities.

Several measures used in Europe and elsewhere, and described as "adjustment assistance" measures, are in reality instruments of regional policy which provide substantial incentives, often on a non-selective basis. Such incentives are given by central, regional or local authorities to attract any industry willing to settle in a region or locality considered as "backward." In certain areas of the Community this practice has resulted in overbidding to such an extent that an agreement now limits such incentives to 20 percent of the initial investment in central regions of the Community to avoid waste of resources and distortions of industrial location.

So much for the policies of the various member states of the EEC. As far as the Community as an entity are concerned, certain instruments for adjustment assistance measures are to be found in the EEC Treaty, and in the Treaty establishing the European Community for Coal and Steel. These instruments are Social Funds

---

4. Ibid., Supplement 1 (New York, January 1972).

which operate to alleviate the social consequences of integration. Between 1953 and 1970, over $600 million was expended from these funds. This sum accounts for 50 percent of the cost of government programs for retraining and resettling workers who had become, or were to become, unemployed as a result of increased competition within the Community. Retraining programs provided workers waiting for new jobs with a tide-over allowance equal to between 80 percent and 100 percent of their last average wage, and with differential allowances to make up, for up to two years, any difference between previous and new wage levels. Resettlement grants were made available to those willing to move to take new jobs. The aid of these funds had no *direct* relation to helping industries adjust to imports from nonmember states.[5] However, it can be argued that these funds, which have helped to retrain and resettle 1.7 million workers, have had a favorable influence on the EEC member states' import policies by avoiding social troubles that otherwise could have arisen.

As the experience with the Social Funds of the Coal and Steel Community and EEC were positive, it has long been felt that the intervention of these funds in favor of the Communities' workers should be increased. When the EEC Social Funds' rules were revised in 1969, the Commission, backed by the trade unions of the member states, put forward proposals to increase the powers and the scope of the Fund. These proposals were adopted in outline form by the Council of Ministers in July 1970. The aim was to change the fund from a limited, and rather inflexible clearing house, to an effective instrument of the Communities' employment policy. The details of the new scheme were agreed in October 1971, became operative by May 1, 1972 and can be summarized as follows:

Activity of the Social Fund

The new Fund will operate in two distinct ways, with about half the resources available being spent on each. Under the first formula authorization can be given for assistance to be granted from the Fund (a) when the employment situation is affected or in danger of being affected either by special measures adopted by the Council in the framework of Community policies, or by jointly agreed operations to further the objectives of the Community; or (b) when the employment situation calls for specific joint action to improve the

---

5. The reformed EEC Social Fund can, however, in the future, address itself to such a specific objective.

balance between supply of and demand for manpower within the Community. When situations of this kind arise, and the Council thinks fit, it will be able to grant assistance from the Fund in a new field by taking a specific decision on a Commission proposal. In this decision it will also lay down the special conditions which must be fulfilled by operations carried out in this field.

The second formula makes it possible for assistance to be provided from the Fund when the employment situation in certain regions, in certain branches of the economy, or in certain groups of undertakings, is affected by difficulties which result indirectly from the working of the Common Market or impede the harmonious development of the Communities.

Three sets of cumulative conditions must be fulfilled by operations designed to remedy this type of situation:

1. They must help to solve employment problems arising:
   a. in areas which are less developed or where the main activities are in decline,
   b. in branches of economic activity where technical progress is bringing about major changes in manpower and professional knowledge and skill,
   c. in groups of undertakings which are forced to cease, reduce or change their activity because of substantial changes in the conditions of production or disposal of products.

2. They must also:
   a. assist the unemployed, or those who will become so after a specific period, and the underemployed to eliminate long-term structural unemployment and underemployment, or
   b. train workers to enable them to pursue occupations requiring high qualifications, or
   c. facilitate the integration or reintegration into the labor force of workers having difficulty in finding another job because of their age, that is, women over 35 and young people under 25 years of age.

3. They must be part of an overall program directed at remedying the causes of imbalance affecting employment in the area, branch of the economy, group of undertakings or category of persons involved.

Assistance from the Fund can be granted not only to public authorities and bodies governed by public law, but also to joint public-private social institutions entrusted with tasks in the public interest and to bodies or other entities governed by private law, on condition, in the latter case, that the public authorities of the member state or states concerned guarantee the completion of such operations and also share in the financing.

It should be pointed out that the amount granted from the Fund will be fixed in a different manner according to whether the operation is undertaken by the public, semipublic or private sector. In the first case, the amount granted to the body undertaking the operation will be 50 percent of eligible expenditure. On the other hand, an operation undertaken by the private sector will be financed jointly by the Social Fund, the public authorities and the private entity. In this case, the amount granted from the Fund to the body undertaking the scheme will be equal to the part of the eligible expenditure provided by the public authorities, with the further condition that part of the costs must be paid by the private entity itself. Thus it is now possible for assistance to be granted from the Fund for operations in the private sector; this is one of the major innovations of the reform.

Henceforth it will be possible for the Social Fund to be used to help all persons, including nationals of a nonmember country who belong to the working population of the Community and who are normally engaged in wage-earning activities. Furthermore, in special cases to be designated by the Council, the Fund can be used to help persons who wish to take up self-employed activities.

The special cases eligible to benefit from operations carried out under formula A of the Fund's activities will be determined as a result of Commission proposals, in ad hoc Council decisions which will open up fields in which assistance may be granted from the Social Fund.

Plans have to be drawn up and submitted beforehand by member states to the Commission for each operation. These plans must indicate, among other things, the nature of the various measures envisaged, how they are to be carried out and how they are to be financed. They are subject to approval by the Commission after consultation with the "Social Fund Committee."

The money granted from the Fund will be made available as the approved operations proceed, although the Commission reserves the right to carry out audits.

The initial list contains four forms of aid. (1) Aid for the preparation, operation and management of training courses, including training of instructors. The main types of aid here, in addition to the traditional aid for personnel remuneration and allowances for trainees, is aid towards the accelerated depreciation of buildings for operations carried out in less developed areas, aid to help recruitment in firms being set up in these areas and aid to cover expenditure on vocational aptitude tests and examinations. The Fund can facilitate all types of training, enabling workers to acquire, increase, adapt or improve job knowledge and skills, regardless of the kind of teaching given. There is only one restriction. The Fund cannot be used to finance the initial training of young people immediately on the completion of their compulsory schooling. (2) Aid for persons obliged to change their place of residence within the Community in order to take up a new job. The aid is to cover transport costs and various resettlement allowances generally granted in the member states. (3) Aid to encourage integration of these persons and members of their families into the new social and working environment, and in particular aid for information schemes, hostels for young people and language teaching. (4) Aid to eliminate obstacles which make it difficult for certain categories of workers who are at a disadvantage to take up available employment, that is, handicapped persons and persons aged over 50.

Additional types of aid can be decided at any time by the Communities' institutions if the necessity is felt. No time limit is fixed for the retraining programs cofinanced by the Fund. In practice, these programs can run over three to four years in exceptional cases, especially where handicapped persons are concerned.

To round off this description of the new Social Fund, it should be further noted that the Commission is empowered to promote, carry out or give financial assistance to studies and pilot schemes, and also that special credits will be earmarked for this purpose. Such studies financed by the Fund have, however, limited importance and must not involve more than thirty jobs. They have to be approved in advance by the government or governments in whose territory they are to be carried out.

Formula A of the fund is, of course, an instrument par excellence for adjustment assistance. The decisions taken by the Community, for example, authorized the Fund to help governments pay the social cost of trade liberalization measures, which the Council may adopt. Formula A also permits the Council to give such aid for liberalization measures it has taken in the past. It should be stressed, however, that the Fund's activity is limited to helping workers. The Fund can thus neither accord capital grants for conversion, nor initiate economic analyses that might help to devise an "early warning system."

It is, of course, too early to see whether the Communities' institutions will make appropriate use of this instrument to facilitate imports from developing countries. There is, however, little doubt that this new and comprehensive Social Fund will intervene in cases where a liberal import policy threatens the jobs of the Communities' workers, especially if this happens in regions in which no other employment is available in the short run. Experts have estimated that after a starting period of three or four years, the new Fund's expenditures will total some $250 million to $300 million annually, compared to an annual rate of about $50 million before 1972.

When the new Fund's operations have been discussed with the representatives of developing countries, the issue whether the Social Fund could help member states grant what is generally called "anticipatory" adjustment assistance has been raised. Knowing member states' views on the subject, I think that it would be unrealistic to presume that any government, and even less the EEC institutions, could select firms or sectors to be phased out to make room for developing country imports. The practical problems of identifying firms or industries for elimination are insoluble, and the political difficulties would be insuperable. Artificial measures of this kind are not, in any case, likely to foster economic efficiency. They threaten a risk of freezing patterns of production, leaving the developing countries with low productivity, labor-intensive production.

For all these reasons, "anticipatory" adjustment assistance appears to be delusion rather than a real contribution to the discussion of how a more reasonable division of labor and resources between developed and developing countries might be achieved.

Finally, in discussing adjustment assistance, several important corollaries with a major impact on the process of structural adjustment of industries in developed countries must be mentioned.

State Assistance Policies

It is evident that, to obtain the structural results necessary to achieve a better international division of labor, governments should abstain from granting subsidies which maintain production lines that would normally be condemned by outside competition. It should be noted in this context that state aid operated by the member states of the EEC is a "Community matter." Aid has to be authorized by the Commission, which over the years has developed a policy which is likely to have a favorable impact upon adjustment of the EEC's members' industrial structures. The principles of this policy can be outlined as follows: (1) Assistance to preserve a given industry can only be allowed for a limited period if it is a question of preserving jobs, or of helping a less developed region of the EEC. (2) Assistance must decrease over time to force the industry concerned to make the necessary adaptation. (3) Assistance must be selective and may be granted only to industries which have a chance of becoming viable on their own. (4) Assistance must not allow the state to carry the risks of the industries concerned. (5) Assistance must be framed so as to have the minimum distorting effect on competition and inter-Community trade.

These principles, as enforced, indicate a major step toward the elimination of subsidies which are granted only as a substitute for tariff protection.

Regional Policy

Efficient regional policies which insure that the disparities between highly developed and less developed regions of a country or of a regional grouping do not increase, but diminish in the long run, must be considered as a precondition for liberal import policies. As indicated, some of the sensitive industries affected by imports from developing countries are situated in less developed regions with no or little other sources of employment. The closure of enterprises in such regions creates almost insurmountable political difficulties; serious threats of unemployment are likely to result in protectionist measures or in ad hoc state aid permitting existing enterprises to maintain traditional production.

Regional policy should also aim not only at the creation, but also at the diversification, of production structures in less developed regions to avoid the social unrest and political pressure which inevitably arise when a region has only one major source of employment, and when this source runs into problems. Such production diversification needs very careful long term planning to avoid the kinds of mishaps that some member states have experienced. For example, ten to fifteen years ago it was assumed that the light electronics industry could be used to diversify less developed regions where the textile industry was running into difficulties because it was rather labor-intensive, employed a large percentage of female labor, and had a favorable growth rate. This reasoning was correct, but one decisive factor had been forgotten. The availability of a more qualified and adaptable labor force in less developed countries such as Hong Kong and Singapore, combined with large scale foreign investment, substantial managerial skill and western technology, was able to build up a light electronics industry which, as a result of lower wages, was able to undercut its European competitors. As a result, this industry is now running into difficulties similar to those of the textile industry, much to the embarrassment of regional planners who are now starting to question seriously the possibilities of building up any new labor-intensive industries in central Europe.

The alternatives for developing the backward regions of industrialized countries have thus become more restricted. The choice is usually limited to either finding capital-intensive industries willing to move away from the large centers of consumption and from their sources of highly qualified labor, or the discovery of servicing industries which are at the same time labor-intensive and unaffected by world market competition.

Both alternatives will be doomed to failure unless the unqualified labor force of the less developed regions undergoes comprehensive training financed by public funds. Furthermore, it has to be borne in mind that regional investment incentives are mostly granted by paying a certain percentage of the initial investment out of public funds. It is obvious that the cost of the public investment incentives will increase if capital-intensive industries are to be attracted. But the public funds available for purposes of regional policies are limited, and the cost problem is causing considerable consternation to regional planners. The dilemma planners are facing has led to other forms of regional planning. Direct physical control of industrial investment has attempted to bar new investments from areas of excessive urban concentration, thus trying to compel investors to go to less developed areas. This system is promising, but requires an administrative infrastructure few industrialized countries can provide at present. If it were applied in the central areas of the Community it would necessarily imply application by all the member states concerned to insure that firms barred from establishing factories in the urban concentration areas of one member state cannot merely move to a similar area in another member state.

Individual member states of the EEC have all pursued, and are

pursuing their regional policies by different instruments and to varying degrees of intensity, with the frictions described arising from
overbidding in investment incentives. On the Community level, intervention has been limited to raising loans through the European
Investment Bank at a level of $300 million per year. Most of this
sum has been spent in developing the infrastructure of the less
developed regions.

With the EEC's plans for economic and monetary union, and
with the accession to the EEC of new partners battling with difficult
regional problems, it is being found necessary to define a more efficient regional policy on a Community level.

Modern economic theory suggests that the freezing of exchange
rates leads to the accentuation of existing regional imbalances unless
appropriate compensating measures are taken. Member states with
special regional problems are therefore insisting on a substantial
Community's Fund for regional policy which would operate side by
side with national instruments of this type. It is becoming increasingly clear that such a Fund will be a condition sine qua non for
those Community members' movement towards monetary union.
Such a Fund, and the coordination of national regional policies in
the EEC, are likely to ease regional frictions, and thus create the political conditions for proceeding with full scale liberalization of imports from less developed countries, without a growing risk of political crises arising from unemployment caused by the closing down of
uncompetitive production units situated in backward regions.

Measures to Encourage Investment in Developing Countries

If the opening of markets of industrialized countries for imports
from developing countries is to be of maximum benefit to the "third
world," it must result in a transfer of investment to less developed
countries. The Generalized Preference Scheme will constitute a major incentive to do so if it succeeds in opening up the markets of all
the industrial countries to imports of manufactures from less
developed countries. That is, success would require all the major industrial countries, and in particular the United States, to apply the
scheme, and the product coverage of the scheme to be more or less
identical for all developed countries.

This alone, however, would not be sufficient to obtain what the
EEC Commission in its Memorandum on Industrial Policy has
called "the progressive and orderly transfer of certain activities to
the developing countries." Political risks in developing countries

have been increasing over the years. Every major wave of nationalism sweeping a developing country and resulting in the nationalization or expropriation of foreign firms without, or with insufficient
compensation, has negative repercussions on investment from industrial countries. Medium-sized firms which realize that comparative cost advantages would justify a transfer of their production to
developing countries in particular often refrain from doing so
because of the risks of expropriation. They prefer instead either to
appeal to their government to subsidize them, or to apply protectionist measures.

For this reason a guarantee of investment in less developed countries against political risk should be made available to all firms who
would be willing to transfer their activities. Various guarantee
schemes exist in EEC member states. The EEC Commission is actually preparing proposals to create a Community scheme to close
the gaps existing in national schemes. This could become an instrument of development policy without political strings attached, more
easily than existing national schemes.

The new type of industrial cooperation treaties which the EEC
has started to negotiate, first of all with its preferential trading
partners, but which are also under discussion for other countries,
could also bring about a decisive breakthrough in creating a favorable climate for the industrial activities of firms from industrialized
countries locating in developing countries. These agreements comprise: (1) Mutual information procedures about the possibilities of
investment, joint ventures, subcontracting and related matters. (2)
Trade promotion for developing country products in the EEC market with the creation of trade centers, training of trade experts,
diffusion of information about trade networks and so on. (3) The arrangement of contacts between industrial managers. (4) The coordination of technical and financial aid granted by individual member
states to achieve maximum efficiency. (5) Guarantee for investments. (6) An institutional framework in which all trade, investment and cooperation problems can be discussed.

This kind of agreement is likely to play a major role in the EEC's
"second generation" commercial policy, and might give a new
meaning to the concept of "adjustment."

V. SUMMARY AND CONCLUSION

Whereas adjustment problems have been experienced and tackled by individual EEC member states in the past, notably during the

transition period, the Community's experience in this field is relatively recent. Adjustment problems have not yet come up in the framework of the EEC's preferential agreements with developing countries, to which, in any case, safeguard clauses are attached. Adjustment will become a major policy problem for the EEC if and when new tariff reductions and the elimination of other trade obstacles are realized in the wake of negotiations envisaged for 1973/74.

Adjustment assistance measures of EEC member states have followed the traditional pattern prevalent in most European countries. No direct ties exist between increased imports and adjustment assistance. Adjustment assistance measures are granted by central governments as well as by regional and local authorities. They concern mainly assistance for the retraining and resettlement of workers, and loans to permit conversion of production. Sometimes governments subsidize or sponsor the restructuring of industries to help adjustment by creating bigger and more efficient entities. Adjustment assistance measures are often blended with regional policies granting investment incentives to attract new industries to backward regions and to diversity their industrial structure.

Within the EEC the definition of *problem areas* in connection with imports from developing countries is normally of an empirical nature. The decline of an industry and resulting redundancies, whether or not provoked or speeded up by imports, in itself rarely provokes measures of adjustment assistance. The state does, however, react when such decline causes unemployment in regions where redundant workers cannot readily be put to other activities, taking little account of the factors that have caused disruption. As EEC and GATT rules give little scope for protectionist trade measures the remedies applied usually lie in the financial or fiscal field. So far as EEC as an entity is concerned, the analysis of "problem areas" is rendered difficult by existing national quantitative restrictions for some imports from developing countries. This indicates that although certain member governments consider some sectors problematic, these sectors are not necessarily problematic for the EEC. However, EEC policy in this field will shortly be harmonized, hopefully toward liberalization after a period of transition. Member states are more and more conscious of the fact that the nonselective protection of branches of industry characteristic of quantitative restrictions makes them an inadequate instrument for adjustment, hampering the overall growth of the economy, and implying disproportionately high cost for consumers.

Besides regional problems and unemployment which could, at least partially, be traced to imports from developing countries and against which either protection or adjustment can be sought, the Community and its member states may react with adjustment within the industry concerned or with protectionist devices if an industry, considered to be fundamental to the economic overall balance will, in the future, be menaced by severe shrinkage or by extinction through low-priced imports.

As in other developed economies, the EEC's main problem area is in textiles, where employment has been and is declining by about 40,000 workers per year. Despite this, the EEC had included textiles in its Generalized Preferences Scheme. At the same time, however, it is participating in GATT discussions that might ultimately lead to some kind of limitation of the growth rate of exports of some developing countries. Such an arrangement should be acceptable if it succeeds in avoiding unilateral protectionist measures of certain countries leading to worldwide chain reactions and spreading to other sectors. Certain conditions, however, should be respected. In particular these should include gradual increase of the market share of developing countries leading to liberalization after a specified period, preferential treatment for least developed countries and no precedent for other sectors. The sectors with adjustment problems in the seventies are likely to be shipbuilding, steel and electronics.

In the past the EEC and European Coal and Steel Community's Social Funds have expended about $600 million to retrain and resettle workers who had become redundant as a result of increased competition resulting from the establishment of the Common Market. The EEC Social Fund has undergone a far reaching reform in 1972. The new Fund is an instrument par excellence for adjustment assistance. It is able to carry half the cost of social adaptation, retraining and resettlement programs of member states and private organizations which become necessary as a result of any Community policy, including commercial policy. It can also deal with structural unemployment in the EEC's backward regions and engage in specialized training for industrial sectors lacking qualified workmen. If properly used there is little doubt that it will facilitate liberal import policies from developing countries.

There seems to be little chance that member governments, or the EEC as a whole, will engage in "anticipatory" adjustment measures. The selection of firms or sectors to be phased out to make room for imports from developing countries is inconceivable in a market economy, creates insuperable political difficulties and would tend to freeze patterns of production, leaving the developing countries with low productivity labor-intensive productions.

Adjustment assistance measures cannot be viewed in the narrow context of assistance toward reconversion and subsidy of the social cost of industrial decline. Adjustment is just as much influenced by general policies of state aid, regional policies and active measures to encourage the transfer of investments from industrialized countries to developing countries. State assistance in the EEC is controlled by the EEC institutions. Principles developed over the years are likely to have a positive influence on adjustment.

Regional policy providing for investment incentives in backward regions, and diversifying the economic structure of these regions, can play a decisive role in facilitating liberal import policies. Such policies can avoid political problems which arise when those who become unemployed in declining industries cannot find alternative employment in the region. Regional policy has so far been mainly pursued by individual member states. But in EEC discussions it has become clear that monetary union can only be achieved with a substantial Communities' Regional Fund and an efficient regional policy on the EEC level. These would supplement national policies.

Encouraging investments in developing countries is an indispensable corollary to adjustment assistance measures if developing countries are to reap the maximum benefit from the opening of markets in industrialized countries. Investment guarantee schemes are one means of encouraging such transfers of investment. EEC is about to define new types of trade and cooperation agreements that can be of additional value in creating a more favorable climate toward the EEC in developing countries. This type of agreement might give a new meaning to the concept of "adjustment."

TABLE 7-1

DEVELOPING COUNTRY EXPORTS SUBJECT TO QUANTITATIVE RESTRICTIONS BY EEC MEMBER STATES AGAINST THIRD COUNTRIES APRIL 1972

S.I.T.C. Number	Export	Germany	France	Italy	Benelux
50.01	Silkworm cocoons suitable for reeling			X	
02	Raw silk (not thrown)			X	
04	Silk yarn, other than yarn of noil or other waste silk, not put up for retail sale			X	
05	Yarn spun from silk waste other than noil, not put up for retail sale			X	
06	Yarn spun from noil silk, not put up for retail sale			X	
51.04	Woven fabrics of synthetic and artificial textile fibers	X	X		
53.07	Yarn of combed sheep's or lambs' wool (worsted yarn) not put up for retail sale	X	X		
53.10	Yarn of sheep's or lambs' wool, of horsehair or of other animal hair (fine or coarse), put up for retail sale	X			
53.11	Woven fabrics of sheep's or lambs' wool or of fine animal hair	X	X		
56.07	Woven fabrics of man-made fibers (discontinuous or waste)	X	X		
57.10	Woven fabrics of jute		X		
58.01A1	Other carpets: tufted, kelim		X		
II-B					
58.04	Woven pile fabrics and chenille fabrics	X			
60.05	Outer garments and other articles, knitted or crocheted, not elastic nor rubberized	X	X		
61.01	Men's and boys' outer garments	X	X		
61.02	Women's, girls' and infants' outer garments	X	X		
61.03	Men's and boys' under garments, including collars, shirt fronts and cuffs	X	X		
61.04	Women's, girls' and infants' under garments	X			
61.05B	Handkerchiefs (other than of cotton)		X		
ex 62.03	Sacks and bags, of a kind used for the packing of goods (other than of cotton)		X		
69.07	Unglazed and glazed setts, flags and paving,		X		
69.08	hearth and wall tiles				
69.11	Tableware and other articles of a kind commonly used for domestic or toilet purposes, of porcelain or china (including biscuit porcelain and parian)	X	X		
69.12	Tableware and other articles of a kind commonly used for domestic or toilet purposes of other kinds of pottery (other than of stoneware)	X			
85.15	Transmission and reception apparatus		X		
85.21	Lamps, tubes and electric valves		X		
85.25	Insulators of any material	X	X		

Comment

Haim Barkai

The discussion which has been going on since yesterday has been focused on the rapidly improving export performance of developing countries in the 1960s. It was noted that such performance could have been even better, but for a growing battery of official and unofficial trade restrictions which have been imposed by one industrialized country after another. These developments reflect the developing countries' expansion of manufacturing capacity; the penetration of their products into world markets has been helped by the steady and inevitable erosion of the comparative advantage of the more labor-intensive branches of manufacturing in the industrialized countries.

Employers and unions in these industries, which include many old, established manufacturing activities, have been "naturally" inclined to identify competition from developing countries as the main reason for the squeeze on their profits, wages and working conditions, particularly when these are compared with the booming growth sectors. Such groups have thus been pressing for "action." In practice this generally means quantitative restrictions on competing imports. Indeed, it is the ugly face of protection which appears to have been gaining influence and political muscle in developed countries and which is making some developing country leaders ponder whether a trade oriented strategy for developing countries in the 1970s is practicable.

The quantitative data presented in Ferdnand Braun's paper, which gives an interesting empirical background of the adjustment problems of EEC countries in the 1950s and 1960s, on the whole lends support to the trade optimists. A net annual loss of 40,000 workers in the EEC textile industry through the 1970s, which by common consent has "suffered" most from developing countries competition, can hardly be a major problem. The net separation rate of 1.3 percent for textiles — the principal "declining" activity — cannot be a cause of worry in a full employment economy. The gross separation rate would probably be higher, because the industry undoubtedly has a positive accession rate. It is, however, important to note here that the inflow of labor into this low-wage industry has been heavily weighted by migrant labor from developing countries,

218 / *Haim Barkai*

particularly those of North Africa and Turkey. This, of course, means that nationals of the industrialized countries were moving into better paying and more satisfying jobs which have been created by the growth of these economies.[6]

Yet even if the very large numbers of foreign workers are not taken into consideration, the 1.3 percent annual rate of decrease of the textile industry's labor force, which represents only 0.15 percent of total employment in manufacturing, pales into insignificance in view of the performance on labor absorption by EEC countries. The German Federal Republic not only easily integrated more than 10 million workers from Eastern Europe in the 1950s and early 1960s, it was until recently still subject to labor shortages, though it had pulled several million foreign workers into its work force. France easily absorbed more than two million repatriates and an almost similar number of—mostly North African—workers during the 1960s. Similar statements apply to other EEC countries with the exception of Italy (which has, however, drawn on its south) and to several EFTA countries, too.

Thus, given full employment, even a significantly greater penetration of developing country imports would not appear to be a cause of major problems but rather necessitate only minor adjustments. Retirements and voluntary departures would appear likely to be large enough to allow for the necessary reduction of the size of the labor force in labor-intensive industries, which would have to carry the brunt of import penetration from the developing countries during the 1970s.

Yet though this is to my mind a reasonable interpretation of Ferdnand Braun's figures, and of other relevant data, the drift of his argument is rather different. He seems to suggest that the EEC countries and, by the same token, other industrialized countries do face difficult adjustment problems if the export potential of developing countries is allowed to manifest itself too rapidly in EEC markets. Branch concentration, closely related to geographical concentration, is identified by him as a major ground for the expected difficulties. The regional concentration of declining industries to

---

6. We may note in passing that a study on employment patterns of migrant labor and their relative role in various industries classified by capital intensities, wage rates and employment stability in EEC and EFTA countries would be an interesting piece of research in this context. Its relevance to the discussion on developing country export trade with industrialized countries and the debate on trade restrictions is obvious. Thus, the employment of several million workers from developing countries in the Community at the very time at which EEC governments attempt to make a case in favor of trade restrictions in view of hardships allegedly wrought on local labor by imports from developing countries is surprising.

which he alludes means that such monoindustrial regions are not only far behind the present growth foci, but lag significantly behind the average for a developed country as a whole. The distributional effects of the differentials in growth performance are obvious. So also is the political appeal of employers' organizations, unions and regional representatives for immediate relief, which in practical terms means the imposition of more restrictions on foreign, "cheap labor" competition.

These points, some of which are implicit in Ferdnand Braun's paper, have been strongly endorsed by Nat Goldfinger. Although Mr. Goldfinger has been referring to the scene in the United States, and represents presumably the present frame of mind of United States unions only, his forceful presentation does convey in essence labor fears and attitudes toward imports from developing countries in most industrialized countries. In all but identifying full employment as a situation in which any specific employment figure ever reached by an industrial branch is either maintained or improved upon, Nat Goldfinger stressed the fear of unemployment. This is certainly reasonable within a frame of mind still subject to the memory of the 1930s. These presumptions can, however, be rejected out of hand in this discussion. Surely nobody would consider strategies for developing country export drives except in a full employment context, which economists, whatever their political persuasion, believe can be maintained by what is by now a well-known mix of macroeconomic policies. Given full employment, which also means growth sectors with growing demand for labor, employment problems of stagnant industries can be handled more easily, though this would require retraining and similar adjustments. Thus, unless one believes in a Byzantine-like ossification of economic sectors suggested by Nat Goldfinger's implicit definition of full employment (in terms of specific branch employment levels), a claim that developing country imports might have a significant effect on employment in industrialized countries does not seem very persuasive.

Yet, coming down to brass tacks, the so-called regional argument in favor of trade restrictions has not only strong political appeal, which it indeed has, but also economic rationale. It is not only based on distributional grounds, it is also pegged to the perplexing issue of social benefits versus private costs.

It is this facet of the case in favor of trade restrictions, closely intertwined as it is with the distributional argument, which is not only morally and socially appealing, but which is also reasonable in purely economic terms. The case for a laissez faire policy on imports from developing countries—and indeed from any country of origin—is obviously derived from first principles of trade theory. These suggest that the phasing out of industries which are in the process of losing their competitive position together with the substitution of imports for home production, is beneficial to the (fully employed) economy which pursues this policy.[7] The corresponding movement of resources into its own growth industries—the rapid productivity gains which were the major cause of the shifts in the positions of activities on the scale of comparative advantage in the first place—would offer material benefits due to overall productivity gains to the economy as a whole. The phasing out of an industry however involves a social cost, which *ex definitio* is necessarily lower than the benefits. If only market forces are relied upon to bring into effect the required restructuring of industry, the entire social cost would be imposed on the factors of production most specific to that industry. This is mainly the labor force which has been employed in its firms. Furthermore, the more concentrated the industries subject to the phasing out process, the greater the social and therefore also the private costs imposed by the market on the individuals engaged in such industries. Since most of the benefits of the overall rising productivity would go to consumers, the benefit cost ratio to producers—that is, to the personnel employed in a declining industry—would be smaller, and inevitably significantly smaller than unity.

These private cost benefit calculations do suggest the rationale of the pressure which workers (and employers) in such industries bring to bear for policies intended to prevent or to delay the phasing out of such industries. Their campaigns for import restrictions are indeed warranted if they are expected to bear the full social cost. Furthermore, since these groups of workers are more often than not also the economically weaker elements of society, the economic argument is strengthened by considerations of equity. After all, why should they, of all people, bear all the costs while others reap almost all the benefits of growing overall productivity?

In this way it is possible to reduce Ferdnand Braun's "problem areas" argument and labor's case, usually couched in terms of equity

7. It goes without saying that the fact that developing country and other exporters would benefit from such policy, is a point in case too. Yet the benefits to "others" is evidently not a strong point in an internal debate which for some participants is an immediate bread and butter problem.

only, to the welfare economics externality argument. It then becomes clear that market forces on their own cannot be relied upon to offer an efficient, not to mention an equitable solution to this conundrum.

This inference from Pigovian welfare economics is not a matter of theory only. It is indeed the economic rationale of the adjustment assistance programs insofar as they have been attempted in the EEC, in the United Kingdom and in the United States. Such programs were devised as an attempt to overcome the social benefit-private cost impasse by means of transfer payments to labor (and to property owners), to compensate for the private cost of moving away from declining industries.

This indeed was hoped to offer the required compensation for the private costs involved in changes of the branch composition of an economy, and the corresponding reorientation of its foreign trade. And in any case, it is hard to see why labor should object to such a policy. Nevertheless, Nat Goldfinger suggested that adjustment assistance is "flim flam." He did not elaborate though he did refer to the "small change" which has been offered as compensation in the United States. Though probably not intended for that purpose, Ferdnand Braun's data for the EEC upholds this deprecating view of the programs as carried into effect. According to Braun's estimates, the EEC has been disbursing $50 million annually in the 1960s for this purpose. The enlarged "Social Fund" of the Community which is to finance structural adjustments in the 1970s is about to rise to an order of $200-$250 million.[8] This budgeted flow, which is prima facie a breakthrough, amounts to only 0.05 percent of the Gross National Product of the Six. The funds allocated for this purpose in the United States through the 1960s were probably even lower in relative terms. Now as trade restrictions cost consumers, say, at least one-quarter to one-half of one percent of GNP in the EEC and in the United States, disbursements of this order are "peanuts" indeed. It is thus easy to see why trade unionists believe that adjustment assistance programs have failed and should be conveyed to the scrap heap. My reading of these figures, of course, suggests something quite different. They indicate to my mind that adjustment assistance in the genuine sense of the term has never yet been tried.

---

8. It goes without saying that most of the expected adjustments are due to the growing integration of the economies of member countries and not due to branch restructuring induced by competition from developing country imports.

Adjustment assistance moreover also implies the need for a proper framework for programs which are to facilitate interbranch factor mobility. Since for the larger industrial countries, the productivity gains from more rapid adjustments can be easily counted in billions of dollars, the funds which are to "bribe away" factors from activities which are losing, or are about to lose their comparative advantage, must be of similar orders of magnitude. Moreover, the policy must also be conceived within the general context of the dynamics of the industrial structure, and not only within the context of adaptation to growing imports in certain lines.[9] It must therefore also be devised accordingly. Thus, the real hope for the reduction of barriers to developing country exports depends on the industrialized countries' application of a "grand concept" to the economic and social problems generated by their own growth.

Comment

Juergen Donges

This paper by Ferdnand Braun is particularly rewarding, largely because it gives a very detailed picture of the practical problems which the adjustment process in the EEC may involve, and of the possibilities of overcoming these problems. There is not very much I can find to quarrel with in this statement. Much has already been said by Haim Barkai, so I propose to restrict my remarks to the case of the Federal Republic of Germany. As Ferdnand Braun's paper shows, there is obviously some diversity of opinions of policies among the EEC members, so that it seems worthwhile to me to concentrate on the one country with which I am most familiar, and to make some amplifying remarks on the paper. I do it with the full knowledge of Ferdnand Braun's apparent comparative advantage in this topic, derived from his fifteen years of international service in the European integration movement.

The Federal Republic's policy-makers seem to be aware of the fact that the country must allow manufactured products from developing countries into the market if developing countries are to

9. It goes without saying that the term *adjustment assistance* is unfortunate, not only because it smacks of "welfare," but also because it fails to convey the economic and social rationale of the program.

succeed in their industrialization efforts. Interestingly enough, the Federal Government officially stated in February 1971 that structural adjustment constitutes an indispensable requirement for the improved international division of labor. It also emphasized that structural changes caused by the process of integrating the developing countries in international trade should not be delayed, but encouraged by appropriate structural adjustment measures. This is a serious—and within the EEC a unique—commitment; the question is, will the government succeed or will it fail in fulfilling it? That is, provided it is not in any case a question of lip-service, how does the present trade, structural and regional policy fit in with such a commitment?

The tariff structure in the Federal Republic of Germany (as in many other industrial countries) is still biased against imports of manufactures from developing countries. Among the labor-intensive industries we found (for 1970) effective rates of tariff protection of 23.4 percent for paper manufactures, 21.5 percent for clothing, 21.2 percent for textiles, 16.4 percent for ceramics, 15.5 percent for leather manufactures, 15 percent for wood products and 13.2 percent for footwear. The industrial average is 11.9 percent. In addition, there are still important quantitative restrictions in force, and likely to be increased, particularly for the benefit of the domestic clothing and textile industries whose growth has become stunted because they are no longer able to compete with foreign producers. Furthermore, the extensive, and sometimes prohibitive nontariff barriers on processed agricultural products, in which many developing countries might have comparative advantages, are too well known to need further comment. The system of tariff preferences for developing countries introduced by the EEC in mid-1971 surely can be regarded as an attempt to open more of the market. But I hesitate to share Ferdnand Braun's positive evaluation of this attempt. The scheme suffers from several shortcomings, which are reflected in the fact that it is the more generous the less competitive the preference-receiving commodities are, and/or the more inelastic the export supply is. Manufactures which are of greatest export interest to developing countries because of their supply potential, such as textiles and shoes, must from year to year expect to become fully dutiable again. Such regulations seem to be of economically dubious wisdom because they provide relatively higher incentives for activities in which the developing countries are not likely to have, under given factor endowments, any comparative advantages.

So far as structural and regional policy is concerned, there is also discrimination against developing countries. Investments of all kinds undertaken in so-called backward (mostly peripheral) areas enjoy a subsidy equivalent to 25 percent of the outlay. There are also some additional, more or less hidden incentives given to industries in these areas. Thanks to these provisions, branches which have to compete significantly with imports of manufactures from the developing countries are able to continue production and to delay structural adaptation to the changing external circumstances. We find ourselves in the paradoxical situation that, while manufacturers in developing countries are inhibited from entering the German market, there is no impediment to free immigration of cheap labor (whose number now amounts to 10 percent of the Federal Republic's labor force). There can hardly be any doubt that it would be more advantageous to substitute labor-intensive products for labor: the Federal Republic of Germany would be able to avoid additional environmental costs; in the emigrant areas the chances to mitigate the existing unemployment problems would improve.

This apparent inconsistency between official commitments and actual policies in the Federal Republic results from the very effective pressure toward protectionism exerted by domestic producers and labor unions. The main arguments of both groups are five in number: first, it is said that unhindered imports from developing countries will lead to severe disruption of domestic markets; secondly, it is stressed that developing countries have anomalous competitive advantages because of their relatively low wages; thirdly, it is asserted that many developing countries derive competitive advantages from price dumping; fourthly, it is emphasized that only a few developing countries would benefit from a nondiscriminatory opening of markets; and fifthly, it is contended that while other industrial countries, particularly the United States and Japan, do not facilitate access of developing countries' exports to their markets, the Federal Republic of Germany would have to absorb the lion's share of these exports. Obviously the arguments are rather similar to those of Nat Goldfinger. The economic logic of most of these arguments is unsatisfactory, but Ferdnand Braun is correct in emphasizing that ignoring these arguments could cause substantial political problems, which every government wants to avoid.

What can be done? The crux of the problem is the fact that structural changes caused by increased imports from developing countries can be supposed to be in the form of interindustry, rather than intraindustry, specialization. This aspect of the problem is now well recognized. It means that more imports from lower-wage countries will have an impact on particular domestic industries and in particular regions or localities. This may be felt as an unjust hardship, because of the contraction of sales, reduction of profit margins, and the loss of jobs, particularly by female workers. On the other hand, historical experience clearly shows that the capability of an economy to adjust its production and employment structure to the changing structure of demand, technical progress and shifts in the international division of labor, is a necessary condition for economic growth. The Federal Republic's profound reallocation of resources during the last twenty years of rapid economic growth is, moreover, an excellent example of the possibilities of a positive reaction to changing comparative advantage. In comparison with these structural changes, the extent of structural adjustment associated with increased manufactured imports from developing countries is most likely to be within manageable orders of magnitude. For example, calculations carried out recently by Gerhard Fels and Jurgen Horn in the Kiel Institute conclude that an increase of manufactured imports from developing countries to the Federal Republic of Germany, at least at the historical rate of the sixties, would cause a reallocation of about 400,000 jobs within the next ten years, affecting five primary material-intensive branches and ten labor-intensive ones. The annual rate of labor turnover would lie in the order of one percent of employment in these sensitive sectors. This is much less than the substantial displacement of workers from the European coal industry in the fifties which took place rapidly and without causing too many strains to those affected.

However, although the impact of increased imports from developing countries is not likely to be very sizable in terms of production and employment, I agree with Ferdnand Braun that some assistance should be provided by the government to neutralize resistance against increasingly liberal import policy, and to enable the process of structural adjustment to take place. The question then arises, what kind of assistance and for whom? I would like to add three remarks to Ferdnand Braun's on this point. First, it would probably be a mistake if assistance is extended to "damaged" owners of fixed assets in the form of socialization of losses. Such assistance would reduce the risk of investment carried out today or in the future, thereby delaying rather than encouraging the process of structural readjustment. Secondly, it makes more sense to provide capital grants at preferential terms or investment subsidies to "damaged" entrepreneurs who are willing to engage in new ventures. If the shift of production occurs within the Federal Republic of Germany, assistance should only be given for those activities in which that country has comparative advantages. If production is shifted to developing countries financial help for this purpose should be linked with the number of jobs created there, in order to promote actively the use of labor-intensive techniques. Thirdly, assistance to affected workers should focus on their resettlement and their retraining for new jobs so that they command better income possibilities in the future, and on premature retirement for older workers. The Vocational Training Law and Law for the Promotion of Work, both enacted in the recent past, contain several provisions of this type; what is needed now is that these laws are consistently applied. Assistance to capital and labor should be limited in time in order to avoid it becoming a permanent device for the collectivization of private risks.

I agree with Ferdnand Braun that regional policy is an indispensable complement to any adjustment assistance program. But there is no need to think only in terms of alternative industrial activities which have to be created in areas affected by increased imports from developing countries. At least in the Federal Republic of Germany, the service sector lags behind overall economic development. This can be shown by cross-section analyses according to which the share of this sector in the Federal Republic's gross domestic product is lower than one would have expected of a hypothetical country with similar per capita income and population. Under these circumstances it seems worthwhile to think about the possibility of promoting certain service activities, such as tourism, training centers, and hospitals, in the sensitive regions. These activities are not only labor-intensive, but also capable of absorbing a large, relatively high proportion of female workers.

Whatever the assistance measures applied, I would plead for as many anticipatory actions as possible. Ferdnand Braun is probably right in his assumption that the practical problems involved are tremendous. However, economic history is full of examples where the fear of the "tremendous practical problems" has induced policymakers to do the right things too late, if at all, and therefore at high social cost. I think that it is possible to identify industrial activities which are likely to come under increasing competitive pressure by exports from developing countries. If the government makes it definitely clear to producers and workers that international competition in a well-functioning market system never takes place under conditions of equality, and if it provides the whole industrial community with structural guidelines including structural benchmarks, there is no reason to doubt that entrepreneurs will try to adapt themselves in advance to forthcoming changes in order to survive. Adjustment assistance measures could then be more effective and less expensive than if the government waits until specific industries have become sick and can only be kept alive through protection and government subsidies. In practice, of course, it normally proves difficult to apply an anticipatory trade, structural and regional policy because of the existence of nationalistic or neomercantilistic philosophies which justify the preservation of actually or potentially "old" industries. The Federal Republic of Germany currently shows a strong tendency toward economic nationalism. Fortunately for the policy-makers this can be concealed somewhat by pointing to a loss of sovereignty, since such actions can only be carried out under the auspices of the EEC. But it is well known that the EEC policy is strongly influenced by less liberally oriented trade policies, such as those of France and Italy, and that it is more related to producers' than to consumers' interests.

A final remark as to the administrative difficulties and the budgetary costs of a program of adjustment assistance may be in order. Ferdnand Braun rightly refers to them, but it seems to me that the scope of the problem is generally overestimated. Highly industrialized countries have, by definition, the administrative infrastructure for applying even the most complex regulations; the EEC bureaucracy in fact provides many examples in this respect. The costs of adjustment assistance may be high, but they have to be weighed against the contribution which structural change can make to economic growth and welfare in industrialized countries as well as in developing countries. To explore this more might be an interesting field for further research.

8

The Japanese Experience and Attitudes Toward Trade Adjustment

Kiyoshi Kojima

The international economy has run into another period of uncertainty. There is a challenging need for a new stimulus to trade expansion and for the growth of economic interdependence to project it forward once more. Steady and dynamic development of the Third World should provide one such force; another is likely to derive from the enlargement of the EEC.

The creation of new products and technologies and the transformation of each country's industrial structure as part of an expansive and harmonious international division of labor should be complementary to these forces. Japan's aim throughout the coming decade will be to expand the new technology-based, or so-called knowledge-intensive industries which consist of more sophisticated heavy and chemical industry products and software. Such expansion will open up wider opportunities for increased imports of processed raw materials and metals, both from advanced and developing countries, and of textiles and other labor-intensive manufactures, mainly from developing countries.

Japan should undertake positive, hopefully dramatic policy measures to promote the developing countries' economic progress. Japan has accumulated substantial foreign exchange reserves, trade with advanced countries cannot be expected to grow as smoothly as it has in the past, but assistance to the developing countries to insure the expansion of mutually beneficial trade is promising. Trade between the Japanese and developing economies is already basically complementary. There is plenty of scope for Japan to adjust its industrial structure, thus to increase imports of developing countries' primary as well as manufactured imports. How to "live on trade with developing countries" may be one of the main foci for Japanese economic policy in the 1970s.

The establishment of a new international division of labor between advanced (the North) and less developed (the South) countries is a task for Japan, the United States and other advanced countries.

However much involved they are in their own troubles, once they develop a common purpose, they can find new solutions to their mutual trade adjustment problems. Reorganization of the North-South trade is a major target in the 1970s for Japan as well as other advanced countries; here Japan's role and responsibility is crucial. This will require cooperation in development assistance programs fostering their own structural adjustment in accordance with the developing countries' growing comparative advantages, and in expanding trade with developing countries. It may be that among advanced countries, those of the Pacific have the most incentive for such cooperation.

This paper first explores Japanese attitudes toward the changing international division of labor from the viewpoint that structural adjustment in developed countries is essential to reorganization of the trade between developed and developing countries. Section II examines the origins of Japan's successful industrialization with the aim of drawing policy implications for developing countries. In Section III, Japan's aid and foreign investment policies are discussed and evaluated alongside American policies. Finally, in Section IV Japan's trade policy towards developing countries is examined, and experience with adjustment assistance policies reported. The conclusion stresses the need for an integrated aid, investment-*cum*-preference and structural adjustment policy.

I. THE REORGANIZATION OF NORTH-SOUTH TRADE

Japan's optimum and government-declared policy is to expand mutual trade with every trading region. The country's present stage of industrialization, dual pattern of trade with developed and developing countries, and geographic location dictate such a choice. But it is also true that Japan's main interest continues to be directed toward the Asian-Pacific region. Japan hence sees its role in the coming decade as promoting a harmonious reorganization of the North-South trade in this region; this will require a large-scale aid in-vestment-*cum*-preference structural adjustment scheme.

Japan's economic growth in the 1970s may decelerate somewhat compared with growth performance in the 1960s, but it will con-tinue at about 9 percent per annum in real terms, or 17 percent per annum in current dollar price terms. Thus, gross national product could be $957 billion by 1980, compared with $200 billion in 1970. This is not an excessively optimistic forecast since there was sus-tained growth in Japanese real income of around 11.4 percent per annum on average throughout the last decade, and considerably higher growth rates were achieved after 1965. In 1970, Japan's ex-ports amounted to $19.4 billion and her imports to $15.7 billion. By 1980, Japan will have become the largest trading nation after the United States, with exports around $92.2 billion and a 10.8 percent share in total world trade.[1]

Trade with Southeast Asian countries and with the United States is equally important for Japan, each direction accounting for a third of total trade. Japan's trade with Southeast Asia has provided, and will continue to provide a large export surplus. In 1970, Japan's ex-ports to the area amounted to $4.9 billion, and imports were $2.4 billion in return (both in f.o.b. values), the imbalance ratio being 2:1. Even if Japan tries to increase its imports faster than its exports to the area, in 1980 exports will be $19.1 billion and imports $10.3 billion, the imbalance ratio still being 1.85:1. Filling this gap is a task for Japan. Moreover, because of the rapid increase of Japan's trade with Southeast Asia, Japanese goods will account for 40 percent of the area's total imports. This might well invite Asian antagonism towards Japanese domination.

Coupled with heavy trade dependence, the increased aid and in-vestment flows presage a testing time for Japan's economic relations with Asian countries. This will be a major challenge to Japanese eco-nomic diplomacy in the seventies and it will require a new under-standing of Asian problems and aspirations. Japan's policies toward developing countries should be focused on how to increase trade between Japan and developing countries, especially in the Asian

---

1. *Japan's Economy in 1980 in the Global Context* (Tokyo: Japan Economic Research Center, 1972). This projection seems to be mildly overoptimistic, but is used in this paper as a reasonable reference point.

region. Through trade growth, Asian economies are able to benefit from the rapid growth of the Japanese economy and promote their own economic development. How can Japan increase her imports from developing countries much faster than the growth rate of gross national product however? Further trade liberalization and the provision of general preferences and other incentives favorable to the exports of developing countries are required. It is crucial for Japan to foster an industrial readjustment policy aimed at the contraction of those industries in which developing countries already have or are gaining comparative advantage. On the other hand, export capacity should be created and increased in developing countries. To accomplish this, Japanese aid and investments should play an important role in the efficient reorganization of the North-South trade in the Asian-Pacific Area.

Currently, the North-South problem seems to be facing a turning point: there is a shift in emphasis from aid and trade expansion of a "surplus disposal" type to that of a "structural adjustment" type.

Structural adjustment in developed countries is an essential element if new development policies are to be successful. Multilateral and nondiscriminatory free trade is most important if world trade is to be increased. How to provide the basic conditions necessary to realize and maintain the free trade system is an important problem to be explored at present. The international monetary system must be revised so that balance of payments disequilibrium is quickly and frequently adjusted by *a more flexible adjustable-peg system.* Then, many tariff and nontariff barriers to trade which have been introduced, mainly for balance of payments reasons, can be eliminated. However, as a prerequisite for trade liberalization and smooth adjustment of balance of payments, *structural adjustment is needed* in each country's industries in response to changes in comparative costs. Inefficient, old industries which have lost comparative advantage should be contracted and capital and employment must be transferred to other growing sectors through adjustment assistance policies. To do this development centers will have to be created. How to cure overall unemployment is another difficult task in structural adjustment.

The need for industrial structural adjustment, and for new trade relations, has been more keenly recognized in Japan in recent times. Five factors support the emergence of a new structure in production and trade. First, the availability of land and harbor facilities suitable for heavy industrial expansion is extremely limited. Secondly, the problems of environmental pollution are extremely serious, mainly because of inadequate governmental control but also because of the constraints of geography. Thirdly, the logistic problems of supplying basic heavy industries with raw materials and energy from abroad will become too large to manage economically. In consequence it will be necessary to restructure production toward activities which require less basic raw material and energy fuel. This implies a relocation abroad of basic industrial capacity to service Japan's requirements for intermediate manufactured goods. In part, this relocation can be assisted by Japanese participation in investment abroad, and it can also proceed through the establishment of links with reliable independent suppliers. Fourthly, Japanese labor-intensive manufactures, including traditional light industries such as textiles, will lose their competitiveness in international markets as Japanese wages rise in step with national income. It can be confidently expected that by 1980 the Japanese worker will enjoy a thirty-five-hour, five-day working week and that wages will be about four times their present level. Fifthly, because of labor shortage in manufacturing and service sectors and rapidly rising wages, inefficient and small-scale farmers will have to be transferred to these sectors, with only modern large farms being retained.

Throughout the coming decade, the Japanese aim will be to expand the new technology-based, or so-called knowledge-intensive industries. They are not yet well identified, but in the early 1980s, research and development-intensive industries such as computers, aircraft, electric cars and other transport systems; complex assembly industries, such as communications equipment, office machinery, pollution control instruments and equipment, and construction machinery; fashion industries, such as sophisticated clothing, furniture and musical instruments; and the information industry, will all become important and competitive sectors of the Japanese economy.[2] Such industries may be seen as belonging to the more sophisticated heavy and chemical industry product groups.

These structural adjustments will take place gradually by the early 1980s, creating a huge outlet for developing country products. But the heavy and chemical industries will continue to dominate export specialization throughout most of the seventies; and raw materials will remain a key factor in import specialization until late in the decade, when there will be larger imports of intermediate goods. Meanwhile, a huge amount of industrial raw materials and

---

2. *Trade and Industrial Policies in the 1970s* (Tokyo: Ministry of International Trade and Industry, 1971).

fuel will be required to service Japanese industrial growth; in 1980, Japan will represent 30 percent of the world market for these commodities. Securing stable supplies at reasonable prices is now a major task. Increasing imports of cheaper foodstuffs will be another. New sources of supply both of raw materials and foodstuffs will have to be developed all round the world, but Asian-Pacific countries will hold a large share in the growing market. In the coming decade, it is quite certain that, as structural adjustments proceed successfully on both sides, a large market will be opened in Japan for labor-intensive manufactures from nearby Asian suppliers.

Knowledge-intensive industrialization has several important implications. Because of the lack of natural resources and availability of able and industrious manpower, the Japanese economy has developed for the last 100 years basically through "processing trade," that is, importing raw materials, manufacturing them for domestic use and export except for the exports of staples such as tea and silk in the early days. Concern about balance of payments problems, among other things, has produced policies aimed at maximum domestic processing, protection of infant industries and restraint in the import of consumer manufactures, although machinery and equipment necessary to import-substituting industrialization remained an important element in imports.

Successive new industries have been nurtured in the process of Japanese industrialization over the past 100 years, but there were two major structural changes.[3] The first was light industrialization, which began around 1900 and accelerated after World War I. The second was heavy and chemical industrialization, which started in the late 1930s but succeeded after World War II, 1955-65. These structural changes and diversification and upgrading of industrial structure contributed to a decrease in the import-GNP ratio from 21 percent in the 1920s to 8 percent in 1970 due to the lower imported raw material content of the heavy and chemical industries as compared with the light industries (mainly cotton textiles) and to the substitution of imported machinery and equipment for domestic production. In other words, to save import content and to increase domestic value-added have been the major objectives in industrialization of the processing trade type. Now, it is felt that there should be a shift towards knowledge intensive industrialization, a third significant structural change.

---

3. Kiyoshi Kojima, *Japan and a Pacific Free Trade Area* (London: Macmillan, 1971), pp.9-12.

In the 1960s, the industrial structure of Japan shifted rapidly towards heavy and chemical industries catching up with the pattern of more advanced economies. In Japan's exports, foodstuffs and raw materials and fuels are unimportant. Almost all exports are manufactured goods (Table 8-1). The share in total exports of light industrial goods decreased from 53.5 percent in 1955 to 22.4 percent in 1970 and is expected to decline further to 11.9 percent in 1980, according to the latest Japanese Economic Research Center (JERC) projection. On the other hand, the share of heavy and chemical goods increased rapidly from 38.0 percent in 1955 to 72.4 percent in 1970 and will rise to 86.3 percent in 1980.

A somewhat different classification of export commodities (Table 8-2) shows that the share of commodities originating from technology-intensive industries in Japanese exports increased, and will increase further.

How are these changes reflected in import structure? In 1955, more than half of total imports consisted of raw materials (Table 8-3). Besides raw materials, foodstuffs and mineral fuels were essential imports for Japan's development of processing trade. Only 11.9 percent of total imports comprised manufactures, largely essential machinery and chemicals. Heavy and chemical industrialization in the 1960s brought about smaller relative dependence on imports of raw materials but this was almost compensated for by the increased dependence on imported mineral fuels. Further savings in these two items is one of the targets for the coming knowledge-intensive industrialization in the 1970s. On the other hand, the importance of imports of processed manufactures increased from 11.9 percent in 1955 to 30.3 percent in 1970 which is still lower than the corresponding ratio for other advanced countries; for example, 50.7 percent for the United Kingdom, 59.2 percent for the Federal Republic of Germany and 66.2 percent for the United States. It is expected, if the knowledge-intensive industrialization is successful, that processed manufactures will amount to about half total imports, resulting in increased horizontal trade in machinery (imports in 1980 are estimated to be $16.9 billion) and chemicals ($5.1 billion) mainly with other advanced countries and also the increased vertical trade in other manufactures ($22.3 billion) with developing countries and natural resource processing nations. The JERC estimated that in 1980, 37 percent of Japan's imports from Southeast Asia will consist of other manufactures (textiles and other labor-intensive products), amounting to $4.1 billion.

THE JAPANESE EXPERIENCE / 235

Before 1965, the Japanese trade balance (or current account balance) was generally in deficit, and business expansion was checked on three occasions by balance of payments problems. Government policy therefore sought to restrain imports and promote exports. Not only agriculture but almost all manufacturing industries, old as well as new, were protected from foreign competition through tariffs, quota restrictions and other nontariff barriers, and they were encouraged through lower interest subsidy and tax incentives. A first phase of Japan's trade liberalization came from 1960 to 1963. The trade balance turned to surplus in 1965, and another liberalization phase began in 1969-1971.[4]

The shift in the trade balance position has, indeed, seen a change from protectionist attitudes toward a new philosophy. The change, however, takes a long time. First, it was thought that the trade surplus was merely a short-run phenomenon and not a long-run trend. Secondly, the economic community was not ready to accept the new philosophy overnight, since protectionist policies had been so intensive, and so successful in assisting exports to grow almost twice as rapidly as world trade. Although a change toward a new philosophy has been taking place gradually since 1965 and dramatically in the last two years, the Japanese economy is not yet ready to open its market more widely for developing countries' manufactures and semimanufactures. Before this can be done a third structural change is urgently required to upgrade Japanese industries. It seems to me that the delay in structural adjustment of the Japanese economy vis-à-vis developing countries is hindering the latter's industrialization and trade growth. The economic position of Japan today may be compared with the United Kingdom in 1932 when it decided to favor textiles and other manufactures of a labor-intensive type under the Imperial preference scheme.

Structural adjustment policy usually focuses its attention on contracting old, comparatively disadvantageous sectors of the economy; however, promoting the growth of new, comparatively advantageous sectors is equally important. The cure of overall unemployment is another problem which relates directly to the degree of flexibility and cost of adjustment programs. This may be the most serious problem for such "mature" economies as the United States and the United Kingdom, but not for Japan which is still "young" and suffers from labor shortages. Structural adjustment in declining,

---

4. For more detailed analysis, see below, section entitled Japan's Trade Policy and Structural Adjustment.

inefficient sectors is undertaken successfully only in a dynamic economy in which the growth sectors' expansion is rapid enough so that resources from contracting sectors may be absorbed smoothly. Japan's structural adjustment has a number of facets.

First, knowledge-intensive industrialization implies a partial shift from the processing type of trade pattern to the export of products based upon human resources with little import of overseas raw materials. This is applicable to pure knowledge products such as information services, technological know-how, computer programming, fashion design and managerial skill on a contract basis. Exports of more sophisticated heavy and chemical products decrease dependence on overseas raw materials per unit of production and export. Thus, increased export of knowledge-intensive products itself contributes to the reduction of the import to gross national product ratio.

Secondly, heavy industrial expansion in Japan will slow down for the various reasons already mentioned. This implies a relocation abroad of basic industrial capacity and increased imports of intermediate manufactured goods. There will thus be wider markets for countries with abundant natural resources.

Thirdly, if knowledge-intensive industrialization is successful it will become possible to transfer resources from traditional industries, mainly textiles and other labor-intensive type industries. This will result in the opening of a wide market for manufactures from developing countries. It is expected that knowledge-intensive industrialization will accelerate the transfer of resources from small- and medium-scale industries, which is the hard core problem for structural adjustment policy, because many knowledge-intensive industries are suitable not only to large-scale but also to small- and medium-scale enterprise.

Fourthly, if the expansion of exports in knowledge-intensive products is sufficiently large, the Japanese economy will be able to continue to grow rapidly with a lower import/GNP ratio. There is a reconsideration of policies designed simply to foster export expansion and restrain imports, resulting in a waste of domestic resources and neglect of social welfare. There is a need to increase public investment in infrastructure, antipollution measures, housing, social security and the like. This will also contribute to a reduction in export growth and the import/GNP ratio. Too fast a growth of Japanese exports is criticized increasingly and orderly marketing is urged upon exporters. Knowledge-intensive industrialization will make it possible to overcome these problems.

Thus, there is a strong belief that upgrading the industrial structure in Japan (and other advanced countries) through knowledge-intensive industrialization would also favor the industrialization of developing countries and as such facilitate the reorganization of North-South trade. But this solution crucially depends upon the prosperity of horizontal trade in knowledge-intensive products between advanced countries. The promotion of this trade also needs serious consideration. In this sense, the North-South trade problem cannot be separated from the problem of maintaining harmonious growth in trade among advanced countries.

II. INDUSTRIALIZATION AND TRADE GROWTH IN JAPAN

The success of Japan's knowledge-intensive industrialization is not only important to its own economic development but also for the creation of a new division of international trade both with developing and developed countries. Although such industrialization may not be an easy task, it can be undertaken determinedly and with the prospect of rapid progress, since the Japanese economy has had plenty of experience in fostering structural change successfully in the past.

In Japan, Dr. Akamatsu, Professor Emeritus of Hitotsubashi University, propounded a "catching-up product cycle" theory as early as the mid-1930s, preceding Professor Vernon's "product cycle" thesis.[5] He originally called it "the wild geese-flying pattern" *(Ganko keitai)* of industrial development in developing countries since, as shown in Figure 8-2, the time-series curve for imports of a particular product is followed by that of domestic production and later by that of exports, suggesting, according to Prof. Akamatsu, a pattern like "wild geese flying in orderly ranks forming an inverse V, just as airplanes fly in formation."[6]

The concern of Vernon and others[7] was to explain how a new product is invented and manufactured on a large scale in leading industrial countries (Figure 8-1). Exports of this product grow insofar

5. Raymond Vernon, "International Investment and International Trade in the Product Cycle," *Quarterly Journal of Economics* LXXX, no. 2 (May 1966): 190-207.

6. Kaname Akamatsu, "A Historical Pattern of Economic Growth in Developing Countries" in *The Developing Economies* (Tokyo: The Institute of Asian Economic Affairs, 1962), p.11; idem, "A Theory of Unbalanced Growth in the World Economy," *Weltwirtschaftliches Archiv* 86, no. 2 (1961): 205-8. This theory is widely recognized by now. For examples, see Benjamin Higgins, *Economic Development: Problems, Principles and Policies,* rev. ed. (New York: W.W. Norton, 1969), pp.623-24; Miyohei Shinohara, *Growth and Cycles in the Japanese Economic Development* (Tokyo: Kinokuniya Ltd., 1962), pp.57-58.

7. For example, Gary E. Hufbauer, *Synthetic Materials and the Theory of International Trade* (London: Gerald Duckworth and Co. Ltd., 1966).

as a "technological gap" exists between the product developing country and foreign countries. Foreign producers imitate the new technology and follow suit. Then exports slow down and through direct investment an attempt is made to secure foreign markets. When the technology is standardized and widely disseminated and the limit of scale economies is reached, trade based on wage costs, or factor proportions, starts and the country turns to import this product from abroad.

In a developing, or catching-up country, the product cycle starts from the importation of the new product with superior quality. "Imports reconnoiter and map out the country's demand," and once increased demand approaches the domestic production threshold, domestic production can be economically started.[8] A learning process follows and is assisted by the importation of technological know-how and/or foreign direct investment. The expansion of production then leads to the exploitation of economies of scale, increases in productivity, improvements in quality and reductions in costs. This involves an import-substitution process. But as domestic costs reach the international competitive cost threshold, foreign markets are developed, the scale of production is extended further and costs are reduced again. Thus, the expansion of exports that is originally made possible by the growth of domestic demand, in its turn, provides a stimulus to industrial development.[9] In sum, it may be appropriate to call such successive development of imports-domestic production-export the catching-up product cycle. It should be noted that such a product cycle takes place only for standardized, rather than new products, and in developing, rather than in industrialized countries.

What factors contributed to successful development along catching-up product cycle lines in Japan? It is taken for granted that each successive product enjoyed the increased demand, domestic as well as foreign. The key to successful catching-up product cycle development was long-run decreasing costs of the nature revealed clearly for steel, automobiles and so on. Foreign direct investment and technological know-how were certainly important but the technological adaptability, active management and industrious skill of the Japanese were much more important. Foreign technology was often amended and assimilated in a way which made its application in Japan more efficient.

---

8. Albert O. Hirschman, *The Strategy of Economic Development* (New Haven, Conn.: Yale University Press, 1958), p.121.

9. Cf., Kojima, op. cit., p.13.

In the stage of import-substitution, various types of protection for infant industries were granted, including protective tariffs and subsidies.[10] For certain key industries (especially steel, shipbuilding, trucks, and so on) government purchases assured demand in the early stages of development.

To grow successfully from the import-substitution stage to the exporting stage costs have to become lower than international prices, and good quality has to be achieved. Even then there are a number of difficulties of the kind now being faced by developing countries in the barriers to new entry into advanced country markets. Policy-makers may justify assistance to "infant trade," instead of to infant industry.

Barriers to new entry in advanced economies include, besides tariffs and other ordinary barriers, (1) economies of scale which advanced country enterprise has but developing country enterprise has not realized; (2) advanced technology which advanced country enterprise monopolizes and developing country enterprise can only use with royalty or through foreign direct-investment; (3) product differentiation in brand or design which makes adaptation by developing countries difficult; and (4) other barriers such as marketing and information networks, vertical and horizontal integration in production and sales are only possessed by large multinational corporations. Because of these barriers developing countries may be wise to utilize the advantages of multinational enterprises through direct investment.

Japan's unique general trading firms[11] played an important role in the expansion of trade. Their hundreds of subsidiaries and branches throughout the world were able to identify where Japan's comparative advantage lay, and to participate substantially in Japan's direct investments abroad. Developing countries could establish similar organizations, use Japanese trading firms facilities, or do both.

After World War II, the Japanese government established the Japan External Trade Organization (JETRO) for trade promotion and information. The government also provided effective incentives for export promotion[12] through tax reductions for export earnings

---

10. See Ippei Yamazawa, "Industry Growth and Foreign Trade: A Study of Japan's Steel Industry," *Hitotsubashi Journal of Economics,* forthcoming; idem, "Industrial Growth and Tariff Protection in Prewar Japan," *[Hitotsubashi Daigaku] Keizai Kenyu* 24, no. 1 (January 1973): 22-34, indicates how such industries as computers, automobiles and steel in postwar Japan have developed in close cooperation between business and government.

11. The ten largest firms, in the 1970 fiscal year, handled $21.9 billion or 55.6 percent of Japan's imports and exports.

12. See Kiyoshi Kojima, "Nontariff Barriers to Japan's Trade," *Hitotsubashi Journal of Economics* 13, no. 1 (June 1972): 1-39.

and subsidized interest rates for export financing, long-term export credit on a deferred payment basis, and subsidies for export and export-oriented production which were designed to encourage exports by influencing the profitability of enterprises engaged in export activity. Reparation payments and tied aid were managed to give exporting activity extra profit. Export interest subsidization worked particularly effectively. Incentive interest rates are accorded to foreign exchange bills which conform to the rule of standard settlement. Such trade bills become eligible to be discounted by, or qualified as collateral acceptable to the Bank of Japan, and enjoy the benefit of discount or borrowing at interest rates lower than those prevalent in the country.[13] Early availability of export earnings discounted with lower interest rates is a significant benefit for an enterprise compared to longer deferred payments in domestic marketing. Total export incentives made it profitable to export goods at, say, 10 percent to 15 percent less than domestic prices. This, however, led to some waste of resources, as well as to accusations of "dumping" from abroad. Such practices should be fully rectified as soon as possible.

Marginal pricing practices in exports, particularly of mass production type goods, is common in Japan and is even encouraged by the government, as can be seen from the *White Papers* of the Economic Planning Agency and the Ministry of Trade and Industry.

To diversify and upgrade the industrial structure of an economy is another difficult task which needs much broader macroeconomic consideration than the present paper can cover. I believe that the structure of comparative advantages is basically regulated and changed by factor-proportions à la Heckscher-Ohlin theory.[14] Diversification and upgrading of the industrial structure usually implies progress toward more capital and technology-intensive industry and production processes. To accumulate capital (inclusive of such human capital as scientists, engineers, managerial skill, skilled labor and so on) and to raise the capital/labor endowment ratio is the major force for economic development.

The Japanese economy accumulated capital by limiting the demonstration effect on consumption in the early period of industrialization, and attaining a high rate of saving. A comparison of the

---

13. In fact, the Bank of Japan raised interest rates on export-related loans to the level of interest rates on domestic-related loans effective August 10, 1971, thus eliminating export incentives with regard to interest rates. However, the system itself which gives special treatment to export credits has been retained.

14. Cf., Hal B. Lary, *Imports of Manufactures from Less Developed Countries* (New York: Columbia University Press, 1968).

capital/labor endowment ratio with those abroad should dictate the choice of industries with appropriate factor intensities. When the economy expands excessively through structural change, it must choose production processes with lower capital-intensities in all industries, resulting in a setback in per capita income. But once the structural change is accomplished and capital accumulates further, then the economy can enjoy a steady growth. It is also usual for an economy to suffer from trade deficits in periods of structural change and enjoy trade surpluses in later periods.[15]

The Japanese economy has perhaps been fortunate because its industrial take-off was relatively early. The economy could find markets abroad for its industrial output, its domestic market rose with incomes, and it was large enough to enable large-scale intermediate capital goods industries to be established.

Compared with the Japanese experience, developing countries now confront two basic problems. First, many developing countries already have a clear comparative advantage in labor-intensive goods such as in textile and clothing, and there is a considerable danger of oversupply of these goods and a consequent fall in the commodity terms of trade unless advanced countries foster accommodating structural change, thereby opening wider markets for developing country exports. This can be clearly understood when Figures 8-1 and 8-2 are compared.

Secondly, developing countries tend to be overambitious in wishing to establish intermediate capital goods industries. Some countries' economies have reached a stage where this is economic, but others must reconsider whether their factor endowments allow the establishment of such industries, or whether such investment is not overambitious. Many have to overcome the smallness of their domestic market either through economic integration among neighboring developing countries, or through production integration with advanced countries.

III. JAPAN'S AID AND FOREIGN INVESTMENT POLICY

The Japanese economy's move towards knowledge-intensive industrialization implies a basic switch from the type of development characterized by the catching-up product cycle to the creation of its own product cycles. The Japanese economy should enter into in-

---

15. Such a model is presented in Kiyoshi Kojima, "Capital Accumulation and the Course of Industrialization, with Special Reference to Japan," *Economic Journal* LXX (December 1960): 757-68.

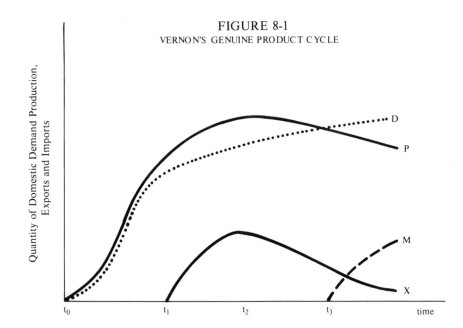

FIGURE 8-1
VERNON'S GENUINE PRODUCT CYCLE

Quantity of Domestic Demand Production, Exports and Imports

D

P

M

X

t_0 t_1 t_2 t_3 time

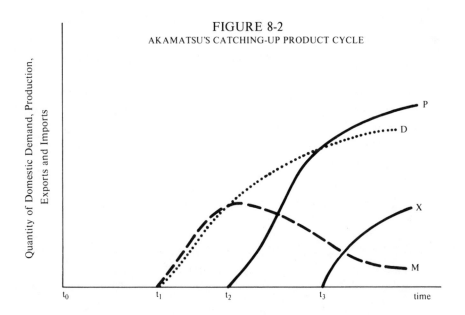

FIGURE 8-2
AKAMATSU'S CATCHING-UP PRODUCT CYCLE

Quantity of Domestic Demand, Production, Exports and Imports

P

D

X

M

t_0 t_1 t_2 t_3 time

novative competition in new products on an equal footing with other advanced countries and promote horizontal trade with them in new products. The successful reorganization in the international division of manufacturing production depends on such a trend. Although the patterns in Figures 8-1 and 8-2 look similar, the genuine product cycle is basically different from the catching-up product cycle. Imitation and learning are much easier than invention and innovation. The Japanese research and development investment in 1967 was 1.7 percent of the gross national product which was far smaller than the 3.6 percent in the United States, 3.0 percent in the United Kingdom, and 2.8 percent in the Federal Republic of Germany. Making the coming structural changes effectively is therefore not easy for Japan. In addition, international specialization and coordination in innovation of new products is needed among advanced countries for the benefit both of advanced and developing countries.

Another new task for the Japanese economy in the coming decade is how to increase its aid and direct investment to developing countries in such a way as to facilitate harmonious structural change both in Japan and developing countries, with the aim of successful reorganization of the North-South trade. Current trends in aid flows make for a pessimistic outlook on the chances of fulfilling the Pearson Commission's recommendations that "the one percent target . . . be fully met by 1975, at the very latest," and that "official development assistance should be raised to 0.70 percent of donor gross national product by 1975, and in no case later than 1980."[16] On the other hand, in Japan there is a growing realization both at the public and government level, that the country must assume a greater responsibility in aid-giving. A healthy balance of payments will render additional transfers relatively painless.

Increased foreign aid and investment will be major factors in curbing the growth of Japan's international payments surplus. The political will to mobilize larger resources for foreign aid is growing. According to the New Social and Economic Development Plan of 1970, Japan will be able to attain the one percent aid target by 1975, with $4 billion worth of total aid (although the amount in terms of the dollar ought now to be somewhat inflated owing to revaluation of the yen).

16. Lester B. Pearson, *Partners in Development* (New York: Frederick A. Praeger, 1969), p.18; the Tinbergen Report, Committee for Development Planning, *Preparation of Guidelines and Proposals for the Second United Nations Development Decade, 1970* and UNCTAD III set even more ambitious targets.

It may be more realistic for Japan to increase official development assistance at 15 percent to 20 percent annually, with a higher growth rate than in the gross national product. If official development assistance on this scale is efficiently utilized in close combination with direct investment, total outflows will nevertheless surpass the one percent target in 1975.

Although there is a commitment to a substantial increase in official aid, foreign investments will play a more significant role in assisting the growth of developing countries. At the end of 1969, Japan's total foreign investments abroad (including advanced countries) amounted to $2.69 billion (Table 8-4). Total investment will rise to $11.5 billion by 1975 and $27 billion by 1980[17] and the outflow in those years will be $2 billion and $3 billion respectively. Of this, in 1980, $1.9 billion will be directed to Asia, accounting for 20 percent of the total foreign investment flow to this area. By 1980, there will be an accumulated Japanese investment in Asia of around $7 billion. These rapid increases in Japan's investments may also arouse Asian nationalism against Japanese domination.

Direct foreign investment is a potential agent of economic transformation and development.[18] A large increase in Japanese direct investment in developing countries, insofar as it is welcomed by them, will contribute significantly to developing their natural resources, agricultural production and processing industries, and will as well transfer manufacturing industries which are suitable to each developing country.

Japan has endeavored to invest in developing countries with the object of securing increased imports of primary products which are vitally important for its economy. This is called "development assistance for import." It was first directed (and is still being directed in increasing amounts) toward natural resource development projects such as oil, natural gas, iron ore, coal, copper bauxite and other metals. Wood and timber also have high priority. Benefits of such development assistance are limited, however, to those countries where abundant natural resources are available, and the employment and training effects are small insofar as the goods are exported in the form of raw materials. If we can extend our development investment for import to agricultural products, benefits will be spread more widely in developing areas. Thailand's successful develop-

---

17. *Japan's Economy in 1980 in the Global Context,* pp.45-51.
18. Harry G. Johnson, "The Multinational Corporation as a Development Agent," *Columbia Journal of World Business* V, no. 3 (May-June 1970): 25-30.

ment of exports to Japan of maize is a good example. Since February 1970, the Asian Trade Development Corporation has been providing subsidies to development assistance for the import of various agricultural products produced in the wider Asian area. The government is also considering whether to provide low interest rate foreign exchange loans to those enterprises which venture to develop new natural resource deposits.

However, developing countries have strong nationalistic fears against foreign ownership in natural resource development and they sometimes nationalize such enterprises. New forms and new codes of behavior should therefore be devised for foreign investment. Joint venture with local capital is preferable. Import-linked investments and production-sharing methods, which have been adopted by Japan, may also be recommended, and progressive transfer of ownership may be necessary.

The development of natural resources, including timber, in developing countries is not only highly risky, but also expensive for private enterprise since it has to provide infrastructure related to the natural resource development, such as roads, railways, harbors and towns, which are usually provided by the host government in advanced countries. A close combination of private investment and official development assistance should be considered so that the latter accommodates needed infrastructure, making private investment more attractive. Otherwise, natural resource development in advanced countries will go ahead and that in developing countries may be delayed. Also, a risk-insurance system should be introduced by governments or international organizations.

Processing natural resources within the developing countries is desirable from the point of view of both developing countries and Japan, but it is not necessarily economical. More careful case-by-case study is required.

Japan's direct investment in manufacturing capacity in developing countries is important, and plays a harmonious role for both sides if appropriate manufacturing industries are selected. The industries to be chosen should be those in which Japan is losing its comparative advantage while developing countries are gaining it, or are expected to gain it. Such industries should be export-oriented, and not merely serve the economically privileged local classes.

Japanese foreign investment has to date been "trade-oriented." It was aimed at complementing Japan's comparative advantage position. The major part of investment was therefore directed toward natural resource development in which the Japanese economy is comparatively disadvantaged. Even investment in manufacturing has been confined either to such traditional industries as textiles, clothing and processing of steel in which Japan has been losing its comparative advantage, or the assembly of motor vehicles, production of parts and components of radios and other electronic machines in which cheaper labor costs in Southeast Asian countries are achieved and the Japanese firms can increase exports, substituting for exports of final products, exports of machinery and equipment for the factory and technological know-how.

Japanese foreign direct investment has thus been quite sensitive to change in its comparative advantage position.

The bulk of Japanese foreign direct investments in manufacturing is undertaken by small- and medium-sized firms which transfer technology suitable to local factor proportions, with larger employment and training effects than those characteristic of "enclave" investments. Joint ventures have been preferred to wholly owned subsidiaries. Transfer of only parts of the package may be considered, if the recipient country desires, through loan-*cum*-management contracts or transfer of technology through licensing arrangements rather than direct investment.

Suppose that textiles which are losing comparative advantage in Japan move away from Japan through increased direct investment in developing countries. This will promote structural adjustment in Japan and open wider markets for developing country products. If other advanced countries do the same, markets for developing country products will become very large. The Japanese textile industry has long experience of excellent management and technology which is more suitable to developing countries than that of America or Europe. When abundant relatively cheap labor is combined with this in developing countries, the joint venture products will certainly succeed in international competition.

The point is that it is better for Japan to transfer, one by one as it has, out of those industries in which it is losing its comparative advantage, and to invest in developing countries which are gaining a comparative advantage in the same industries.[19] In other words, foreign direct investment to developing countries should be, as

19. Here the importance of selecting the right kind of industry in foreign direct investment is stressed. Certainly there is another problem of behavior and performance of direct investment with which, however, it is not possible to deal here. A new modality of foreign direct investment to developing countries should be seriously considered. This was discussed intensively at the Chile Pacific Conference recently. See H.W. Arndt, "Economic Cooperation in the Pacific: A Summing Up" (Paper delivered at the Conferencia del Pacifico, Vina del Mar, Chile, September 27–October 3, 1970).

Japan's was, "trade-oriented," that is, aimed at complementing and strengthening comparative advantage in investing and receiving countries respectively.

In Asia, the success of a free trade and investment zone in Kaoshiung, Taiwan, and the development of a similar area at the Jurong Industrial Estate, Singapore, as well as the successful industrialization of Korea and Hong Kong is impressive. These demonstrate the need for step-by-step transfer of manufacturing industries from advanced to developing countries.

Foreign direct investment in harmony with changes in comparative advantages will accelerate structural adjustment in Japan, contracting traditional industries of the labor-intensive type. It is in the mother company's interests to make the invested activity prosperous by opening markets both in Japan and other advanced countries even by taking advantage of general preferences provided only for developing country products. The mother company's marketing facilities are indispensable, as mentioned above, for the new entry of developing country products to advanced country markets. Foreign direct investments for Japanese small- and medium-scale firms, which played a major part in past manufacturing investments, are a promising outlet for their survival and a great accelerator to internal structural adjustment.

In contrast to Japan, it seems to me that the United States has transferred abroad those industries which ranked in the top of her comparative advantage and has thus brought about balance of payments difficulties, unemployment and then need for protection in her remaining industries.

According to Raymond Vernon, "the United States position in manufactured goods is based heavily on a comparative advantage in the generation of innovations, rather than on the more conventional notion of relatively cheap capital" and "the big postwar increase in United States overseas investment in manufacturing subsidiaries has come about mainly in the kind of industry that would be expected to have participated in such a process: industries associated with innovation and with oligopoly. It explains why so much of the investment is found in the chemical industries, the machinery industries, the transportation industries, and the scientific instrument industries."[20] They are "highly innovative and strongly

---

20. Raymond Vernon, "The Economic Consequences of U.S. Foreign Direct Investment," in *United States International Economic Policy in an Interdependent World*, vol. 1 (Washington, D.C.: U.S. Government Printing Office, 1971), pp.929-52. A similar view is seen by Stephen Hymer, "United States Investment Abroad," in *Direct Foreign Investment in Asia and the Pacific*, ed. Peter Drysdale (Canberra: Australian National University Press, 1972).

oligopolistic," and "multinational enterprises are found principally in industries that devote a relatively high proportion of their resources to research and advertising and that tend to be dominated by very large firms."[21]

Thus, the American economy is split into a dualistic structure: (a) those innovative and oligipolistic industries or, in brief, new industries, and (b) traditional industries (textiles, steel, agriculture and so on) which are price-competitive and stagnant. The genuine product cycle and foreign direct investment takes place successfully only within the innovative and oligopolistic industry group. Foreign direct investment from such new industries which ranked at the top of American comparative advantage are "antitrade-oriented" or involve foreign direct investment which works against the structure of comparative advantage. Those new industries should strengthen exports of their final products if they were conscious of national economic interests, but actually they set up foreign subsidiaries, cutting off their own comparative advantage and inducing increased imports of those products from abroad where they invested. Both lost foreign markets and reverse imports later on resulted in balance of payments difficulties and the "export of job opportunities."

It may be true, as many researchers[22] claim, that the new industry sector on balance contributed to foreign exchange earnings because of the increased exports of intermediate goods and equipment, the return flow of earnings from past investment and the like. It should be stressed, however, that if they had been conscious of national economic interests, by refraining from foreign investment and strengthening export promotion, those new industries would have earned greater export surpluses and covered import surpluses in other sectors.

If American foreign manufacturing investment was "trade-oriented," rather than new industry oriented, it would be welcomed by developing countries and accelerate the reorganization of North-South trade, as in the case of Japan's investment.[23]

---

21. Vernon, op. cit., p.930.

22. For example, see Emergency Committee for American Trade, *The Role of the Multinational Corporation in the United States and World Economics,* 2 v., reproduced from typewritten copy, February 1972.

23. An American labor union researcher states that "U.S.-based multinational operations may adversely affect host countries as well as the U.S. The balanced economic and social development of developing economies, for example, is not necessarily promoted by the establishment of electronic subsidiary plants, with high productivity and low wage—with production for export from countries that urgently require basic educational, health and housing facilities, as well as balanced growth of domestic investment and consumer markets." Nat Goldfinger, "A Labor View of Foreign Investment and Trade Issues," in *United States International Economic Policy in an Interdependent World,* vol. 1 (Washington, D.C.: U.S. Government Printing Office, 1971), p.927.

Moreover, since innovations and foreign direct investment cycles have been confined to the new oligopolistic industry sector, much inflow of resources from the traditional sector was not allowed and structural adjustment was hindered. An increased labor force was available for employment in traditional industries but they have been losing comparative advantage. In consequence, there has been a rise in protectionist attitudes. Thus, the American economy has fallen into a vicious circle due to foreign direct investment of the antitrade type.[24]

It may thus be concluded, first, that foreign direct investment should be trade-oriented and that, since this is most beneficial for both sides, this type of investment should be much encouraged from advanced to developing countries to accelerate the reorganization of North-South trade. Secondly, as far as new manufactured goods are concerned, horizontal trade mainly among advanced countries should be promoted instead of direct investment. The decisions and performance of United States-based multinationals may be rational and perhaps wise, in terms of the firm for its profit-maximization. But such investment of the antitrade type is in conflict with national economic development as explained above. Labor is still immobile internationally and, therefore, economic development and welfare should be considered in terms of the national economy. The monopolistic or oligopolistic nature of multinationals internally as well globally should be rectified, for it results in a wastage of world resources. If all the advanced countries liberalize imports of new goods and exporting countries make concerted efforts at exporting, mutual trade in these goods among advanced countries certainly will expand, and there is no need to undertake foreign direct investment. If a firm still dares to undertake direct investment, it is because it expects a certain monopolistic profit which should not be allowed.

Technological know-how should genuinely be a public good, provided that there is enough incentive for innovation, and should not be the source of monopolistic or oligipolistic gains. Innovation of new goods is required for the reorganization of, and new dynamism in, the international division of labor. Innovative human resources are relatively scarce in the world as a whole. It might be desirable for advanced countries to arrange an agreement of specialization in the

---

24. Dunning makes an interesting comment on British investment: "there is probably too much U. K. investment overseas in traditional-type industries and not enough investment at home in the newer technologically based industries." See John H. Dunning, *Studies in International Investment* (London: George Allen and Unwin, 1970), p.91. Perhaps a proportionate increase in investment of both types is desirable.

line of innovation in which each country concentrates its effort. Assurance of specialization and accompanying economies of scale will promote liberalization of trade in these commodities.[25]They might also be able to spare innovative human resources to create technology which is more suitable to developing countries.

As in the case of direct investments, aid should also be provided in a close combination with investments so as to facilitate the donor country's structural adjustment although major aid is directed towards infrastructural investment. Untying aid is also an important objective.

IV. JAPAN'S TRADE POLICY AND STRUCTURAL ADJUSTMENT

It becomes very clear that Japan and other advanced countries should develop an integrated aid, investment-*cum*-preference, structural adjustment policy in order to establish harmonious and expanding North-South trade relationships in the 1970s. Although the key factor is structural adjustment in advanced countries as has been stressed repeatedly, a brief survey of Japan's trade policy, especially in relation to developing economies, is in order since the provision of wider market access in advanced countries to developing country manufactures is a crucial problem.

Japan's trade liberalization made its first spurt from 1960 to 1963, enabling it to move to GATT Article XI and IMF Article VIII status. A second liberalization period from 1969 to 1972 was prompted by the desire to bring the liberalization of trade and capital movements to completion rather than to revalue the yen, since large surpluses of international payments had been accumulated. However, from 1964 to 1969, the pace of liberalization lagged. During this period residual import restrictions were maintained with few positive initiatives, overprotecting some industries.

Paradoxically, the Japanese government was too busy with the Kennedy Round tariff negotiations to give attention to its own trade liberalization. Import quota restrictions are the most important non-tariff barriers in Japan. In April 1969 there were 120 items under residual import restriction.

They were rapidly reduced to thirty-three items: twenty-four agricultural, one mineral (coal) and eight manufactured items, in

---

25. This is an application of my "agreed specialization" to the innovative activities. See Kiyoshi Kojima, "Towards a Theory of Agreed Specialization: The Economics of Integration," in *Essays in Honour of Sir Roy Harrod,* ed. W.A. Eltis, M.F.G. Scott and J.N.Wolfe (Oxford: The University Press, 1970).

terms of the BTN four-digit level by April 1972. The problem of the residual import restrictions on manufactured goods might be said to have come nearly to an end with only eight items remaining unliberalized.[26]Of these, four items are raw hide and leather (bovine cattle leather, equine leather, sheep and lambskin leather, goat and kidskin leather) and one is leather footwear. The liberalization of these items is said to be difficult because of the protection that will have to be accorded subsistence producers in the so-called dowa districts, where these industries provide the main support for minority tribes. The other four items consist of digital-type electronic computers, their machinery and parts, and integrated circuits. The protection for these items is justified by infant industry arguments. No major nontariff barriers in manufactured goods remain. In the agricultural field, in addition to the twenty-four items, several other items—such as rice, wheat, butter and tobacco—are controlled by state trading.

Japan's agricultural imports have been, and still are, restrained by quota, while manufactured goods at present are protected mainly by tariffs. Recently, Japan reduced tariffs to a fairly low level in accordance with the Kennedy Round reductions. That reduction is currently being completed, and tariffs on dutiable nonagricultural products will then average only 9.9 percent in the United States, 8.6 percent in the EEC, 10.8 percent in the United Kingdom and 10.7 percent in Japan.[27]

Although the average level of Japan's tariffs on manufactures is not high, tariff revision in 1961 took escalation as its principle, and tariff escalation is obvious. Some examples of tariff escalation in nominal rate and estimates of "effective rate of protection" are shown in Table 8-5.

Tariffs on finished consumer goods, moreover, remain high even after the Kennedy Round reductions, for heavy protection once imposed on infant industries has not been reduced sufficiently. For example, tariffs on automobiles were 20 percent to 40 percent in the 1960s. They were reduced to 18 percent to 24 percent in 1970, and to 10 percent in 1971. Tariffs on traditional labor-intensive products on the other hand have remained high. In 1971 tariffs on laces and

---

26. See Kojima, "Nontariff Barriers to Japan's Trade," loc. cit.; Ryutaro Komiya, "Japan's Nontariff Barriers to Trade in Manufactures," in *Obstacles to Trade in the Pacific Area,* ed. H.E. English and Keith A.S. Hay (Ottawa: Carleton University School of International Affairs, 1972).

27. See Ernest H. Preeg, *Traders and Diplomats* (Washington, D.C.: The Brookings Institution, 1970), pp.204-36, 249-55.

tulles were 24.5 percent for cotton, and 15 percent to 17.5 percent for others; the knitted underwear tariff was 24.5 percent for cotton and 15 percent to 17.5 percent for others. Hong Kong-made flowers had a tariff of 25 percent and plywood of 15 percent to 20 percent. However, these defects of our tariff structure will be revised within a year by the Tariff Committee of the Finance Ministry.

Following the EEC, Japan since August 1971 has begun to provide general preferences to developing countries. Before the introduction of the system, we tried to estimate its effects. First, on twelve sensitive commodities of importance to all developing countries, the increase of Japanese imports in consequence of the extension of 100 percent tariff preferences would amount to 24.7 percent of these imports, but only $0.91 million, on 1964 trade figures.[28] Secondly, in consequence of preferential tariff elimination, Japanese imports would increase by $3.7 million, or 5.3 percent of its dutiable imports, from nine Southeast Asian countries (the Philippines, Indonesia, Singapore, Malaysia, South Vietnam, Cambodia, Laos, Thailand and Burma) on 1967 trade figures and $15.6 million, or 11.8 percent of its dutiable imports, from the developing countries in ECAFE.[29]These show that although the percentage increase appears large, the absolute increase is almost insignificant when compared with annual increases in Japanese exports of the order of $3-$4 billion.

The actual benefits of Japan's general preferences have so far been rather limited because the range of commodities under the scheme is limited, and the quota ceiling is so small that it was mostly filled within one or two months. The system should be improved, as the government has already promised, so that the preference margin is more generous.[30]

The general preferences to developing country products are not sufficient for opening wider markets in advanced countries, although the longer-term effects might be more significant. Thus, it should be stressed again that extension of trade preferences is unlikely to be practicable or effective unless complementary, adjustment policies are implemented in both advanced and less developed countries.

Where tariffs remain important, advanced countries should work towards the adoption of a system of value added tariffs on imports

28. Kojima, *Japan and a Pacific Free Trade Area,* pp.107-8.
29. Kiyoshi Kojima, Saburo Okita and Peter Drysdale, "Foreign Economic Relations," in *Southeast Asia's Economy in the 1970s* (London: Longman, 1971), pp.297-99.
30. On the EEC preferences, see Richard N. Cooper, "The EEC Preferences: A Critical Evaluation," *Intereconomics,* April 1972, pp.122-24. Japan's system is basically similar to the EEC preferences and is subject to the same critical evaluation.

from less developed countries.[31]Value added tariffs involve the levy of duties solely on that portion of the value of an imported commodity which is added to materials and components in the less developed country itself. This concession is important where manufacturing activity in less developed countries depends heavily on foreign capital equipment, and on parts and components imported from advanced countries. Value added tariffs would minimize the impact of tariff escalation in advanced countries, and encourage the migration of inefficient advanced country industrial capacity to efficient locations within less developed countries. United States Tariff Item 807 permits this kind of concession, although its terms are too restrictive. The Australian preference scheme for less developed countries can also be used to this effect. Japan has also recently extended value added tariff concessions to Korea on a limited number of items. Perhaps the most promising means of achieving generalization of value added tariff systems is by negotiation among groups of interested countries. It is important to establish now regional forums through which these negotiations might take place.

While Japanese trade policy has been reluctantly changing in favor of manufactured exports from developing countries, our imports have increased rapidly in terms of their growth rate. For instance, imports of textile goods from other Asian countries increased from $5.8 million in 1965 to $178 million in 1971; imports of machinery from $2.2 million to $45 million; and raw silk was an important export item for many decades for Japan, although four years ago Japan became a net importer. However, the size of total imports of manufactured goods from developing countries is yet very limited.

What is Japan's basic attitude to the rising ability of developing countries to export manufactured goods? Many interests in Japan think that it still maintains a strong comparative advantage in traditional labor-intensive manufacturing industries of the type most competitive with potential export industries in developing countries and that there is no scope to import them because of employment and social problems. Thus, Japanese structural adjustment continues to lag.

In liberalizing Japanese trade, no voluntary and positive action is taken unless pressure is exerted from foreign countries. Once a certain target has been established under foreign pressure, great

---

31. Kojima, Okita and Drysdale, op. cit., p.302.

progress is made. The rapid progress of the liberalization since 1969 was forced mainly by pressure from the United States; it duly came in those items in which the United States is seriously interested. Thus, developing countries' interests have been rather neglected, and this is coupled with the fact that they lack counter-offers for reciprocal concessions.

Undertaking structural adjustments effectively therefore becomes a central issue for advanced countries if really wide markets for manufactured goods of the developing countries are to be created. Strong resistance, both economic and political, can be expected. Various steps will have to be taken to assist the adjustment, along the lines of those under the United States Trade Expansion Act of 1962 and the amended act of 1968.[32]

The Japanese economy has only limited experience of adjustment assistance policy. The first example is a recent policy of adjustment in rice cultivation, which should be examined since it is most important although it is not directly concerned with manufacturing. Heavy price supports have been provided for rice production, while imports of rice have been controlled by a state-trading system. The implicit tariff rate on imports of rice is at least as high as 70 percent and probably higher than 100 percent, depending on the rice type and price quotations in Japan and abroad selected for comparison. Coupled with rapid productivity improvement, this has brought about overproduction of rice in Japan, resulting in difficulties for Asian rice-exporting countries. A land-retirement scheme has been introduced since 1970. The government provides compensation for those farmers who contract rice production acreage in the hope that they may switch to other occupations. This has not worked as expected. "Rice is far more profitable than other farming enterprises, which prevents desirable shifts in the production pattern, and also more profitable than most nonfarm employment: this discourages farmers from making a complete shift to nonfarm work.[33]The rice price was raised every year to take into account increases in nonfarm wages. Such price determination should be changed and the rice price should be lowered. Even if the rice price is lowered, the full-time farm unit, can make enough profit if it attains a sufficient

---

32. U.S. adjustment assistance policy is critically evaluated, and needed improvement is suggested by *U. S. Foreign Economic Policy for the 1970s: A New Approach to New Realities,* National Planning Association planning pamphlet no. 130 (Washington, D. C. , November 1971), pp.194-211.

33. Michael Tracy, *Japanese Agriculture at the Crossroads* (London: Trade Policy Research Centre, 1972), p.21.

size. Agricultural pressure groups in Japan are still strong, but have declined substantially, and a more determined agricultural policy may be expected in the not too distant future.

How can job opportunities be created for those farmers who are discharged? The farm is diversifying its production from rice to dairy industries, cattle growing, poultry and fruit, which also necessitate protection. Many farmers already obtain income from outside farming. A Law for Promoting the Introduction of Industries into Rural Villages was introduced in 1971; retraining schemes for farmers and a farmer's pension scheme were also introduced. But structural reform has not yet been made effective. One hope is that natural contraction of the farm population will take place. Michael Tracy concludes, "The age distribution of the farm population is heavily biased toward the upper age groups: in 1970, out of 4.0 million males engaged mainly in farming, 1.3 million were aged over 60 and 0.7 million were aged 50-59. It seems likely, therefore, that during the 1970s the control of nearly two-fifths of the farms in Japan will pass to the next generation."[34] Agricultural reform in Japan is clearly a political and social problem rather than an economic problem.

In a second example of Japanese experience with adjustment assistance policy, the Japanese coal industry has undergone dramatic structural adjustment since World War II. Immediately after the war, in December 1946, coal and steel industries were taken up as a priority industry for recovery. Governmental funds, steel and other inputs, including labor, food and clothing for labor were allocated with top priority to coal mining. The production of coal increased from a mere six million tons in 1945 to thirty million tons in 1947 and to fifty million tons in 1951.

The situation completely changed after the switch in policy toward the importation of oil in 1949. The change occurred because the price of coal was too high, and oil was more efficient in various uses. Perhaps also, the major international oil companies were interested in expanding markets in Japan. The coal industry changed to rationalization and contraction under a law enacted in 1955, and amended in 1960. The law aimed at scrapping three million tons of old inefficient capacity and another twelve million tons later by using tariff revenue levied on imports of oil. The coal mining firms were confronted with strikes and other resistance from laborers who had to move to other jobs. The scrapping of old, inefficient

34. Ibid., p.25.

mines were nevertheless rapidly accomplished during 1963 and 1964. The firms were keen to switch to other lines of activity because the superiority of oil to coal was obvious, and workers waited to find other jobs while the Japanese economy was growing dramatically.

A third example is the textile spinning industry. This industry was originally very capitalistic and depended little on government assistance before the war. It grew through the growth of small firms, their integration into big firms, the control of production through a cartel and the diversification of production from cotton to synthetic and chemical fibers. However, after the war, government intervention in spinning was introduced through the Textile Structural Adjustment Law of 1956, and the amended Law of 1964 and 1967. Those laws aimed at scrapping old, inefficient spinning mills and building new, more efficient mills of optimum size. Governmental moneys were provided as compensation for scrapping old spinning facilities. New spinning capacity was limited. But because of the superior efficiency of new capacity, the volume of production increased. In other words, the governmental assistance to the spinning industry contributed to increased production, to modernization of the industry and to the strengthening of its international competitiveness, rather than to a reduction in production capacity and to the reallocation of resources to other industries. Since it consists of large firms, the spinning industry is more alert and adaptive to do structural adjustment than smaller processing textile firms.

There is, as a fourth example, some experience in undertaking structural adjustment for small- and medium-sized firms, but this is a most difficult problem in Japan. Numerous adjustment assistance policies have been established. There are many laws, financial organizations, semigovernmental corporations and so on, specifically to assist the vast number of small- and medium-sized firms. They are perhaps too piecemeal, cumbersome and ad hoc, so that firms cannot make effective use of governmental assistance. They might well be better integrated into a single, comprehensive law and organization. These policies intend to overcome the disadvantages or handicaps which, it is believed, small- and medium-sized firms have compared with large, modern firms. Their intention is to allow small- and medium-sized firms to survive, sometimes leading to their modernization and rationalization, but they are usually not assisted to move into growing industries. There is a tendency for new laws to be added to compensate unadaptable firms for whatever loss they suffer. For instance, the revaluation of the yen in December 1971 led to such legislation.

Other difficulties arise when a certain district is entirely specialized in producing specific export goods. For example knives and forks are produced in the Tsubakuro area, and certain types of processed textiles in the Japan Sea districts. The problem is similar to that in agriculture. However there are good prospects for Japanese small- and medium-sized firms in establishing subsidiaries and joint ventures abroad, and moving to knowledge-intensive industries. The United States adjustment assistance policy is confined to cure unemployment caused by increases in imports, along the same lines as general unemployment insurance. Japan and other industrialized countries of Western Europe deal with the difficulties of business firms and works in a much broader and longer-term context. For them the adjustment problem is one of industrialization and development.[35]Such a broader but well-integrated policy is advisable since successful structural adjustment heavily depends upon the dynamic upgrading of the country's whole industrial structure.

Structural adjustment assistance policy for inefficient, declining industries should consist of two aspects.[36]The first is comprised of measures to promote the running down and transfer of inefficient industries to other sectors. For this purpose public infrastructural investment, low-cost loans, investment grants and subsidies, tax benefits, technical assistance and training programs, should be undertaken in a much more systematic way. Secondly, some safeguards for the gradual running down of inefficient protected industries are needed. But this safeguard should not be abused for protectionistic purposes. It should assure the transfer out of inefficient industries. Therefore GATT Article XIX should include obligations to implement structural adjustment and to specify the duration within which the safeguard expires.[37]

There is one particular measure that would assist the adjustments desired. A fund for assisting structural adjustment should be estab-

35. *U. S. Foreign Economic Policy in the 1970s,* p.202.

36. "The optimum policy for bringing about the graceful retirement of uneconomic industries would be a 'package' of subsidies to allow uncompetitive production to continue over the retirement period and of a cash grant to finance the closing down of productive capacity. Facilities should be provided, in addition, for the retraining and movement of redundant labor." David Wall, *The Third World Challenge, Preference for Development* (London: The Atlantic Trade Policy, 1967), p.51.

37. Gerald Curzon has proposed the adoption of an international adjustment assistance code. See Gerald Curzon and Victoria Curzon, *Global Assault on Nontariff Trade Barriers,* Trade Policy Research Centre Thames Essays, no. 3 (London: Ditchling Press Ltd., 1972), p.32.

lished in every advanced country. This should become an international obligation similar to the one percent of gross national product foreign aid target. A certain percentage (say, a half of one percent) of gross national product could be collected through taxation for this purpose.[38] The fund should be used to eliminate gradually uneconomic industries and transfer factors of production to more productive activities where the advanced country enjoys a comparative advantage.

These funds would be more efficient than direct aid to developing countries, for they would serve to raise incomes and efficiency in developed countries as well as promoting industrialization in the developing countries. From the point of view of advanced countries, there is a clear parallel between the reclamation of uneconomic industries suggested here and the urban renewal already widely undertaken by governments.

Trade preferences for developing countries are justifiable if divergence from the principle of nondiscrimination within GATT is temporary, and if they foster liberalization of world trade. They are positively desirable if they encourage transformation in the international division of labor in such a way as to strengthen specialization in the export of labor-intensive exports from developing countries. However, as already shown, preferences alone may not bring about sufficient benefits. Aid and investment linked directly to preferential tariff and structural adjustment (an integrated aid, investment-*cum*-preferences and structural adjustment policy) could offer more benefits to developing countries. First, directly productive aid and investment in the form of capital goods, advanced techniques of production, managerial know-how and worker training should be provided to developing countries on an increasingly large scale if the efficiency of new export-oriented industries, primary as well as manufacturing, is to be improved to the point where they become increasingly competitive in world markets. Secondly, developed countries should provide preferential treatment to developing country export launched with the help of directly productive aid and investment, coupled with multinational firms' sales promotion. Preferences aimed at insuring wider markets would serve as a kind of aid and investment "after-care," and might well be regarded as indispensable to realizing the full benefits of aid and investment. It is important that the provision of preferences should be closely linked with the provision of aid and investment, since both are likely to be

38. See Kojima, *Japan and a Pacific Free Trade Area*, p.125.

ineffective and wasteful of resources if applied independently. Thirdly, a receptive structural adjustment in advanced countries should be closely linked with the result of the aid and investment.

To conclude, structural adjustment to contract an inefficient sector, if it is done independently, is very difficult. It is most important for advanced countries to succeed in developing new growth sectors in which resources can be absorbed. In order to do this, specialization and coordination in innovation in addition to prosperous horizontal trade in new sophisticated goods are most needed among advanced countries.

The policies of advanced countries for increasing exports of manufactured goods from developing countries should be such as to promote structural change on both sides, and harmonious development of North-South trade. Thus, an integrated aid, investment-*cum*-preference, structural adjustment policy is required. Finally, it is clear that a large scale aid investment-*cum*-preference structural adjustment scheme could be given more effect by a group of like-minded advanced countries. It is also desirable that aid-giving and investment should be multinationalized, and freed as far as possible from bilateral tying. To realize these objectives, the possibilities for and advantages of closer coooperation among advanced countries in the Asian-Pacific region should be studied.

TABLE 8-1

COMMODITY COMPOSITION OF JAPAN'S EXPORTS

Year Commodity group	1955	1960	1965	1970	1980
	Percentage				
Foodstuffs ....:..............	6.6	6.6	4.1	3.4	1.4
Raw materials and fuels	1.9	1.6	1.5	1.0	0.4
Light industrial goods (Textiles, non-metal ore, and others)	53.5	48.4	31.9	22.5	11.9
Heavy and chemical industrial goods (Metals, machinery and chemicals)	38.0	43.4	62.5	72.4	86.3
All commodities	100.0	100.0	100.0	99.3	100.0

SOURCE: Japan Economic Research Center, *Japan's Economy in 1980 in the Global Context* (Tokyo, 1972), p.29.

TABLE 8-2

COMPOSITION OF JAPAN'S EXPORTS BY TYPES OF INDUSTRY

Year Type of Industry	1955	1960	1965	1970	1980
	Percentage				
Labor-intensive industries	58.9	55.1	36.5	27.7	15.3
Resource-consuming type industries..................	22.3	14.9	21.3	18.9	11.5
Technology-intensive industries..................	18.6	29.6	41.6	52.7	73.2
Total........................	99.8	99.6	99.4	99.3	100.0

NOTES: Labor-intensive type—Foodstuffs, textiles, other light industrial goods and metal goods.
Resource-consuming type—Raw materials and fuel, nonmetal ore, iron and steel and nonferrous metal.
Technology-intensive type—Chemicals, general purpose machinery, electrical machinery, transport machinery and precision machinery.

SOURCE: Japan Economic Research Center, *Japan's Economy in 1980 in the Global Context* (Tokyo, 1972), p.31.

TABLE 8-3

COMMODITY COMPOSITION OF JAPAN'S IMPORTS

Commodity group \ Year	1955	1960	1965	1970	1980
	Percentage				
Foodstuffs	25.3	12.2	18.0	13.6	9.5
Raw materials	51.1	49.2	39.4	35.4	21.9
Mineral fuels	11.7	16.5	19.9	20.7	18.8
Chemicals	4.5	5.9	5.0	5.3	5.7
Machinery	5.7	9.7	9.3	12.2	19.0
Other manufactures*	1.7	6.5	8.4	12.8	25.1
Subtotal: Processed manufactures ...	11.9	22.1	22.7	30.3	49.8
Total	100.0	100.0	100.0	100.0	100.0

*Other manufactures consist of iron and steel, textiles and nonferrous metal.

SOURCE: Japan Economic Research Center, *Japan's Economy in 1980 in the Global Context* (Tokyo, 1972), p.34.

TABLE 8-4

BALANCE OF JAPAN'S DIRECT OVERSEAS INVESTMENTS BY INDUSTRY

Type of Industry	Balance of Investments (Mns. US$)		Percentage of Total	
	1969	1980	1969	1980
Resource-oriented	1,092	13,881	40.7	50.8
Labor- and Market-oriented	620	7,148	23.1	26.2
Finance and services	969	6,280	36.2	23.0
Total	2,683	27,309	100.0	100.0

NOTES: Resource-oriented—Agriculture, fishery, forestry, etcetera.
      Labor- and market-oriented—Foodstuffs, textiles, chemicals, iron, nonferrous, machinery, electrical machinery, transport machinery and construction.
      Finance and services—Commerce, finance and insurance.

SOURCE: Japan Economic Research Center, *Japan's Economy in 1980 in the Global Context* (Tokyo, 1972), p.50.

TABLE 8-5

EXAMPLE OF TARIFF ESCALATION IN JAPAN

	Rates of Protection (%)	
	Nominal	Effective
Yamazawa's estimate for the period before the Kennedy Round reductions		
Cotton	free	—
Cotton yarn	5.0	9.9
Cotton textiles	16.0	36.2
Clothing	27.8	48.8
Pulp woods	free	—
Pulp	5.0	3.3
Paper and paper board	13.6	30.2
Manufactured paper and paper board	15.0	16.7
Iron ore and scrap	free	—
Pig iron	10.0	24.4
Steel ingot	12.5	47.0
Rolled steel	15.0	35.1
Automobiles	36.0	66.5
Wantanabe-Muto's estimate for 1968 after partial Kennedy Round reductions		
Raw materials	3.9*	0.9*
Capital goods	15.2*	22.3*
Intermediate goods	14.1*	21.7*
Finished capital goods	16.9*	23.2*
Consumer goods	23.6*	35.8*

*The unweighted average rates for several commodities belonging to each category.

SOURCES: *Sekai Keizai Hyōron* (June 1967) and *Kansei Chosa Geppo* (April-June 1971) respectively.

Comment

David Wall

People slotted to be a late speaker at a conference always suffer from some nightmares. One is that by the time they get around to speaking, people have started leaving. The second nightmare is that if they have not gone, the participants will have fallen asleep. The third and worst nightmare is that, by the time they come to speak, all their main points have been made by earlier speakers. I have been watching all three nightmares come to life this afternoon. But one major issue has been left untouched and I will concentrate on this in the context of Kiyoshi Kojima's paper. As with all policy-orientated papers, I read it with three simple questions in mind: what is it that we want; how do we intend to get it; but more important, I think, how do we sell the idea that we should have it? Before turning to Kiyoshi Kojima's paper let me remind you that we were told earlier in this seminar that we should not be too positive in our analysis, that we should be openly normative and that (we were told at several points) we should be blunt and frank. Let me, then, be blunt and tell you frankly what my normative reaction is to the results we have seen here of throwing positive analysis out of the window: it is a mixture of a little anger and a little sadness. I will keep the little sadness to myself to mull over at nights, but I will share with you my anger.

Let me try to explain this anger in the context of Kiyoshi Kojima's very interesting and useful paper. Refer to the most crucial sentence in the paper, indeed in the whole adjustment assistance debate: "Structural adjustment in declining, inefficient sectors is undertaken successfully only in a dynamic economy in which the growth sectors' expansion is rapid enough so that resources from contracting sectors may be absorbed smoothly" [p. 235f]. I think this is the fundamental issue, the key point, to use two clichés. (We can excuse Kiyoshi Kojima for not being entirely accurate in his use of the world *inefficient,* even God makes mistakes.) I think this sentence is crucial because it identifies what is in the minds of the people who determine the policies in the country with which we are concerned. Mr. Kojima thus meets a prerequisite for trying to figure out how to get from them what we want and how to sell it to them as being in their own interest. This brings me to the "major issue" I

referred to above which has not received much attention at the conference. This is, that you do not sell anything to anybody in this
world unless you convince them it is in *their* interest to buy it. This
has been a basic theme of mine for some years.

The Japanese government wants the Japanese economy to grow
as rapidly and smoothly as possible. What *we* want is to insure that
that growth is as beneficial to the trade interests of poor countries as
possible. Now we have answers to our first two simple questions—and an implied answer to the third. We want to expand exports from poor countries to Japan; to achieve this we have to
devise methods of gearing such expanded trade into the Japanese
growth process; to sell it we have to convince the Japanese government that the structural adjustments their economy requires in
order to grow rapidly can best be based—partially at least—on expanded imports from poor countries. Kiyoshi Kojima is aware of all
this. He devotes a considerable proportion of his paper to arguing
that future Japanese growth will depend on a reorientation of the
economy towards what he calls "knowledge-intensive industries" (a
euphemism for capital-intensive industries—to be sure *specialized*
capital, but still capital). He proceeds to show that such reorientation
would depend on the availability of five factors, four of which could
be designed to incorporate increased imports from poor countries.
The five factors, the first four of which could clearly be embodied in
imports from poor countries, are: land and harbor facilities of other
countries; the atmospheric environment of other countries; the raw
materials of other countries; the cheap labor of other countries; and,
one that is not as important and has a different dimension, increased
labor mobility within Japan.

I think that Kiyoshi Kojima has the right approach. That is, he
has sought to identify the *domestic* goals of Japanese policy-makers
and sought to find a way of demonstrating to them that it is in their
interests to expand Japanese imports from poor countries. In his
paper, Mr. Kojima has shown how Japanese domestic objectives
can be more easily attained by drawing on increased imports from
poor countries. The wrong approach—which has prevailed in this
conference and has led to my anger—is to start with *our* objective
and then try to convince rich countries to modify *their* domestic objectives so that we might more easily obtain ours. It is easy to see
how following such an approach to the adjustment assistance debate
can lead to the sort of irresponsible defeatism expressed earlier by
Mahbub Haq. Mahbub Haq implied that as sectional protectionism

is currently a strong feature of domestic politics in rich countries, the poor countries would be well advised to "seek their own salvation" and give up an attempt to obtain trade concessions from rich countries. Such advice, if accepted, would (and Mahbub Haq is in a better position than most to appreciate this) commit the majority of the inhabitants of poor countries to perpetual poverty. As justification of his defeatism, Mahbub Haq referred to the comments made by Nat Goldfinger. Nat Goldfinger, however, was simply doing the job for which he is paid, and to my mind he was doing it very well. Those of us here whose job it is to seek ways of enhancing the welfare of the poor countries were not doing their jobs very well when they sought to prove Nat Goldfinger wrong, or simply ridicule him. Kiyoshi Kojima has shown us, in his paper, how to cope with people such as Mr. Goldfinger. *We* have to seek ways of making our objectives mutually consistent and not ways of forcing the Goldfingers in the rich countries to give up their objectives in favor of ours. I am almost alone, it seems, among participants in believing that our objectives and Nat Goldfinger's can be made mutually consistent. I agree with Max Corden who said (amidst some strange controversy) that increased imports of developed countries from poor countries necessarily lead to a reverse trade flow. I also believe that it is not beyond the wit of man to arrange things in such a way that these two-way trade flows (combined with some sort of adjustment assistance program attractively packaged) help the Goldfingers and governments of the rich countries to achieve their objectives concurrently with our achieving ours. I get angry when I see people, whose job it is to devise such arrangements, throwing their arms up in the air at the first sign of resistance, giving up hope and advising poor countries to let the Goldfingers inherit the world.

Once we, as economists, have devised programs for grafting increased exports from poor countries into the domestic objectives of developed countries we have to design ways of convincing opponents in those countries that we are right. We have not spent much time on either of these fundamental questions in this conference. We certainly cannot convince our opponents simply by telling them that they are wrong and by appealing to them in the name of morality. When Nat Goldfinger said that "workers are people," he only had the United States's workers in mind. He cannot comprehend a morality based on treating all human beings as equals just as he did not understand the economic logic of arguments made against his points yesterday. To sell our programs to Nat Goldfinger we have to start by convincing him that we wish to increase employment and welfare *in America* by stimulating profitable exports *from America*. For other opponents we have to use other arguments—and it is in the nature of things that they will seldom be based on morality. Kiyoshi Kojima clearly realizes this and does not moralize too much about Japanese responsibility towards less-developed countries. Indeed, he shows that it would be silly in a Japanese context, because the Japanese policy-determining group are not concerned about the welfare of the poor countries. They are only concerned with how to take advantage of the poor countries' resources and facilities in order to increase their *own welfare*. Rightly so. So we have to wrap our programs up in such a way that our opponents see something in it for them and for the people whose welfare it is their responsibility to look after. I am not overpessimistic about the difficulties of convincing our opponents. After all, if they can be convinced that the space race, Concorde, the Vietnam war and the Agricultural Fund are in their interest, convincing them to accept something clearly in their own interest should not be too hard.

Comment
Jo Saxe

I will be a trifle more empirical and direct and will take as the verse for my sermon, what Kiyoshi Kojima says about a major challenge, to which I subscribe in general. For Japan, he says, there will be a major challenge to Japanese economic diplomacy in the seventies because of some of the measures which he proposes. I would like to suggest that these measures, seen against the background of the present Japanese institutions and policies, will pose an absolutely insurmountable challenge to Japanese economic diplomacy, unless the Japanese authorities have changed, and rather radically changed, the ways in which they do business abroad. I will just take up a few specific points on which I believe that this general proposition rests. First of all consider Japanese concentration in the Asian-Pacific region. The way to avoid the obvious dangers (and to an American milieu at least this may suggest how the United States might deal with Latin American affairs) is to diversify geographically and to broaden the definition of national self-interest at least in the geographical sense of the word. In saying that I do not necessarily suggest that Japan do anything less in Southeast Asia. Indeed I think Kiyoshi Kojima's suggestion that Japan reduce its export surplus with many of these countries is absurd; one wants to increase that gap, if one wants to transfer resources to those countries. But the modalities are what seem to me to be important here. I think that one has to strike a somewhat different balance between direct investment and the provision of assistance to governments for essentially the same purposes. In passing, I still, despite Mahbub Haq's persuasiveness and my friendship for him, believe that transfers of financial, and then real resources are pretty important to developing countries and that they will continue at some level, or rather more than less, although not as much as some of us utopians would have it.

So I would suggest that one way out of the dilemma of Japanese dominance, and reactions to it, is to give some of the money away, rather than investing it in Japanese enterprises. I also suggest that the absorptive capacity problem is not as serious as Kiyoshi Kojima seems to think it is. The figures indicate that there is no difficulty whatsoever in absorbing $1.5 billion in Japanese private investment and export credits, so I do not see why there should be any great difficulty in absorbing a like amount of money for essentially the same purpose in the form of grants or something like International Development Association credits. I agree with him that the purposes which he wishes to be served by these transfers are eminently sensible purposes for Japan and for the recipient countries. So I would not worry about the absorptive capacity quite so much. It seems to me that it is a matter of arranging financing in a sensible way, for which there are precedents.

It also seems to me, and here perhaps I am repeating something that David Wall already has said, that the question of knowledge-intensive industries needs just a word or two of elucidation. From all that I know of what will happen in Japan and is happening elsewhere in the industrialized countries, there will be a shift, not only toward the service sector and toward a higher standard of living, but toward a rather different style of living. I do not think it is just cotton textiles or gray cloth or that sort of thing, I think it is a lot of the things that he suggests ought to be produced in Japan, and I would ask that he rethink the definitions of the categories of industries he is using.

What I am saying is, do not lend the money or buy up half the neighborhood, give some of it away; do not be too narrow in your view of the geographical area in question; do not be too narrow in the view of areas in which developing countries have a comparative advantage. These are my conclusions. I would also wish, just by way of afterthought, to take exception to Mr. Kojima's classification or description of the process of the United States' oligopolistic movement of enterprises into Western Europe and elsewhere. That seems to me to be a very much more complex phenomenon and the rationale or motivation for it is rather different than he has described it.

9

Summary and Conclusions

Helen Hughes

Some twenty-five years of growth and development since World War II have changed the structure of the world economy. Developed and developing countries, and the international institutions founded in the early postwar years, are now concerned with adjusting their economic policies to the new trends emerging in international economic relations. Industrial and associated trade policies are only one of the many areas in which rethinking is taking place. The social impact and objectives of economic growth are being reviewed. The international monetary system is in the throes of fundamental change. Agricultural policies of both developed and developing countries require reconsideration. Changes in the world's production structure have, however, been greatest in manufacturing in the last two decades. It is thus in improved relations in trade in industrial goods that developed and developing countries are likely to gain most from radical adjustments of policy; it is also, unfortunately, the area of trade where the danger of confrontation between them is most acute. This was the principal theme discussed at the seminar reported in this book.

I. THE WORLD STRUCTURE OF
MANUFACTURING INDUSTRY IN THE 1970s

The industrial production structure of the developed countries has become markedly similar in the last twenty years. This is particularly true of the three major trading blocs comprising the United States, the European Economic Community and Japan. The developing countries, in contrast, increasingly display a widening range of industrial production from the least developed countries to those which are in effect already semi-industrialized. Indeed, for small- to medium-sized semi-industrialized countries such as Taiwan and Mexico manufacturing industry contributes as much to gross national product as it does in some high income countries. The technological characteristics of manufacturing industries in these countries are very close to those of developed countries. Even in other, lower income and larger developing countries, notably Brazil and India, where manufacturing industry still contributes a relatively low proportion of the gross national product, there are now highly sophisticated, large industrial concentrations.

The last twenty-five years have thus seen a process of industrial maturation in developing countries, and this has been reflected in the industrial goods being traded. Until the end of the 1950s developing countries' industrial exports consisted largely of semi-processed raw materials. During the 1960s exports of relatively simple, labor-intensive products led to a 12 percent to 14 percent average annual increase in all developing countries' manufactured exports. The few small countries responsible for most of this increase reached average annual growth rates of 40 percent and more. Since the late 1960s not only have many new developing countries become manufactured product exporters, so that the overall rate of manufactured exports from developing countries has tended to accelerate, but a greatly broadened range of products, much of it departing from the labor-intensive end of the industrial production spectrum, has entered world markets. On the basis of 1960s developing countries' export growth trends, it may be expected that manufactured exports, which accounted for less than 20 percent of total developing country nonfuel exports at the end of the 1960s, will represent more than 40 percent of such exports by 1980. These estimates are likely to prove a conservative indication of the export supply potential because the changes in industrial and trade policies which lie at the back of the developing countries' export effort have not yet been fully reflected in trade.

The developing countries' capacity to export manufactured products is being augmented by changing world trends in capital and labor markets. The rapid postwar growth of developed countries provided multinational corporations with resources for investment in developing countries. In the 1950s this was principally for import substitution, but by the 1960s multinational corporations were also looking for low cost sources of semifinished and finished goods for their developed country markets. This type of export takes a variety of organizational forms ranging from direct manufacturing by wholly owned subsidiaries of multinational corporations, to independent local manufacturers' subcontracting for large retail and wholesale firms in developed countries. In this type of export the purchasing firm characteristically takes care of all marketing problems, and usually also extends varying degrees of technical and managerial assistance in production.

In recent years additional capital has become available through indirect private investment to all but the lowest income developing countries (and those with chronic political or economic instabilities) through international capital markets. The 8 percent to 9 percent interest rates for loans of up to ten years duration are considerably lower than the social price for capital in most developing countries; the relatively low rates indicate that international capital is seeking investment opportunities in manufacturing in developing countries.

Labor trends are also contributing to the changing international structure of manufacturing. The pressure of labor supply on industrial employment opportunities in developing countries is likely to reach a peak in the next twenty-five years. Even on the most optimistic assumptions of containing population growth, there will be a continually increasing flow of new entrants into the labor force in the next twenty years. The movement from the countryside to urban areas is likely to accelerate with population growth. Employment considerations are being underlined by the emerging concern with alleviating poverty. Creating new employment opportunities is an important, and in some countries the most important way of improving the standard of living of poor people. This is putting new pressures on policy formulation in developing countries. Economic policies and administrative policies are becoming better geared to development. Export orientation is becoming more prevalent. In a number of developing countries, and particularly in the semi-industrialized ones which now have a greatly improved physical infrastructure and considerable administrative capacity, there has been a healthy lift in the rate of economic growth in recent years and there are good prospects that it may be maintained. There is frequent talk of "half a dozen Japans around the corner."

In the developed countries the situation is markedly different. The recovery and growth of Europe, and more recently the coming of age of the Japanese economy, have led to new trading and investment relations which are still in the process of adjustment. Twenty-five years of rapid development have led to high living standards, but also to some intransigent economic and social problems. The developed countries are finding it increasingly difficult to control inflation in a full employment environment. Structural rigidities are leading to inefficiency in all sectors of the economy, and in the allocation of resources among sectors. Social welfare measures have alleviated extremes of poverty in most developed countries, but depressed regional pockets persist. The natural environment is threatened by careless exploitation, and the man-made one is increasingly seen to be inadequate to human needs. The policy and institutional measures required to remedy these problems are lacking.

The changed economic climate in Europe, together with pressures to provide social infrastructure facilities for immigrants, is also leading to a new look at European temporary migration policies which eased the employment problems of several Mediterranean countries in the 1960s. The substitution of labor-intensive imports for immigrant labor is likely to become an increasingly attractive policy alternative in the 1970s.

The changing composition of the world's industrial structure is reflected in the framework of international trade. The principal adjustments are taking place among the three developed country trading blocs, but developing countries, largely because of their greater participation in trade in manufactures, are being affected to an increasing degree.

The Kennedy Round tariff reductions, the most important trade agreement of recent years, failed to reduce tariffs on "sensitive" products, that is, on primary processed goods, textiles and leather goods. The extension of the EEC reduced the preferences hitherto enjoyed by Commonwealth countries in the United Kingdom. The Generalized Preferences Scheme to some extent offset this loss, but the Scheme does not apply to "sensitive" products, thus excluding the bulk of manufactures currently exported by developing countries, and relies on country quotas to limit low duty market access. Further tariff reductions by industrialized countries are likely to eliminate developing countries' preferential access to rich markets.

Privileged market access is largely important to the least developed countries which find it difficult to compete with the more industrialized developing as well as with developed countries. For the more industrialized developing countries it is not tariffs, but nontariff import barriers which inhibit exports. The reduction in tariffs among developed countries, and the developing countries' growing ability to export manufactures, have been matched by the growth of "restrictive practices by the high income countries fearing the "cheap" labor imports of developing countries (and Japan). Some eight hundred such measures have been identified by GATT.

Nontariff barriers are not restricted to simple, labor-intensive goods; they are being used against basic materials such as steel, and against capital goods. Such trends are leading developing countries to a new mood of pessimism about trade prospects: they are matched by fears of "cheap" labor imports in high income countries.

II. THE MUTUAL INTEREST IN TRADE EXPANSION

A deep-seated paradox confounds the international trade debate. The theorems of the pure theory of international trade continue to be used in "textbook" demonstrations of the benefits to be gained from increased international trade. This approach, however, fails to take into account the "realities" of international trade. The pure theory of trade is static, it assumes pure competition, and it ignores income distribution. Yet international trade is essentially dynamic, it is widely known to be very imperfect, the income distribution effects of a change in trade are immediately felt and, at least in psychological terms, a tendency to factor price equalization is perceived as a threat to labor in developed countries. The result is a disbelief in the textbook theorems, and a retreat to protectionism. The pure theory of international trade is undeniably a useful departure point in the analysis of costs and benefits of trade. However, unless it can be clearly shown that the benefits of increased trade in industrial goods will exceed the costs for all productive groups—workers as well as the owners of capital (and land)—in developed and developing countries under actual trading conditions, the protectionist trend will not be stemmed. This means that the assumptions usually swept under the rug in theoretical expositions have to be brought out into the open.

The dynamic nature of trade has been examined and demonstrated in the product cycle approach to the explanation of trade trends, principally with reference to the United States and Japan. The focus of this approach has been on the role of technological innovation, but there are other, not yet adequately explored aspects of trade growth and change. The "infant industry" argument applies to the export of individual products, and to the export of manufactured products as a whole. Manufacturers and countries need time for their export capability to mature, but once such a capability is established, the composition of exports will be determined by shifts in international comparative advantage broadly interpreted as resulting from changes in all the factors which in a dynamic sense affect comparative costs. The capability to export may in fact be defined as the capability to adjust to such shifts.

The imperfect nature of international trade has received little systematic attention though it is increasingly evident in the erosion of "international prices" for manufactured products. There are two types of imperfections. One is of economic origin and relates to such practices as product differentiation, vertical and horizontal integration and various "dumping" practices. Imperfect competition does not only apply to the market for manufactured products, but also to the market for associated services such as shipping and insurance. Secondly, government policies which include tariff and nontariff protection for domestic markets, and direct and indirect subsidies for exports, have created a neomercantilist world in which benefits accruing from trade, and actual comparative advantage, are extremely difficult to estimate. Current exercises in shadow pricing indicate the complexity and indeterminateness of such estimates.

An extensive literature devoted to domestic resource costs, effective protection and project evaluation has sought to analyze the effects of policy created barriers to trade, but its reliance on "international prices" is now leading to some second thoughts. The joint application of the theory of imperfect competition and the theory of trade, which is essential to an understanding of trade trends and potentials, is only beginning to evolve, mainly around the role of the multinational corporation in international trade.

Multinational corporations have come to play an important and, in some product groups, dominant role in international trade during the last decade. They are estimated to account for more than half the international trade in manufactures. They are able to exploit the economic rents created by market imperfections and by government policies in developed and developing countries through internal transfer pricing. Their budgets and political power sometimes exceed those of the countries in which they operate. Multinational corporations are therefore tending to attract attention, but at a somewhat superficial level, whereas a more profound analysis could be more usefully directed to those economic conditions which enable them to thrive at the expense of smaller, "national" as distinct from multinational enterprises. There is general agreement that most developing countries to a large measure have the ability to control the operations of multinational corporations by eliminating excessive import replacement and export incentives, particularly if they are biased toward the use of capital rather than labor, and by policing transfer pricing. It is also agreed that developed countries should exercise better control over multinational corporations. There is less agreement that an international "code of behavior" to control multinational corporations is practicable. Indeed, it seems likely that the monopolistic profits being earned by multinational corporations, and their excessive economic and political power, can only be curtailed effectively by a more competitive international trading framework.

The lack of attention to the income distribution effects of changes in trade has been more clearly recognized as a weakness of the textbook approach. It is in fact now usually argued that the underlying reason for developed countries' opposition to increasing trade with developing countries is that those groups which benefit are not well organized, while those which bear the burden of the change, principally the workers and firms directly affected, have strong political representation.

The principal beneficiaries of trade are the consumers. It is true that they are not a strong political group.

The second group of beneficiaries are the workers and firms engaged in exports. Provided exchange rates are set at the right level, and provided the economic structure of a country is flexible, higher imports will stimulate exports. Such groups cannot be said to be unorganized, but their gains from trade are less apparent and so they have less interest in making their views felt than the firms and workers displaced by imports. These groups feel an immediate, considerable and genuine loss. In a democratic society they are likely to be very vocal and, in the absence of appropriate social policies, very protectionist.

It is well recognized that the opposition to change is strongest when the workers and firms displaced are the least privileged in a community so that they find it difficult to move to new occupations. Opposition to change is particularly strong if the industries affected by increased imports are concentrated in one geographical area, and they are stronger still if there are few alternative business opportunities in such an area. This tends to be the case where labor-intensive products are imported from developing countries to developed countries. The diversification of developing countries' manufactured exports out of labor-intensive products is thought to be conducive to a lessening of such pressures. So is the move toward intraindustry trade characteristic of trade among developed countries, for then the problem of displacing whole industries, typical of interindustry trade, is likely to be avoided and workers and firms can move and specialize within existing industries and within existing geographic locations, considerably reducing the costs of dislocation.

The objections to increased imports from developing countries need not be rational in the economic sense to be effective. There is thought to be a strong psychological element in opposition to such trade which is absent in the reactions to trade among developed countries. The cause of such a reaction is the fear of "cheap labor." Psychological factors are no doubt an important aspect of economic motivations, but little is known about them, and they are often contradictory. Thus while some groups appear to fear imports, other groups are accused of an irrational preference for imported goods. Such preferences may, of course, be held by different economic groups, or the preference for imported products may be only for products from high-income countries. It is agreed that the psychological fears have to be understood to be countered. This requires at least a closer look at the fear of "cheap" imports.

It is clear that while capital, technology and managerial skills are highly mobile, the mobility of labor—unskilled, semiskilled and skilled—is very limited in relation to total labor supply in developing countries. Population pressure and the outflow of labor from rural areas, together with improved education facilities in schools and on the job, are likely to keep industrial labor costs low at least for the next twenty years in developing countries. A free trade, free factor movement world would tend to absorb labor in countries where labor costs are relatively high. This would lead to a more equal distribution of income throughout the world in the way that nineteenth-century migration from Europe tended to relieve poverty in the surplus population countries. This safety valve is no longer available. The ratio of the "poor" to the "rich" labor force is overwhelming, and in the poor countries the population of working age is still growing rapidly.

The pattern of international adjustment has to follow a new path. The availability of capital and technology to the developing countries is leading to a situation in which they are becoming increasingly competitive in a widening range of industrial (and in some cases agricultural) production. The principal economic activities into which workers and firms displaced by low-cost imports can move in developed countries are those industries and associated activities which are somewhat imperfectly defined as "science industries," and service activities tied to specific localities. Some of the latter activities, for example repair services, are however also being ousted, by the competition of low-priced manufactured goods. Given the wage differentials between developed and developing countries, it is no longer economic to repair a domestic utensil; it is cheaper to replace it.

The degree to which overall employment problems in developed countries are likely to result from increased trade in manufactures will partly depend on the movement at the margin, that is, the developing countries' ability to accelerate industrial efficiency and export growth. Paradoxically it is also affected by the degree of protection afforded to industrial activities in developed countries. While the short- and medium-term benefits of protection are generally stressed by the groups affected by imports, the costs are rarely discussed or quantified. A protected national market encourages imperfect competition and hence technical as well as economic inefficiency, it slows down innovation, and makes adjustment to world production conditions progressively more and more difficult. The costs of adjustment increase through time, and they appear to increase exponentially. Evidence of excessive protection is emerging in some developed countries in increasing structural rigidities, persistent unemployment and the inability to control inflation. The developed countries need an injection of momentum to regain their economic competitiveness and maneuverability. Such momentum need not be devoted to increased personal incomes. Public expenditures or increased leisure may be thought to be more desirable. However, momentum is needed, and growing, more competitive international trade can supply it.

III. ADJUSTMENT ASSISTANCE

The concept of adjustment assistance for firms, workers and communities affected by structural changes in the economy, whether due to internal or external causes, is relatively recent, and experience of adjustment assistance policies is fragmentary and varied. One of the two principal industry specific adjustment schemes, the Ruhr coal adjustment program, was the result of internal rather than trade-induced changes, but the other, the Lancashire cotton textile industry scheme, was intended to provide assistance to workers and firms displaced by textile imports, principally from developing countries. Sweden and the United States have had some experience of industry-wide schemes intended to deal with problems caused by trade. The EEC has provided adjustment assistance for hardship caused by the creation of the Community in the past, and it is now beginning to introduce Community-wide adjustment assistance measures to deal with structural change due to foreign trade. Japan has encouraged firms to move out of labor-intensive production, particularly in textiles, through capital incentives, and provides a variety of other assistance schemes. However, full employment has made assistance to workers largely unnecessary.

A priori, it can be argued that there are strong tendencies against automatic adjustment in both full employment economies, and in those with high unemployment. In a full employment economy inflationary pressures usually lead to balance of payments difficulties, and hence to a demand for protection. Workers believe not merely that they are entitled to a job, but that they have a specific right to the job they hold. A full employment, inflationary economy is one in which the case for an "optimum tariff" might be expected to be valid. These arguments carry some conviction, but the experience of the 1950s and 1960s suggests that structural change is easier to accomplish, and increased imports from developing countries are hence easier to accommodate, in a full employment than in an underemployment environment. The mere threat of higher overall unemployment rates is usually enough to strengthen protectionist lobbies, and there is evidence that the higher unemployment rises, overall, or within a region, the more difficult structural adjustment becomes. The administrative agencies dealing with retraining and other services become swamped.

Although the evidence is limited, it does appear that full employment, particularly in the context of a dynamic economy, with upward mobile labor, is much more conducive to the success of adjustment assistance policies than a sluggish economic environment. In the Ruhr, in Lancashire and in Japan, full employment was important in providing new opportunities for entrepreneurs and workers. The United States has faced a different situation in recent years. During the 1950s, adjustment was relatively easy, and the rigorous interpretation of adjustment assistance legislation which severely restricted its effectiveness attracted little comment. At the beginning of the 1970s, with a sharp rise in unemployment, conditions changed. The ineffectiveness of adjustment assistance became a matter of debate, and the interpretation of the law was changed to enable assistance to be granted under less rigorous conditions. By this time, however, total unemployment had risen to some 5 percent to 6 percent of the work force, and it was heavily concentrated in the very regions being hit by new imports from developing countries. Adjustment assistance policy provisions could not be brought into effect because the regional offices in the badly affected regions were unable to deal with the increase in work caused by high overall unemployment. In retraining programs for example, unemployed war veterans received priority over workers displaced by imports in obtaining places at limited training centers. But while the workers displaced by trade were generally treated as other unemployed, they could, unlike them, point to a distinct external cause of their plight—imports of goods from "cheap" labor countries—and press for an immediate remedy in the form of protection. Adjustment assistance had become "burial assistance," and organized labor became heavily protectionist.

It is usually argued that all factors of production, entrepreneurs, and the owners of capital, land where appropriate and labor, should be eligible for adjustment assistance. Entrepreneurs and owners of risk capital are, however, engaged in business on the assumption of risk, and they may therefore be expected to bear the risks as well as the profits of their endeavors. In the case of these factors of production it thus appears to make little sense to distinguish between "internal" and "external" causes of industrial dislocation. The principal argument for assisting firms to adjust to imports rather than allowing them to go bankrupt is that they will otherwise become protectionists. Providing assistance may result in reducing their competitiveness, because once it is known that they will be helped, they will lose much of the incentive to help themselves. Nevertheless this may be a sensible price to pay as an alternative to heavy protectionist lobbying.

The case of the workers is somewhat different. They are not primarily risk-takers and, as a matter of common experience, they have less resources than entrepreneurs and owners of capital to tide them over a period of unemployment. Their training is often largely socially conditioned, and if they require retraining, in order to move and find new jobs, they require assistance.

There are a number of preconditions for the success of adjustment assistance policies. First, the economy has to be vigorous; private enterprises, and public institutions and policies have to be able to respond to the need for structural change. Secondly, basic social as well as economic policies are of considerable importance to the adjustment process. Swedish experience suggests that workers' initial industrial training is an important factor in the ease with which they find jobs when they have to move to a new industry. Most displaced workers failed to move to more productive jobs. In the United States displaced workers who find it most difficult to obtain new employment are those with poor education and few industrial skills. Their skills, moreover, are plant specific. They are trained to maintain particular types of textile machines rather than being all-round skilled mechanics. Retraining then often has to make up for an initial lack of skills. If this is not undertaken, then the condition that workers in industrialized countries are easily upward mobile, in contrast to those in developing countries, does not apply. In some instances upward mobility may be easier in developing countries, where workers in labor-intensive industries tend to be better educated and more devoted to their tasks than in developed countries. Low skills not surprisingly tend to create hard core protectionist attitudes. Thirdly, the more adjustment assistance policies are "early warning" policies, the more successful they are likely to be. As inefficient or "senile" industries decline, the best firms and workers tend to leave them. This often means physically leaving an area or region. The entrepreneurs and workers remaining are those who are least energetic or mobile, making the process of adjustment very difficult. If a region's economy is to be upgraded, it is wise to do so before the most enterprising members of the work force leave.

In economic terms there may be a considerable disparity between the private and social costs and benefits of letting "senile" industries run down. Thus a long-established firm with depreciated equipment may wish to stay in business as long as returns are sufficient to cover running costs. However, from a social point of view, this is a low-productivity industry hampering forward movement, and one likely to become a strong supporter of protectionist pressures. The movement of entrepreneurs, capital and workers out of the "senile" industry and into more productive economic activities will be worthwhile in terms of social cost at an earlier stage than it will pay firms and workers to move out. Adjustment assistance subsidies should thus be available before an industry is fully in decline.

One of the problems of adjustment assistance is that there is a considerable danger that entrepreneurs and workers will wish to use adjustment assistance funds to reequip "senile" industries on the grounds that factor intensity reversal will then make them competitive with low-wage countries. There is some doubt whether this is indeed likely as capital intensity is gradually rising in the same industries in developing countries, not necessarily under the pressure of rising wages, but for technical reasons. Even if this were not so, and it would thus be profitable for firms in developing countries to engage in capital intensive reinvestment, it would not be justified in social terms. Comparative advantage in industries in which alternative technologies are in use, would still be likely to be found in low labor cost developing countries.

The most intransigent cases of "senility" are associated with problems of regional development. Regional employment has been a problem even in Japan, where structural change has otherwise seen few difficulties. It is likely to be characteristic of many developed country industries hit by low-cost imports in the future. In this situation the problem of adjustment is not one merely for a firm and its workers, but for the community as a whole. Without appropriate assistance measures, the community tends to lose young and vigorous people, and become aged. Assistance measures are however difficult. The alternatives are to find new, more productive occupations for the labor force, or to assist people to migrate out of the area. The former is likely to be costly, at least initially, and it requires long range forward planning if it is to be effective. Moves out of a "senile" industry into another one with low requirements in skilled labor have been counterproductive in both the United States and the EEC because of the rapidly rising competitiveness of developing countries. Growing opposition to the multinational corporations' shifts of production out of these developed countries has accompanied this trend.

Regional policies may involve heavy environmental restoration costs. Many of the industrialized countries' "senile" industries are located in areas which originally had a comparative advantage based on water power, and later coal. The countryside was often destroyed in the pursuit of economic growth. The much wealthier communities of today can afford to restore the environment with a view to replacing manufacturing by labor-intensive service industries in such areas, providing interim employment in construction, encouraging reforestation and similar labor-intensive works and laying a basis for tourism and similar industries.

Social policies are a particularly important aspect of long-term regional policy. Communities which have been declining for many years are usually marked by poor educational facilities and standards. Whether it is thought desirable that the labor force should move, or whether it is planned to introduce more productive industries, workers require improved basic training and retraining. Where it is thought desirable to have at least some migration from a declining employment area, the lack of appropriate housing facilities in other regions may be an important reason for lack of mobility. Providing housing in areas chosen as being desirable for new industrial concentrations may therefore be the crux of an effective adjustment policy. A migration policy must also take account of the service industries, small businesses and public services which served the previous community.

Marginal farming and low-skill industrial employment for farmers' wives and daughters are typical of many depressed regions in industrialized countries. Such industrial problems are difficult to handle because labor is both untrained and immobile. If it is not possible to increase skills substantially and to introduce new productive industries, the adjustment assistance that may be required may be to the farmers to improve productivity of agricultural units to the point where they can absorb more family labor either directly or through associated processing facilities.

The nature of adjustment assistance varies with the problem being dealt with, the extent of supplementary social and welfare services provided by a country and similar factors. There is no optimal set of measures. Swedish experience suggests that the most efficient, if not politically most acceptable form of adjustment assistance to workers may be lump sum cash payments which they may use to undergo retraining, move or otherwise make an independent adjustment response. At worst, if workers are not able to take advantage of such assistance, a cash payment is at least some compensation for the dislocation of personal life caused by the loss of employment in a particular firm and industry. Similarly, if it is desired to maintain a community in a given region for social or political reasons, cash grants may be the least costly way of doing so.

A somewhat special situation prevails in the EEC because of the possibility of substituting imports for immigrant labor. The education, housing and other social service costs of migrant labor are increasing with greater pressure from the labor-supplying countries which at present bear the bulk of such costs. There are thus considerable opportunities for increasing imports from developing countries with minimal adjustment costs by substituting imports for migrant workers.

In general, however, there can be no doubt that adjustment assistance programs will be costly if they are to be effective. In the short to intermediate term, the direct adjustment cost may be higher than the direct benefits of lower prices of imports, though higher export earnings also have to be taken into account. In a more dynamic setting, the total costs are likely to be considerably outweighed by the benefits. Thus while it has been estimated that some $500 million should be spent annually on adjustment assistance programs in the United States at current levels of trade, the costs of protection are estimated to run to $10-$15 billion annually.

IV. DEVELOPING COUNTRY ALTERNATIVES

The handful of countries which followed successful export-led strategies during the 1960s had an important effect in turning the predominantly import-replacing industrialization strategies of many developing countries toward exports. The exhaustion of import replacement opportunities was also a factor. Entrepreneurs were ready to explore new markets. The resulting diversification of developing country manufactured exports is likely to lead to a relative lessening of pressure on the narrow range of developed country markets penetrated by developing countries during the 1950s and 1960s. Such diversification is, however, not likely to be helpful to the least developed countries, or to some of the largest low-income countries. The latter include Bangladesh and Indonesia. The evolution and introduction of effective adjustment assistance policies would take time even with strong political goodwill. The market for developing country labor-intensive manufactures is thus likely to expand less rapidly than the supply.

Sole reliance on export-led growth based on developed country markets cannot, in any case, be regarded as a satisfactory strategy for most medium-sized and large countries. For countries such as India, Brazil or Nigeria exports can make a substantial balance of payments impact, but they cannot be regarded as more than a component of a strategy designed to provide reasonable minimum living standards for the bulk of the population in the foreseeable future.

The employment and income effects of policies encouraging the growth of manufactured exports are beginning to receive attention as part of the overall interest in the welfare aspects of economic growth. Heavy subsidies to exports are increasingly being regarded with scepticism because the same urban groups—entrepreneurs and an elite of factory workers—that benefit from import substitution incentives tend to benefit from incentives to exports. Where import substitution subsidies are high, with a consequent highly distorting effect on the domestic economy, export incentives have to be equally high to make exports viable in spite of high local costs. Agricultural and traditional service sectors are discriminated against by excessive incentives to export as well as by import-oriented development. In extreme cases, if, for example, subsidies to foreign investors are very high, there may even be adverse foreign exchange effects. Leading developing country economists are therefore reexamining export-led growth in the context of the reassessment of overall development policies.

During the 1950s and 1960s most developing countries pursued industrialization policies which were heavily biased toward meeting the demands of middle- and upper middle-class consumers, at the expense of balanced development for the mass of the population. Most countries therefore saw a worsening distribution of income in this period. The industrial products which were produced involved relatively capital-intensive production technologies so that the direct and indirect employment effects of such industrialization were smaller than they might have been. The production of goods for upper income groups required high quality standards and involved significant economies of scale, so that there was a tendency toward a concentration of ownership in industrial production at the expense of small-scale enterprises. Industrialization took place at the expense of agricultural development, and low-cost inputs into agriculture both in the form of producer goods and consumption goods were by and large ignored. On the contrary, the agricultural population and that engaged in urban traditional services were, in actuality, severely discriminated against by the high cost of manufactured necessities.

The rethinking of industrialization strategies for developing countries is therefore focusing on the types of products which industry should produce. If the principal emphasis is on mass consumption goods, then price rather than quality tends to become more important, and relatively labor-intensive and small-scale enterprises can compete over a much broader range of products than is the case in the production of goods aimed at upper income consumption. Regional industrial development becomes more viable. A larger scale of final products output makes backward linkage to intermediate and basic industries more economic. The backward linkages will not be the same as those required for the satisfaction of high income needs. Thus, for example in building construction, bricks and wooden structures for which many countries have indigenous resources are likely to gain at the expense of more sophisticated products. Even in products such as steel, a change in final product mix is likely to have an important effect on the basic industry. Domestic consumer durables and automobiles require mainly flat rolled steel products which are more capital- and technology-intensive than bar steel products.

For many countries a change in the composition of industrial output would mean lower dependence on imports, and hence less balance of payments stress. Reduced dependence on trade is not, however, the long term objective of such a strategy. Rather, with a more economic product mix there would be less reliance on protection, all types of exports would be made easier, and there would be much greater opportunity for trade among developing countries.

Trade among developing countries has unfortunately been neglected in the 1950s and 1960s. The developing countries' tariff barriers are higher than those of developed countries, and nontariff import barriers are also very considerable. Imports often depend on capital or foreign exchange subsidies through suppliers' credits or tied aid from developed countries. The semi-industrialized developing countries which can supply an increasing range of intermediate products and capital goods are often not able to compete because trade is tied by licenses or credit facilities to developed country suppliers. A change in the developing countries' product mix could, with appropriate changes in trade policy, lead to increased trade among developing countries on an intraindustry basis. This would maximize the mutual gains from competition among trading partners, and mean relatively less difficult adjustment problems than interindustry trade. A concentration on labor-intensive production could also lead to a new trade in capital goods among developing countries as they specialize in capital equipment suited to the relative factor prices of low-income countries.

Such a change in development strategy would not mean that developing countries would as a whole trade less with developed countries. On the contrary, world trade growth would be stimulated by the accelerated overall growth, in real terms, of the output and trade of developing countries. An emphasis on low-priced mass consumption goods would tend to keep down living costs in developing countries, and thus accentuate the low labor cost advantage which high protection, which tends to result in high prices to consumers, may seriously undermine.

It has been suggested that the developing countries could achieve a once-and-for-all increase in protection and improve their international competitive position by a substantial devaluation of, say, 50 percent to 100 percent. Such a devaluation would have provided much more advantage in developed country markets than the introduction of the Generalized Preferences scheme. In practice such a proposal would encounter serious difficulties. As already stressed, developing countries are not a homogeneous group, and a uniform devaluation would have given the more industrialized countries an increased advantage in exports. A devaluation would be the equivalent of a move toward an "optimum" tariff, and would thus have the limitations of such a measure. Industrial development is not the only factor which has to be taken into account in balance of payments measures. As a matter of political reality, such a devaluation, whether uniform or tailored to a country's relative level of industrial development, would not be practical. Developing countries would find it a difficult measure to adopt, and developed countries would be likely to retaliate.

The accomplishments of the last twenty-five years together with the developing countries' current rethinking of their industrialization strategies, implies a new view of the "international division of labor." Ex ante predictions of comparative advantage based on a simple factor price international trade model have proved erroneous. Capital and labor markets are very imperfect, and so are the international markets for goods. The countries with the lowest wage rates do not always have low labor costs, and a devaluation to bring industrial labor costs into a realistic alignment internationally is often not politically practicable. The developed country markets for labor-intensive products tend to be inelastic, and structural change tends to be slow because such industries usually employ disadvantaged workers and are heavily concentrated regionally. A sophisticated analysis, taking into account all the relevant factors in international trade is needed to determine where a particular country's comparative advantage and export capability lies.

Developing countries individually, and particularly collectively, need to improve their information base and bargaining position with regard to international trade. The priority areas are a reduction in trade barriers amongst themselves and strong, well-informed pressure to reduce, or at least prevent an increase in nontariff barriers in developed countries. There is general agreement that developing countries largely have themselves to blame if they are exploited by the multinational corporations. A movement to reduce unnecessary incentives to foreign investors, starting with adjacent groups of countries, has been initiated in the Andean Common Market; a rapid extension is required.

To suggest that developing countries have the possibility of improving their industrial growth and trade in their own hands is not to imply that this is easy. A move toward a mass-consumption industrialization strategy, while more acceptable than it would have been a decade ago, would still involve major political shifts in all but a handful of developing countries. While trade among some developing countries is now growing quite rapidly, this is because the base is small. Long range, substantial growth will also require difficult political adjustments as highly protected industries are exposed to competition. Developing countries have more limited resources, and adjustment assistance for industries affected by trade is less feasible than in developed countries. Nontrade factors, particularly the availability of credit, are likely to continue to give developed countries an advantage in trade with developing countries. Developed countries are unlikely to abandon subsidized credit policies or to untie aid to developing countries. Export credit and insurance facilities in developing countries will therefore become increasingly important.

V. PROSPECTS FOR THE 1970s

Seeking to forecast the future is hazardous. A historical analysis of economic development suggests that seers are more often than not wrong. At worst, if their views of the future are taken too seriously, their prophecies can become self-fulfilling at grave cost to development. The belief that developing countries could not compete internationally in industrial goods contributed in considerable measure to excessive import substitution in many countries during the 1950s and 1960s. The current polarization of views of trade prospects for the 1970s suggests similar dangers.

The pessimistic view considers that a growing developing country supply capacity for manufactured product exports will face more and more constrained developed country markets as falling rates of economic growth, inflationary pressures on the balance of payments and trading difficulties among the three principal trading blocs lead at best to "holding the line" at current levels of protection. Tariff reductions will be likely to benefit mainly developed country producers, because as soon as there is a buildup of developing country export capacity in a given product line, "voluntary" or involuntary import restrictions will be used to limit imports into developed countries. In the EEC the less liberal countries will push the more liberal ones toward a greater and more restrictive use of nontariff barriers as these become Community rather than individual country responsibilities. Adjustment policies will remain tokens of appeasement. The inward orientation of the 1930s will be revived within each trading bloc as hard line agricultural protectionists bolster similar views among organized labor and capital groups. Developing country hopes will be frustrated, and the danger of confrontation between developed and developing countries will become acute.

The optimists, on the other hand, point to the way in which protectionism, even in its most acute manifestations, has merely delayed, but not prevented changes in trade patterns in the past. They see an easing of difficulties in the diversification of developing country manufactured exports. Developing countries will begin to penetrate more elastic markets, and interindustry trade will give way to intraindustry trade. The opposition to imports from developing countries will then become less intensive. The multinational corporations will play a strategic role by developing a varied export capability in developing countries, and by disarming the opposition to imports in developed countries. As the semi-industrialized countries' per capita income rises, so will wages, reducing the gap between the developed and developing countries' production costs, and the developed countries' fears of "cheap" labor. Environmental and social concerns will provide a new impetus to developed countries' domestic growth, the problems of inflation will be overcome and the developing countries' increased export capacity will enable them to import more goods and services from the developed countries which will thus be able to support full employment and adequate economic growth rates.

Actual development is likely to fall somewhere between these two extremes. The developing countries' increased participation in the world trade in manufactures is unlikely to be either as difficult as the pessimists suppose, or as easy as the optimists expect. Adjustment to changing world production patterns will require vigorous initiatives. Improvement in trade cannot be achieved without the formulation of better economic strategies geared to social as well as economic objectives in both developing and developed countries. In the context of international trade new "rules of the game" which control and limit the neomercantilist policies of states, and the oligopolistic practices of private firms, will be required. The multinational corporations will have to be subjected to social welfare criteria by both developing and developed countries. Developed countries will have to evolve and apply effective adjustment assistance policies to ensure that the costs as well as the benefits of increased trade are fairly shared. With the establishment of a sound trading framework, both developing and developed countries would have much to gain from increased mutual trade.